CEO-Speak

CEO-Speak

The Language of Corporate Leadership

JOEL AMERNIC

RUSSELL CRAIG

McGill-Queen's University Press
Montreal & Kingston · London · Ithaca

Legal deposit first quarter 2006
Bibliothèque nationale du Québec

Printed in Canada on acid-free paper that is 100% ancient forest free
(100% post-consumer recycled), processed chlorine free.

McGill-Queen's University Press acknowledges the support of the Canada
Council for the Arts for our publishing program. We also acknowledge
the financial support of the Government of Canada through the Book
Publishing Industry Development Program (BPIDP) for our publishing
activities.

Library and Archives Canada Cataloguing in Publication

Amernic, Joel H. (Joel Henry), 1946–
    CEO-speak: the language of corporate leadership / Joel Amernic,
Russell Craig.

Includes bibliographical references and index.
ISBN-13: 978-0-7735-3037-9
ISBN-10: 0-7735-3037-1

    1. Chief executive officers – Case studies. 2. Business communication –
Case studies. 3. Communication in management – Case studies.
4. Corporate culture – Case studies. I. Craig, Russell II. Title.

HD30.3.A54 2006   658.4'5   C2005-907511-2

This book was typeset by Interscript in 10.5/13 Sabon.

Contents

Acknowledgments

It was through a chance telephone conversation in 1989 that we forged the research collaboration that has led to many joint scholarly papers and, now, to this book. We share in the belief that there are considerable benefits to be gained by paying close attention to the words of business leaders and, in particular, to performing a detailed analysis of what CEOs of large corporations write about financial matters.

A book such as this would not have been possible without the encouragement and practical assistance of many institutions, colleagues, librarians, relatives, and friends. Joel Amernic acknowledges the collegial academic environment provided by the University of Toronto's Rotman School of Management, the research support of the Canadian Academic Accounting Association, and the intellectual stimulation provided by colleagues, reviewers, and editors over many years. Russell Craig recognizes the support of the Australian National University, especially its Outside Studies Program. He acknowledges the assistance of the International Commission for Canadian Studies through a Canadian Studies Award and also thanks Canadian National Railway for providing materials that greatly facilitated the completion of chapter 11. Both authors are grateful to Mary Williams, copy editor, for many constructive suggestions.

In some ways this book is a reflective overview of a broad body of work we have conducted over the past decade. Some parts, alluded to or paraphrased in the indicated chapters and written by us, have been published in scholarly journals, as follows:

"Enron Discourse: The Rhetoric of a Resilient Capitalism." *Critical Perspectives on Accounting* 15 (2004): 813–52 (chapters 2 and 3).

"A 'Close Reading' Protocol to Identify Perception-Fashioning Rhetoric in Website Financial Reporting: The Case of Microsoft." *Accounting and the Public Interest* 1 (2001): 1–16 (with an additional author, Lucia Garrott; chapter 4).

"The Rhetoric of a Juggernaut: AOLTimeWarner's Internet Policy Statement." *Prometheus* 22 (2004): 21–42 (chapter 5).

"The Rhetoric of Teaching Financial Accounting on the Corporate Web: A Critical Review of Content and Metaphor in IBM's Internet Webpage Guide to Understanding Financials." *Critical Perspectives on Accounting* 11 (2000): 259–87 (chapter 6).

"Accountability and Rhetoric during a Crisis: Walt Disney's 1940 Letter to Stockholders." *Accounting Historians Journal* 27 (2000): 49–86 (chapter 8).

"Three Tenors in Perfect Harmony: 'Close Reading' of the Joint Letter by the Heads of Aluminium Giants Alcan, Pechiney and Alusuisse, Announcing Their Mega-merger Plan." *Critical Perspectives on Accounting* 12 (2001): 763–95 (chapter 10).

"The Deployment of Accounting-Related Rhetoric in the Prelude to a Privatization." *Accounting, Auditing, Accountability Journal* 17 (2004): 41–58 (chapter 11).

Special thanks go to our wives, Lilly Amernic and Annette Craig, and to our children, Heidi and David Amernic, and Natalie, Steven, and Vivienne Craig. They have been patient, encouraging, and understanding supporters as we pounded away on keyboards, often at odd hours, distracted and absorbed by this book.

Introduction

This book is about the words and language of the chief executive officers (CEOs) of influential, technologically savvy multinational corporations – people like Bill Gates, Jack Welch, Jeffrey Skilling, and Kenneth Lay. Despite the implication of CEOs in the string of high-profile US corporate collapses (such as Enron, Sunbeam, and Worldcom) in 2001 and 2002, and the ensuing reform agenda containing new provisions to improve corporate governance and executive responsibility, CEOs remain largely unbowed; they are the resilient demigods of modern business life and the New Economy.

The influence of the CEO of a large, powerful business is often culturally and socially pervasive: it is not confined merely to the business's own shareholders, customers, and employees. CEOs are often very public figures who engage actively in public debate on what they assert to be important issues of the day.[1] The CEOs of some large corporations (such as Enron's Jeffrey Skilling) are influential for fleeting moments in the great wash of corporate history. Others are influential for a much longer time, possibly decades, and they become cultural icons. Walt Disney, with his wholesome, safe, and sanitized "Uncle Walt" image, is still the touchstone and guiding metaphor of the Disney Corporation more than four decades after his death.

CEOs of mega-corporations often cultivate the dual status of "hero and modern saint."[2] Many are siren-like in their appeal for us to have faith in their judgments and decisions. Some are inspirational, charismatic, and transformational leaders. Most are not. Yet the public often conspires unwittingly with CEOs to raise them to cult status and to imbue them with an aura of wisdom and invincibility. The reason for this seems to be that we live in societies that often construct CEOs as iconic figures, partly through language, including the language of accounting and financial reporting. These iconic figures, or "modern legends," exploit themes anchored deeply in our subconscious, such as those found in frontier myths.[3] For example, a metaphor commonly invoked by CEOs is that of the corporation operating in the "bonanza" climate of the "frontier gold rush" – which they portray with images of "windfall profit, of plenty of magic, of positive transformation."[4]

In the following chapters, we focus on the written words of CEOs, or what we refer to as their "CEO-speak." Our particular attention is centred on the text of prepared CEO-speak, in which CEOs comment in writing on aspects of corporate financial performance. We harness our professional skills as professors of accounting and business studies to reveal how CEOs resort to language (including accounting, the unfashionable but critical "language of business") to create an influential ideology, a sort of insulating cocoon within which the self-reporting of the financial affairs of a corporation should be assessed.

We presume that CEO-speak is a language game, and then we investigate the linguistic, rhetorical, perception-fashioning, and ideology-creating roles that emerge from it. It is important to do so, for all too often the words of CEOs are either neglected or accorded only cursory attention. We show the benefits of a greater concern for words – for why words matter. We interrogate the language of corporate leaders but with a unique orientation towards aspects of the accounting and financial reporting involved. The source CEO texts we have selected for examination lead us to construct a vision of the CEO as a super-manager, a hero, and a warrior chief. The CEO emerges as someone who can engage successfully in "the war of business," despite all of its travails, and who can effect miracles of financial performance and reinvention. CEO-speak is used to construct the modern-day CEO of a mega-corporation as the equivalent of a great military leader of yore, but the battle waged by today's warrior has a single goal: enhanced shareholder value.

The timing of this book seems right. All too often we have allowed ourselves to be blinded by the public relations hype and bluster of the person, a mortal CEO, who has been anointed – implicitly, at least – a corporate messiah, one who will lead us into the land of financial milk and honey. Curiously, the words of the "messiahs" examined in this book suggest that they are reading from a rather perverse and impoverished script(ure). Their descriptions of financial performance are tasty morsels of exaggeration, hubris, delusion, deceit, and manipulation. In many instances, close and careful analysis of the words used by CEOs reveals chilling clues to the way they think.

We devote separate chapters to the written words of the CEOs of major multinational corporations such as Enron, Microsoft, AOL-TimeWarner, Disney, General Electric, Nortel Networks, Canadian National Railway, IBM, Andersen, Pechiney, Alusuisse, and Alcan. Thus, our catchment includes such modern legends of the business world as Bill Gates, Walt Disney, Jack Welch, and Kenneth Lay; their strong supporting cast includes Paul Tellier, John Roth, and Joseph Berardino.

We examine their CEO-speak in a broad variety of corporate strategic contexts, including written text regarding mergers, financial failures, and privatizations. The source documents from which the words are taken include letters to shareholders (found in company annual reports and newspaper advertisements), statements of policy (posted on the Web sites of large companies), a press release (announcing a corporate merger), the transcript of the testimony of a CEO before a US congressional committee, a Web site-tailored homily for those who access the Internet, and CEO-authored articles from a company's in-house newsletter.

Finally, we expose the myth of the CEO as corporate hero and reveal the often unobtrusive persuasive power of corporate Web sites. We clarify the nature of the subtle and not-so-subtle rhetoric that CEOs employ to ensure that their messages and ideological stances are accepted. In general, we show the very powerful nature of the words of CEOs. It is important to do so, for we must not permit CEO-speak to continue unchallenged in its subtle and not so subtle work of constructing our world.

CEO-Speak

1

Why the Words of Business Leaders Matter

Francis Bacon wrote that "the first distemper of learning" occurs when "men study words and not matter."[1] With these words echoing in our (distemper-ridden?) heads, we venture into this book undeterred, although we remain mindful of invoking the wrath of those subscribing to Bacon's view. Our focus, unashamedly, is on words, particularly the words written and spoken by business leaders – especially the CEOs of large multinational corporations. We show why the words of business leaders matter.

We use the expression "CEO-speak" generically to refer to the many incarnations of the words of CEOs: speeches, press releases, interviews, letters to stockholders in corporate annual reports, employee newsletters, and the electronic patois of corporate Web sites. We analyse how CEO-speak is used to sustain mergers, justify privatizations, appeal for equity capital, and endorse published balance sheets, income statements, and prospectuses. Considerable attention is focused on the discourse of the CEOs of Internet-savvy mega-companies that are influential in shaping society – the discourse of CEOs of corporate leviathans in the media, entertainment, telecommunications, and computing industries (companies like AOLTimeWarner, Microsoft, Disney, IBM, and Nortel Networks). But also included is the CEO discourse of Old Economy giants in manufacturing (Alusuisse, Pechiney, and Alcan), together with a large government business enterprise undergoing privatization (Canadian National Railway), and a large multinational professional services firm (Andersen).

In many cases, the words and language of CEOs are chosen carefully, with strategic purposes in mind. They are neither passive nor neutral implements for communication. And they are not chosen in a perfunctory way to report some objective reality. Rather, the words and language are powerful and seductive rhetorical implements for fashioning outlook and opinion. Indeed, CEOs are sometimes criticized when their discourse *disappoints* expectations for rhetoric: for example, America's "CEO," President George W. Bush, was scolded by some critics for his lack of rhetorical leadership following the 11 September 2001 attacks on the World Trade Center and the Pentagon. One wrote: "As he rose before Congress and the world last night, Mr Bush's careful language of recent days had already drawn muted criticism of his leadership skills. The United States and its allies still await a memorable call to action like the words of Second World War leaders Roosevelt and Churchill."[2] There have been similar demands for rhetorical leadership on the part of corporate CEOs during extreme business crises, as well.[3]

However, CEO discourse is also important in times unmarked by crisis. It is a crucial element of the everyday thrust and parry of the business world. CEOs "work with words" very carefully and deliberately,[4] and we must pay attention to what they say, for their language compels our closer attention.[5] "Sharing a language," as we do the language used by CEOs, "provides the subtlest and most powerful of all tools for controlling the behavior of ... other persons."[6]

CEOs choose words, usually in league with advisors and colleagues, to establish an ideological theme that will assist them in exercising control over their companies.[7] Words help them to mediate relations with other key institutions, including governments. As such, the words of CEOs are an instrumental part of a complex communicative act that has symbolic, emotional, cultural, and political overtones. We should view CEO discourse as an essential element in the process that corporations (and their CEOs) ostensibly use to make themselves accountable to their stakeholders, including the broader community. A pressing reason for individuals and communities to observe CEO-speak closely is that CEOs have clout. The views that they expound through their discourse help fashion the way our world is run.

There are many benefits to be attained by developing a keener understanding of the words and language of business leaders. The way CEOs think, talk, and write helps us to comprehend their inner selves, their corporate ethos, their world view – and, ultimately, the motivations for their corporation's behaviour.[8] The need for such an understanding is reinforced by the tendency in contemporary society to elevate the scions of big business to mythic status.[9]

Scrutinizing the words of CEOs is a pursuit with a relatively long history, especially in management literature.[10] This is not surprising, given the considerable power corporate leaders wield within their own organizations and the influence they exert politically and culturally in the broader community. CEO discourse is a "sense-making" window on CEOs' innermost selves.[11] CEOs talk or write in a fashion that reacts to, creates, and justifies the world around them. So how are we to determine the meaning of the following words of Jack Welch, the renowned, recently retired CEO of General Electric? Corporations, he wrote, "are human" and "easy targets."[12]

Two hitherto under-examined aspects of CEO-speak are addressed in this book. The first is the CEO discourse relating to matters of corporate accounting and financial reporting. This seems to have been given short shrift by the stampede of accounting and finance professors, financial analysts, and other pundits who have focused on the numbers of corporate financial dialogue rather than the numbers and the *words*, as well as the interplay between them. The second under-examined aspect is the community practice of viewing CEO discourse on an abstract, metaphorical plane. We respond to the inadequacies of this practice by highlighting important aspects of ideology, rhetoric, and metaphor in the written texts of CEOs.

In the chapters that follow, we conduct close readings of the words and language of CEOs. We reveal a "shared, relatively coherent interrelated set of emotionally charged beliefs, values, and norms" that help CEOs "to make sense of their worlds."[13] We do so without interpreting CEO text as an inevitable component of the "science of doing business" or by dwelling on the incentives for CEOs to achieve budget targets (such as profit and rate of return on investment). Our close readings are similar in concept to Slagell's close textual analysis of Abraham Lincoln's second inaugural address, delivered during the American Civil War. Like Slagell, we consider text in relation to its historical context.[14] However, in contrast to a president's inaugural address, CEO communications (such as annual letters to stockholders) are mundane discourses of seemingly minor importance. But their mundanity and their institutionalized, periodic role in the functioning of our socio-economy make them important documents for scrutiny. Indeed, all CEO discourse seems to hold revelatory potential.

Our close readings do not adhere to any rigid formula. They vary from text to text. But we make good use of five strategies of textual analysis: to dismantle dichotomies and expose them as false distinctions; to examine silences, or what is not said; to fill voids by "attending to disruptions and contradictions [in] places where the text fails to make sense"; to decipher taboos by "focussing on the element that is most alien to a text or a context"; and to interpret metaphors "as a rich source of meanings."[15]

Our close readings are neither exhaustive nor objective, but they are intended to promote awareness of the role of CEO discourse in creating our shared social world. They are also meant to serve as a springboard for much-needed countervailing perspectives on corporate accountability. If, as Boje argues, "corporate writing has been imitated and celebrated by academic writers without much critical reflection on the kinds of issues it raises,"[16] then this book is indeed timely.

Our exploration of the ideology, rhetoric, and metaphor invoked in CEO text pertaining to accounting and financial reporting takes us down a lightly trodden path.[17] We subject selected samples of CEO text to multiple (usually three) close readings, conducted from different (but mutually reinforcing) perspectives.[18] Each close reading constitutes an intensive, almost forensic, scrutiny of the explicit and implicit composition of the text. We typically conduct one close reading for ideology, one for rhetoric, and another for metaphor. Such multiple readings reflect our commitment to uncover "the alternatives that have been effaced by management knowledge and practice," since "things may not be as they appear."[19]

Close readings of the annual reports of large corporations should be conducted routinely, because these reports are a major part of the "battery of belief-forming institutions" that top management uses to define the language in which its self-accounts are written.[20] Letters to stockholders, written by CEOs and published in corporate annual reports, are important instances of the CEO discourse examined in this book. They are a significant part of the ideological paraphernalia of society and should not be brushed aside as mere rhetoric. Such accounting related narratives deserve microanalysis: they are accountability texts offering valuable insight to the motives, attitudes, and "mental models" of top management.[21]

One of our central purposes is to make the discourse of CEOs at least partially comprehensible, thereby providing a basis for counter-discourse on aspects of communication and accountability.[22] Our close readings promote awareness of the role of CEO text in creating, often subtly and unobtrusively, a shared social world and, in turn, being at least partly shaped by it. It would be naive to deny the importance of the language of those who lead the dominant social institution of our time – the multinational corporation. Leaders of mega-corporations, as members of an elite, should not be relied upon to set the public agenda and to determine public policy. For reasons partly of cognitive limitation, conflict of interest, and self-interest, they seem prone to defining the public interest in a narrow, self-serving, and perverse way. Therefore, policy produced by mega-corporations and articulated by CEOs should be analysed critically through careful close readings. It should be challenged vigorously and publicly, as we do here.[23]

In particular, it is vital to cultivate an understanding of the discipline of accounting that is less trite, less misleading, and less naive than that propagated by CEOs. Typically, CEOs portray accounting as being an objective decision-support system that accurately reflects some sort of reality. However, we show that CEOs' views of accounting have been fashioned using subtle metaphoric language influenced by ideological overtones.[24] Indeed, in the post-Enron era – one in which financial accounting is seen as more of a detractor than a facilitator of the social trust needed to fuel social engines – it seems almost de rigueur to view with skepticism the CEO perspective on accounting.

IDEOLOGY

Recognizing the ideology-laden nature of CEO-speak is important. Ideology, or "What persuades men and women to mistake each other from time to time as gods or vermin,"[25] can also be seen as a "shared, relatively coherent interrelated set of emotionally charged beliefs, values, and norms that bind some people together and help them to make sense of their worlds."[26] We need to be alert to the sense-making of CEOs as authors of an ideological discourse: they are potential ideology creators for the various audiences they address. Such a perspective is consistent with the role of discourse "as part and parcel of the reproduction and transformation of any symbolic order."[27] The close reading we conduct to elicit ideological character is important because the ideology inherent in CEO communication is something that is otherwise "apt to be hidden from view."[28]

An example of a CEO discourse laden with ideology is that which surrounds EVA© (economic value added). Gushing platitudes about EVA© have appeared in annual reports and other corporate publications in recent years.[29] EVA© has become firmly ensconced in organizational life, especially in corporate management control and compensation systems. It is beginning to emerge as a contender to such long-standing external financial-reporting indicators as net income and earnings per share.[30] CEO discourse has elevated EVA© to a corporate cultural totem. The ideological (and cultural) characteristics of the EVA© phenomenon have, through CEO discourse, become as important as the technical characteristics of the measure. Indeed, they are likely to be far more important, especially where the EVA© ideology has been subconsciously internalized by managers as they jump aboard the EVA© bandwagon.

We are not arguing for a preferred world view of corporate endeavour. If that emerges, it will be an unintended, and perhaps fortuitous, bonus. Nonetheless, we must inevitably deal with the ideological nature of the text analysed. Indeed, it seems important, at the outset, to acknowledge CEO texts as ideological, for they are human constructions. By urging a critical reading of CEO-speak, we engage in a speech act with subversive overtones. But we need such subversion in our corporatized world if we are to deal forcefully with admonitions that "the trouble with our civilization is that it has stopped questioning itself."[31]

In our reading for ideology we sometimes adopt an interrogatory approach. One question posed is: "What are the assumptions in the text about what is natural, just, and right?"[32] This question is important because "exactly the same piece of language may be ideological in one context and not in another"; and we are very conscious of the need to detect instances in which the inherent ideology "is a function of the relation of [CEO text] to its social context."[33] Additionally, our reading proceeds from the recognition that CEOs hold power over many others and often behave as if they know what is right for those who do not hold power – that is, they seem to adopt the moral conceptual system of a "strict father."[34]

Another question asked is: "What people, classes, areas of life, experiences, are left out and silenced?" We are mindful that success is measured and reported by CEOs using the hallowed (but often hollow) financial accounting indicators of reported net income and rate of return on investment. But such measures tend to induce aberrant behaviour when considered from the perspective of a company's other stakeholders (such as employees, customers, and the general community). Indeed, with hindsight, CEO-speak is often wistfully ironic, as the opening phrase of Enron's 2000 letter to its shareholders demonstrates: "Enron's performance in 2000 was a success by any measure." Of course, we now know that the particular measures adopted by Enron's top management (and duly accredited by the company's auditors) were mere fantasy. By any realistic measure, the company's performance was far poorer than its accounting system indicated.

RHETORIC

In conducting a close reading for rhetoric we are alert to the techniques of argumentation. We ask whether CEO text places the substantial burden of persuasion upon the author's public reputation. Does it allude to a fact or event known to one audience group but not to another? Is metaphor used to establish the presence of an argument in the minds of audience members?[35]

As well, we are particularly mindful of how the Internet, with its trappings of cybertextuality and multi-dimensionality, and its persuasive properties and technological idiosyncrasies, is fashioning a rapidly growing and influential corporate financial-reporting environment. We maintain that the broader public interest will be well served if CEO discourse using this medium is subjected to wide-ranging critical scrutiny: alertness to the rhetorical features of CEO text on the Internet is especially important. Consequently, our close reading evaluates rhetorical features as a device for successful argumentation, especially when diverse audiences (for example, shareholders, employees, and government) are being addressed simultaneously. The restricted opportunity for navigation through Internet-based text (because of constraints imposed by the hypertextual design of Web sites) focuses our attention on the order in which text is presented – an important rhetorical device.

Prominence is given also to the various guises under which CEOs draw upon the rhetoric of religion; the rhetoric of hierarchy; and the rhetoric of development, progress, and journey.[36] Such discourses are "most powerful symbols for rhetorical appeal," since they refer to the things that are "most familiar to us."[37] Kenneth Burke, for example, claims that "religious cosmogonies are designed ... as exceptionally thoroughgoing modes of persuasion."[38] So it is not surprising, that, for example, "The leaders of industrialized countries speak in glowing (almost religious) terms about the potential of the Internet to create prosperity for all."[39] Such religious, utopian rhetoric is often allied with the rhetoric of development, progress, and journey. This rhetorical approach is insightful because it reveals many CEOs to have a "utopic vision of progress ... characterized by a millennialism that conceives of a progressive movement towards ultimate fulfilment ... [in which] the means of progress for the righteous is good deeds and correctly performed ritual."[40] Also apt in this context is Graham's observation that "the Utopias of any age are its most powerful illusions," and his assertion that "Today's official Utopia is said to be located in cyberspace, with its high-tech knowledge and information economy."[41]

The role of CEO-speak in the "(re)production and challenge of dominance" is closely monitored. The World Wide Web is viewed as a dominant discourse, with the capacity to fashion "socially shared representations of societal arrangements ... as well as mental operations such as interpretation, thinking and arguing, inferencing and learning." An implication of this is that Web-based communication is "discourse control": that is, it has the potential to become a form of "social action" control over the minds of CEOs and can be engaged by CEOs in the "management of social representations." The Internet is thus not simply a technology in a mechanistic sense but also an expressive form for the "social relations within which a technology develops and which are re-arranged around it."[42]

This suggests that part of the "immense paradigm" dragged along by the Internet serves that new juggernaut of thought, taste, culture, and control: the virtual corporation.[43] Menzies makes this clear: "virtual corporations are the ultimate fulfilment of ... the bias of communication in the modern commercial era ... towards fast, distance-bridging media of communications and large, monopoly-scale developments around them. The new virtual forms of corporate organization emerging in today's globally networked economy may represent the ultimate in monopoly-scale organization, in which the structures as such disappear into pure digital communications and networking capacity ... They are also inherently unjust in the way they consolidate control into fewer, more remote centres and as they extend inequalities between centre and margin in the systems they create."[44]

One outcome of the growth of the Internet as an expressive form is that hyperreal computer screen images often become a sort of metonymy in which "People take one well-understood or easily perceived aspect of something to represent or stand for the thing as a whole."[45] CEOs might act as if Web pages are a (hyper)real telepresence to their organization's customers, suppliers, fellow managers, employees, and the general public; they might view the Web site as representing the organization as a whole. But on the Internet a physical part does not stand for the whole – instead, the medium emits an evanescent, digital, electronic, hyperreal shimmer.

For many readers of CEO discourse on the Internet, computer-based technology has been a part of life for a decade or more – for some, since the first stirrings of cognitive awareness. It is not surprising that those who regularly access the Internet seem inclined to accept computer-based technology, and everything that appears on Web sites, more or less uncritically. Many view alternative perspectives with suspicion – even scorn. Sensitivity to the social and ideological character of CEO discourse in this fledgling, yet already pervasive, communications medium is difficult to arouse. Nonetheless, undeterred, we focus on how the Internet alters relationships, power structures, and the way we live, organize, and manage.

METAPHOR

Our third approach to close reading analyses the metaphorical features of CEO text to identify underlying cognitive influences. CEOs use metaphors to "conceptualize one mental domain in terms of another." A metaphor is a word, phrase, or sentence that is the manifestation of a "cross-domain mapping" of "everyday abstract concepts like time, states, change, causation, and purpose."[46] We are conscious of the power, and the unobtrusiveness, of metaphoric language and how it "provides a means for ideas nourished in one domain to lend their authority to another domain and simultaneously be enriched by the alliance." When we analyse metaphoric arguments, "spaces may get created ... in which moral and political actions appear to be sanctified by nature."[47] A guiding premise is that accounting is a way of thinking: a language with the potential to influence CEOs subtly and to allow them to express their views on business matters. It affects how CEOs think metaphorically (and subconsciously) in concrete, highly contextualized situations.

There is nothing unique about the notion of a guiding metaphorical paradigm in CEO discourse. Language, in general, and metaphor, in particular, are well suited to controlling thought and behaviour.[48] In the field of industrial relations, for example, there has been debate over the appropriateness of the "trench warfare" or "pioneering journey" metaphors as controlling "root metaphors" or "conceptual archetypes" influencing practice.[49] In business and accounting, metaphors help provide the vocabulary and conceptual tools to identify what are considered legitimate problems and acceptable solutions. Metaphors used by CEOs become a sort of public language or "an external reality that [people] have to adopt if they are to communicate with others."[50]

Metaphor is more than a "frilly and fuzzy adornment to rhetoric and literature."[51] The metaphors invoked by CEOs play an important role in structuring thought, influencing perception, aiding communication, and affecting decision outcomes. In organizations undergoing change, metaphors used by CEOs set the thematic-strategic tone for the new organization by helping people to visualize the imagined-but-soon-to-be-constructed new entity. Most people, CEOs included, make use of metaphor every day, consciously or subconsciously, including in the context of accounting and financial-reporting dialogue and badinage. A poorly performing company might be said to be "haemorrhaging money." A better performer will often be described as having a strong "bottom line."

CEOs deploy metaphor to help them fashion perceptions about how a corporation has fulfilled its accountability to stakeholders. Consequently, there is much to be gained by becoming sensitized to metaphor and to the metaphor-related entailments, implications, contexts, and cognitive models that are used to construct a corporation's accountability. For example, Ziggy Switkowski, the (then) CEO of Australian telecommunications giant Telstra, in commenting on Telstra's results for the 2000–01 fiscal year, described Telstra's balance sheet as "bulletproof." With this militaristic metaphor, the CEO conveyed a powerful opinion: Telstra's balance sheet was accurate beyond reproach, and Telstra was a company of the highest probity. But no balance sheet prepared in accordance with generally accepted accounting principles (GAAP) is unchallengeable. Compliance with GAAP almost guarantees a balance sheet that violates the laws of mathematics by adding together unlike items – that is, assets denominated in dated dollars representing different amounts of purchasing power.

We sensitize readers to metaphor in CEO-speak and explore the potential of metaphors to subtly structure thought, create meaning, and influence decisions. An appreciation of the metaphorical structure of the language used by CEOs provides valuable insight into how they think about business, management, accounting, and related operational settings. Usually, the words of CEOs depict accounting as merely an explicit technical practice. We should recognize that accounting is also a way of thinking, replete with ideological overtones.[52]

Metaphors *about* accounting and *about* the organizational context within which accounting operates are interpreted from samples of CEO discourse that have metaphor embedded in accounting-related narratives.[53] Metaphors are not isolated linguistic phenomenon but are "rhetorically constituted. No metaphor is spoken or written except in the context of a socio-historically bound communicative situation. Therefore, all metaphors are inflected by politics, economics, philosophy, social interests, professional commitments, and personal attitudes – in short by the whole of our cultural and conceptual repertoire. Because metaphors are inflected, we cannot explain how they work unless we consider concrete instances of metaphor, taking into account how inflections constrain the way metaphors are uttered and understood." Accordingly, the metaphors in CEO text are not "atomized," but they are considered in relation to "metaphoric and literal concepts that are already in motion within a culture's (or subculture's) discourse."[54]

CEOs employ metaphors about language, and about the language of business – accounting – and about accountability settings. Their metaphors are about accounting, in general; about specific accounting phenomena (such as balance sheets, income statements, assets, costs, and budgets); and about the financial reporting and accountability settings within which accounting operates.

Metaphors about accounting achieve more than their prime, explicit functions of explanation and communication through the mapping of one domain onto another. Metaphors, in general, have important secondary or implicit consequences or "entailments."[55] That is, metaphors have a subtle connotative meaning as well as an overt meaning. Consider the metaphor "the bottom line." Not only do users and readers equate "bottom line" with "profit" as an end result, but they also associate it with finality (one can go no further in one's financial calculations), and precision (there is no ambiguity in the profit figure reported), and accuracy.

The language that structures the way CEOs comprehend phenomena affects their thoughts and actions regarding those phenomena, as is the case with other, less powerful humans.[56] And since much CEO-speak draws upon accounting language, the often implicit consequences of metaphors about accounting are important because they structure the way CEOs comprehend accounting and, in turn, affect the thoughts and actions of CEOs about real things. The empirical implications are many. For example, are metaphors about accounting coherent within instances of discourse?[57] Or do they differ according to context? Are they shared or idiosyncratic? Are they anchored in broader, society-wide discourse? What are their entailments and other implicit secondary consequences? Do CEOs form attitudes and make judgments about real phenomena consistent with the entailments? We explore all of these matters in the following chapters.

CEOs have metaphor-based mental images of numerous other discourses and phenomena (science, politics, marriage, drugs, and education, to cite just a few). But two important considerations justify our focus on the metaphors CEOs deploy about accounting. First, accounting is implicated intimately in a wide variety of social and economic discourses with profound effects on human welfare. Accounting is used, for example, in debates over whether or not (and, if so, how) to privatize a public utility; and in debates over the design of corporate performance ideologies such as EVA© and the "balanced scorecard." Second, language itself (English, in this instance) relies upon accounting metaphors to structure the way CEOs think about rights and obligations.[58] Thus, a sense of accountability and reciprocation becomes a pervasive and fundamental feature of our thought. Rights and duties are defined metaphorically within the framework of social accounting and moral accounting metaphors.[59] If accounting helps structure non-accounting language (and thus thought), it seems crucial to examine how (non-accounting) language helps structure the way CEOs conceive accounting and its allied paraphernalia, such as financial reports.

HYPERTEXTUALITY

Much of our focus is on CEO-speak found on corporate Web sites, where it has a particularly seductive nature and many rhetorical features. We promote Web–based CEO discourse for several reasons. Web pages are available everywhere at once: they provide managements with access to a worldwide audience. The multimedia and electronic nature of Web pages has resulted in them being regarded increasingly as technologically virtuous and more engaging than identical text on paper. The believability of the overt and covert content of these pages is usually greater than that of non-Internet media. Furthermore, a new electronic "information relationship" has been brought about by CEOs between an accounting entity (such as a corporation) and a reader of an entity's financial information. This new relationship is founded upon the immediacy and hypertextuality of Web sites,[60] and it renders the need to expose the ideological and rhetorical aspects of CEO discourse on the Internet even more urgent.

Corporations have revelled in the communication opportunities provided by a Web site portal. Consequently, the capacity for the Web site paraphernalia invoked in CEO-speak to construct beliefs and shape public discourse warrants close attention. The Internet's implicit suasory potential is exposed through a critical focus on the social influence of this communication medium in relation to its environment.[61] The Internet should not be viewed as mere technology, but rather as the current manifestation of a dominant communication medium. This notion was captured by economic historian and media theorist Harold Innis: "civilization has been dominated at different stages by various media of communication such as clay, papyrus, parchment, and paper, produced first from rags and then from wood. Each medium has its significance for the type of monopoly of knowledge which will be built and which will destroy the conditions suited to creative thought and be displaced by a new medium with its particular type of monopoly of knowledge."[62] There is much to be gained by regarding CEO communication as "a rhetoric of media" intended to persuade one "to see the world with a certain perceptual, social, and cognitive emphasis."[63]

The broader public interest will be well served if Internet-based corporate communication is subjected to wide-ranging critical scrutiny. Such a view is captured poignantly by Gibson, who contends that after the Internet has saturated the cultural landscape people will construct their world views with different tools, since "the Web becomes such second nature that, like print, we hardly notice the immense paradigm it drags along with it."[64] We seem to have reached this saturation point, yet critical inquiry has barely begun.

Close reading techniques are exploited to better understand the influence of perception-fashioning rhetorical features of Web-based financial reporting. We focus on the way in which the hypertext, metaphors, and rhetorical devices influence readers' perceptions of financial and related business information posted on Web sites. It is useful to develop an awareness of the hypertextual conditioning that takes place. We advocate a rhetorical perspective in analysing corporate Web sites – especially pages devoted to financial account-ability. Otherwise, corporate Web sites can create, unchallenged, a seemingly natural, unobtrusive world view, and they can condition perception in such a way that the real features and effects of the emergent New Capitalism will go unnoticed. For example, we are often oblivious to the unpaid labour required to facilitate corporate profitability in the Internet world – labour performed by consumers of Internet media (who operate new and evolving software, do on-line banking and shopping, and so on), by the so-called volunteers who operate corporate Web site facilities,[65] and by the "NetSlaves" who work for Internet companies.[66] It is not surprising that the rhetoric of the Internet also serves as an unnoticed but powerful conditioner of matters we take for granted.

Our three close readings of CEO text for ideology, rhetoric, and metaphor are bound closely together. They help highlight the need for awareness of the rhetoric emerging from mega-corporations through CEO-speak. We must recognize CEO-speak as an important means for influential companies to promote strategic perspectives and to influ-ence public policy and social expectations. We should conceive of the accountability language of CEOs as both a technical and a non-techni-cal phenomenon, replete with rhetorical features and social construc-tion. Accounting should not be regarded as a set of musty, arcane techniques. To better understand corporate behaviour we must under-stand the technical aspects of accounting and its rituals, solecisms, and idiosyncrasies. But we must also accept that accounting is a rich, equivocal, and indeed rhetorical social practice. A healthy skepticism of CEO discourse as it relates to accounting and financial measures and processes is critical. Accordingly, it is important to unmask the ideologies that are often hidden (at least partly) in seemingly objective and quantitative accounting measures.[67] Traditional perspectives of accounting as a sort of modernist reporter of some pre-existing objective financial reality must be challenged in order to expose the "fallacy of misplaced concreteness."[68]

Perhaps not surprisingly, much of the following analysis of the written communication of CEOs is less than flattering. CEOs emerge as elitist and exclusionary propagators of a biased stream of discourse, often based upon the extreme rhetoric of the allegedly "free" market. But, in the marketplace of ideas, it would be surprising if critique did not produce alternatives to the surface message of the discourse of the powerful. The following chapters yield strong examples of the rhetoric of neo-liberalism, extreme individualism, hyper-competition, and global capitalism. They are comingled with rhetorical stances extolling adoration of digital technology in general (and the Internet in particular) and others seeking to fashion a world that seems far removed from an organic society.[69]

This book strives to compel a deeper questioning of the rhetorical moves of CEOs, to extract new meanings from close readings, and to introduce some beneficial new ways of seeing CEO and corporate discourse. Analysis begins with a classic piece of CEO text from Jeffrey Skilling and Kenneth Lay, the CEO and president, respectively, of the Enron Corporation, prior to its fall from grace in 2001.

2

Hyperbole and Delusion at Enron

The second day of December 2001 was a landmark day in American corporate history. On that date, the Enron Corporation, a Houston-based energy, commodities, and services conglomerate, filed for Chapter 11 bankruptcy protection.[1] Enron was no minnow. It had formerly valued its net assets at US$77 billion, reported annual revenues of up to US$101 billion, and had once ranked seventh-largest on the Fortune 500 list of American companies. Enron was the largest declared bankruptcy in American history.

In some quarters Enron's financial difficulties were not entirely unexpected. Enron had already indicated that its financial statements for several previous years were tantamount to fairy stories – debt had been hidden and profits overstated. And the company's share price had fallen considerably (from a high of US$90.56 per share in August 2000 to penny-stock status at the end of 2001). Nonetheless, the collapse sent shockwaves around the world, and those shockwaves became more intense in subsequent months. Events surrounding the collapse became the subject of inquiries by eleven committees of the US Congress and Senate. Allegations of sham accounting, document shredding, and undue political influence issued from the smouldering volcano of the failed Enron.

For media outlets both in the US and internationally, Enron's collapse and its business and political fallout was an irrepressible story. In the early months of 2002, in particular, it seemed that whenever one switched on the radio or TV, or accessed the Internet, or picked up a newspaper, one was assailed with reports and opinion pieces about Enron.[2] Print and electronic news media were pulsating with stories about Enron, its executives, its impoverished lower-level employees, and its accounting firm, Andersen. Also prominent were media accounts of the anger (and sometimes the posturing) of members of the US Congress and the US Securities and Exchange Commission, and the rebuttals of accounting industry representatives. One damning revelation followed another. Suddenly, the modus operandi of accountants and the ethics of CEOs, accountants, and auditors were front-page news. Accounting had achieved an unwanted prominence and had become synonymous with greed and corruption.

Public media exchanges during the months following Enron's declaration of bankruptcy were far from cordial. The stakes were high. The media and various involved parties were in a mood for combat, and they adopted offensive or defensive postures accordingly. When a special investigative committee of the Enron board of directors reported on transactions entered into by the company, it alleged that there were serious shortcomings in Andersen's audit relationship with Enron. Andersen promptly attacked the report, calling it a blame-shifting exercise.[3] But Andersen was not the only target of the special investigative committee's accusations: Enron's senior executives found themselves under even heavier fire, and the main allegation against them was that they had condoned creative accounting. The committee was disdainful of Enron's accounting practices. Acidly, it expressed contempt for the view that Enron's accounting was "a triumph of accounting ingenuity by a group of innovative accountants."[4]

The senior management team at Enron pleaded ignorance of any accounting shenanigans. Indeed, in February 2002, just over two months after the bankruptcy, Enron's CEO from February to August 2001, Jeffrey Skilling, gave evidence before the Energy and Commerce Committee of the US Congress, claiming that "the financial statements issued by Enron," as far as he knew, "accurately reflected the financial condition of the company."[5] But, on 8 November 2001, Enron had massively restated its financial statements and had written off $600 million of shareholder wealth in respect of its financial performance for the years 1997 to 2001. In light of this, Skilling's testimony was somewhat curious, to say the least. Perhaps he had a selective memory.

In effect, there was a disconnection between the accounting reality reflected in Enron's published accounts on the one hand, and the CEO's claims for their accuracy on the other. All of this is quite titillating. What did Skilling say when the original "triumph of accounting ingenuity" was issued to the public? The place to look for his words on the subject is the letter to shareholders that accompanied Enron's last audited financial statements published prior to its collapse. According to Skilling, these statements were a faithful representation.

In this, the first of two chapters dealing with the collapse of Enron, we conduct a close reading of that last formal letter to shareholders. It was included in the company's 2000 annual report and signed jointly by Enron's CEO, Skilling, and chairman, Kenneth Lay. In the following chapter, we focus on the written testimony of Joseph Berardino, CEO of Enron's auditing firm, Andersen, to the Financial Services Committee of the US House of Representatives on 12 December 2001.

The Enron failure was a watershed event in American business, accounting, and regulatory history. There are strong portents that it will have profound consequences, and it will likely lead to an epiphany of sorts in accounting, auditing, and corporate governance practices, which will in turn result in a higher level of CEO accountability. Indeed, on 7 March 2002, President George W. Bush released a ten-point plan that included the requirement that CEOs "personally vouch for the veracity, timeliness, and fairness of their companies' public disclosures, including their financial statements."[6] Attempts at regulation and reform have duly followed.

ENRON'S LAST LETTER TO SHAREHOLDERS

The full text of Enron's 1,768-word letter, downloaded from the company's Web site, is reproduced in appendix 1.[7] We examine its rhetorical character by concentrating on the relationship between the narrative disclosures and the bankruptcy. In doing this, we are consistent with the view that, "Even if managers deliberately attempt to avoid a realistic description of their firm's economic situation (e.g. they attempt to divert attention from financial distress), the words they select may be revealing of their purposes. Therefore, the narrative disclosures of firms approaching bankruptcy may contain words or themes that are unique to this situation."[8]

CEOs do not start from a tabula rasa, but instead they create text and talk within their cognitive and ideological limitations.[9] We can learn much about Enron's CEO and chairman from a close reading of their last letter to shareholders contained in the company's annual report for 2000.

LANGUAGE OF WAR, SPORT, AND EXTREMISM

Enron's performance in 2000 was a success by any measure, as we continued to outdistance the competition and solidify our leadership in each of our major businesses. (lines 2-4)

This first sentence of the letter to shareholders evokes strong images of sport and competition. The (alleged) winner, Enron, is clearly distinguishable from the (alleged) losers. Presumably, this outcome has been decided by explicit quantitative measures: not numbers on a scoreboard, but measures of profit, revenue, and market share.

The assertion "Enron's performance in 2000 was a success by any measure" is arrogant hyperbole, self-reification, and egregiously unrealistic. Is Enron successful by *any* measure? Or is it only successful by the measures that avant-garde capitalism uses to signal success (measures heavily reliant on the financial accounting system)? And just who is contained in the entity "Enron," whose performance is allegedly a success by the universal set of measures? Does it contain just the corporate leadership? Or are lower-level employees also part of "Enron"? In other words, this "success" is for whom? Note that the word "employees" is not used in the letter. Skilling and Lay prefer "people" (used twice, in lines 164 and 185). But Enron's "people" are special. They are "innovative" (line 164) and "talented" (line 185), and they thereby (with the benefit of hindsight) provide ironic counterpoint to the subsequent fate of Enron.

The sport metaphor "outdistance the competition" is invoked to lead us to believe that not only did Enron beat its competitors in 2000, but it has also continued to do so. In the PDF version of Enron's 2000 annual report, the phrase "outdistance the competition" is set off and printed in a thirty-six-point font that differs markedly from that used in the rest of the letter. You can't miss it.

The expression "solidify our leadership" elicits an image of a rock-hard physical structure that would be hard to overcome. "Enron" and its ("our") "leadership" are thereby separated from lesser competitors. The use of "we" (twice) and "our" (five times) in the opening paragraph signals either a team persona ("Enron" as a collectivity) or, perhaps more likely, a top-management cohort (in the extreme, the two signatories of the letter, Skilling and Lay). This blatant touting of "success," "leadership," and achieving a "record" reveals the strong theme of egocentricity that flows through the entire letter.[10]

Enron is laser-focused on earnings per share, and we expect to continue strong earnings performance. We will leverage our extensive business networks, market knowledge and logistical expertise to produce high-value bundled products for an increasing number of global customers. (lines 18–21)

These are words of action and extremism, reminiscent of a major military operation. It is unnerving to observe a human organization proclaim publicly that it (or its leadership cohort) is "laser-focused" on anything. The metaphor connotes an almost irrational tunnel vision. Surely other targets also deserve management's attention.

The term "laser-focused" conjures visions of the so-called smart weapons technology that is part of the American military arsenal and was prominent during the Gulf War of 1990–91. But it should also engender thoughts of mis-targeted laser-guided munitions and death by what is euphemistically dubbed "friendly fire." This term and others (such as "targeted," when referring to markets [line 23], and "break-out," when referring to the company's retail business [line 105]) are usually found in military discourse, and they are effective. For a principally American audience, it has a subtle association with all-powerful US military forces, which have assumed an aura of invincibility since the mid-to-late 1980s, in the post-Vietnam, post-perestroika era.

To be "laser-focused on earnings per share" suggests that the earnings per share (EPS) ratio is a target to be conquered or destroyed, rather than a "measure" by which "success" can be reckoned. Even if it is not a target for destruction, it could be the object of a perverse fixation. It might bias managers' behaviour, for EPS is a measure whose fundamental flaws are well known in accounting and management circles. EPS is calculated according to this formula:

$$\frac{\text{GAAP-based income number (after adjustment for preferred shares)}}{\text{weighted-average of the number of common shares.}}$$

Even though this is the only financial ratio whose computation is regulated by GAAP (generally accepted accounting principles), the numerator (since it is based upon GAAP measures of income) is a perverse signifier of company success or failure. The numerator is past-oriented, historic-cost-infected, and subject to innumerable arbitrary allocations of revenues and expenses (both inter- and intra-temporally). Therefore it serves as the object of "laser-focused" attention only if management is terribly ill-informed – or (perhaps worse) terribly knowledgeable about the capacity for EPS to be manipulated with wild abandon.

HYPERBOLE

The letter is laden with hyperbole. Perhaps this is a special feature of the Houston-based Texan entrepreneurial culture that had consumed (or socially constructed) Skilling and Lay. Their letter portrays Enron as a dynamic, gargantuan, expanding company for whom the outlook is rosy and can only get rosier. This is a company "on a roll," a speeding train with an inexhaustible head of steam – a train that any reasonably perceptive investor should be aboard.

Skilling and Lay use powerful hyperbole effectively to present Enron in a glowing light and with an aura of invincibility. What could go amiss with such a company? Readers are soothed by words like "strong" and "large" (and their derivatives), used five times; "unique" and "enormous," used three times each; and "tremendous," used twice. The letter asserts that Enron has "tremendous opportunities for growth" (lines 11–12), and that its retail unit is "a tremendous business" (line 105). Service deliveries have seen "an enormous increase of 59 percent" (line 5). The company's new markets have "enormous growth potential" (line 15), provide "enormous opportunities" (lines 171–2), and yield "enormous competitive advantages" (line 33). Readers are assured that earnings are (or will be) "strong" (lines 19, 148), that cash flow will be "strong" (line 148), and that shareholders can expect "strong returns" (lines 152–3). Surely, the more astute reader ought to have recognized that the claims made by Skilling and Lay were simply too good to be true.

The talking-up of Enron is very pronounced in the letter's first 33 lines. The 288 words used constitute a barrage of blarney, bluster, and business-suited hucksterism. These lines are somewhat in the

style of the younger Muhammad Ali, who would often tell anyone
who would listen that he was going to knock out his next opponent
in the first round. We sustain the following blows in the opening
barrage: "large" (3 times), "enormous" (twice), "unique" (twice),
"strong" (twice), "highest" (once), and "record" (once). This is a
softening-up, designed to mesmerize. Enron is big, successful, and
growing fast. Nothing can impede it.

Such is its self-referential use of superlatives that readers are given
a clear sense of Enron as a latter-day Midas: everything Skilling and
Lay cause Enron to touch turns to gold. How could such a company possibly fail? We are invited to believe that under the leadership of Skilling and Lay, Enron will be the principal beneficiary of
emerging market opportunities worth nearly $4.7 trillion (line 184).
This would not have surprised those who had unquestioningly accepted earlier assertions about the company's "Robust networks of
strategic assets" (line 34), its "Unparalleled liquidity" (line 37), its
"Risk management skills" (line 39), and its ability to "deliver products and services easily at the lowest possible cost" (lines 41–2).
Competitors are dismissed contemptuously throughout as unable to
"provide high-value products and services" the way Enron does
(line 43-4) and of lacking Enron's "skill, experience, depth and versatility" (line 115); in fact, they are judged unworthy of comparison
with Enron (lines 165–6).

A reader could be forgiven for wondering, "Is there anything this
company cannot do?" The answer ought to have been "Plenty."
Enron's rhetoric was hollow. Within nine months the company was
illiquid and forced to file for bankruptcy protection. Indeed, one
wonders whether the "risk management skills" Skilling and Lay referred to included sham accounting – Enron hid debt in "special
purpose entities" to conceal ("manage"?) investment risk.

The letter is filled with words and phrases that evoke a company
that is always pressing forward. Enron is alert to new opportunities:
it will not rest on its laurels but will "continu[e]" to "outdistance
the competition" (line 3) and achieve "strong earnings" (line 19). It
has "extended" its "successful business model" (line 52) and its
"proven business approach to other markets" (line 99). It is "reaching a greater number of customers more quickly" (lines 58–9), "attracting users" (line 60), "expand[ing]" what it does (line 65), and
streamlining its "back-office processes" (lines 66–7). It is a company

with a capacity to "tenaciously pursue the difficult" (lines 95–6). And it is a "creator," too – having "created a new market" (line 121).

Indeed, Enron is presented as an organism that will grow and change, becoming more intelligent, more formidable. It is a company that has "built ... growth" (lines 11–12). It can "see" its "market opportunities" (line 16), it has "flexibility" (line 35), it can "scale quickly, soundly and economically" (line 64), it is "not sitting still" (line 70), and it has the capacity to "metamorphos[e]" (line 161). Its formidable nature is reflected in the claim that it can provide a "comprehensive solution" and a capacity to "ensure execution" (lines 47–8).

Thus reified, Enron seems more psychotic than energized and more hyperactive than actively healthy. Perhaps it is a victim of a corporate version of St Vitus's dance. Do the words of the letter betray a deep and lasting psychosis? Should a good psychiatrist have been engaged? The words in the annual report letter to shareholders are the words by which the company's two leaders intend the world to know the company. More importantly, they are the words by which the leaders intend the world to know *them*. So the letter, in its role as accompaniment to the 2000 audited financial statements, is more than a piece of corporate puffery. It is, perhaps, in a haunting and dysfunctional way, a Rorschach test through which Skilling and Lay provide an entree to their innermost thoughts – to the way they see Enron, and indeed the world.

This view is disturbing. The letter portrays Enron as smitten with a perverse conception of markets. The result of such affection is portrayed, none too subtly, as leading only to "good" outcomes. Enron's markets are said to have such attributes as "enormous growth potential" (line 15) and enormous capacity to triple revenues (line 16). "[M]arket knowledge" is said to produce "high-value bundled products" (lines 20–1) and to create "sustainable and unique businesses" (line 186). Markets present such good things as "expansion opportunities" (line 150) and sites of successful testing (line 140). Markets are lauded throughout, except in lines 26–8, where there is reference to them "experiencing tighter supply, higher prices and increased volatility" and to "issues of overcapacity." But even this is swept aside by the super-marketers at Enron: the company can overcome these impediments because of its "unique position" and its "size, experience and skills" (lines 31, 32).

Skilling and Lay's love affair with markets was probably inevitable. Their leadership experience with Enron had been in an operating environment characterized by ever-expanding markets and steadily rising revenues. Skilling and Lay deftly portray markets as virtuous, positive, advantageous. They seem intent on conditioning readers to believe in this axiom: Enron must profit enormously because it is market-savvy and market-responsive. Yet, just about anyone who has been in business knows that markets are fickle. They are subject to macroeconomic influences beyond the control of the management of any company. Indeed, the strong notion of "market" that permeates the letter is more akin to a metaphorical market than any real one.[11] This metaphorical market evokes a dream of pure competition and full information, while the real markets in which Enron played were characterized by monopoly power and asymmetric information.

Skilling and Lay seem to have been caught up in thinking that Enron was so influential that it was immune to the effects of recession in the macro economy. Either that or they simply turned a blind eye to the prospect of a market downturn that would compromise the company's financial fortunes. Hubris is reflected in the imperialistic words used in the letter – it is a case of "Enron the Magnificent." CEO Skilling and Chairman Lay claim in this public document to be capable of making "Enron the right company with the right model at the right time" (lines 49–50). They demean their competitors by saying that "No other provider has the skill, experience, depth and versatility to offer" the services that Enron provides (lines 114–15). This seems to be an outward manifestation of a delusion, but the words have gone unchallenged.

We can also reflect upon the personalities of Skilling and Lay. From our close reading, they emerge as egocentric and hubristic. They invite the belief that Enron is unique and so strong, so well placed, and so advantaged that it will prosper without impediment. Enron is praised as a company immune to the economic slings and arrows that threaten its unworthy competitors. This prompts us to wonder whether Skilling and Lay were affected by a delusional psychosis.

No one confronted Enron with the letter's hyperbole and deceit, but had a closer reading been conducted at the time it was issued, and had Skilling and Lay been brought to account for their statements, more socially beneficial outcomes might have resulted. The

CEO-speak in the letter is astounding, provoking us to ponder how, as members of a literate and socially responsible society, we can tolerate such antisocial discourse from corporate leaders. But perhaps we assume too much when we characterize our society, and ourselves, as literate and socially responsible.

3

Framing Andersen

The collapse of the Enron Corporation yielded another rich example of CEO discourse: the written testimony of a prominent, influential CEO to the hearings of the Financial Services Committee of the US House of Representatives into a corporate failure.[1] That testimony, reviewed here, was provided by Joseph Berardino, the managing partner and CEO of Enron's independent auditor, the Big Five accounting firm Andersen (formerly known as Arthur Andersen).

As CEO, Berardino faced a difficult rhetorical challenge in preparing his written testimony. The Big Five accounting firms had been under attack by the Securities and Exchange Commission and a wide range of media commentators for not being truly independent of their audit clients. This was a consequence of large accounting firms providing the companies they audited with lucrative non-audit (for example, management advisory) services. Berardino had good reason to be mindful of this criticism as he prepared his testimony: in the fiscal year 2000 Andersen had earned $25 million from Enron for its audit and $27 million for its non-audit services.

By the time Berardino appeared before the House of Representatives committee, on 12 December 2001, the Enron affair had become an economic and social crisis, and a political hot potato.[2] He would have been well aware that his testimony was likely to be used in future (and pending) litigation against Andersen.[3] The accounting firm had recently paid huge amounts to settle two other accounting and auditing disputes in which they were implicated: it had paid the Sunbeam Corporation us$110 million and Waste Management Incorporated us$220 million. The stakes were high for both Andersen and Berardino. Their reputations and futures were on the line.

Berardino's prospects were bleak. Financial-reporting deficiencies had played an important role in the Enron imbroglio. Income statements and balance sheets dating back to 1997 had been shown to be seriously in error.[4] There had been an appalling lack of fair disclosure. However, the ensuing financial-accounting portrait attested to by Andersen indicated only part of a larger failure of governance. In December 2001 the Web site of the public interest organization Public Citizen published an article containing numerous allegations of monitoring breaches involving us politicians and regulators as well as Enron's senior management and board of directors. It alleged that the "three principles of *transparency, accountability,* and *oversight*" were missing in the case of Enron.[5] Andersen, as Enron's external auditor, was firmly in the spotlight, widely accused of negligence and of failing to exercise its duty of care.

This was the context in which Berardino's written testimony was read to the committee. The testimony is reproduced in appendix 2; each of its 347 lines has been numbered. We begin by analysing how the testimony was framed and then explore the rhetoric of accounting it employed.

FRAMING THE TESTIMONY

The testimony employs framing as a strategy to focus on the issues and to encourage perspectives that are congenial to Berardino's rhetorical objectives. The idea of "framing" is important, since "An audience's interpretation of and reaction to a person, event, or discourse can be shaped by the frame in which that information is viewed."[6]

Framing has been studied in a variety of contexts, including politics,[7] decision making,[8] and assessing how auditors make judgments.[9] The power of rhetorical framing, properly designed, is illustrated by Bill Clinton's 1996 presidential-nomination acceptance speech. In it, Clinton "enacted rhetorical framing through skilful use of [the bridge to the future] metaphor," so that his "metaphors effectively functioned as frames for favorably interpreting himself and his agenda – as well as for unfavorably interpreting Dole and his agenda."[10] The concept of framing (and frames) in a communicating text requires the rhetor (here, Berardino) to "select some aspects of a perceived reality and make them more salient ... in such a way as to promote a particular problem definition, causal interpretation, moral evaluation, and/or treatment recommendation."[11]

"Frames" perform four important rhetorical functions. They define problems, diagnose causes, make moral judgments, and suggest remedies; and they function at the level of the "communicator," the "text," the "receiver," and the "culture":

Communicators make conscious or unconscious framing judgments in deciding what to say, guided by frames (often called schemata) that organize their belief systems.

The *text* contains frames, which are manifested by the presence or absence of certain keywords, stock phrases, stereotyped images, sources of information, and sentences that provide thematically reinforcing clusters of facts or judgments.

The frames that guide the *receiver's* thinking and conclusion may or may not reflect the frames in the text and the framing intention of the communicator.

The *culture* is the stock of commonly invoked frames ... [it is] the empirically demonstrable set of common frames exhibited in the discourse and thinking of most people in a social grouping.[12]

The opening twenty-one lines of Berardino's written testimony highlight how framing can be used effectively.

I am here today because faith in our firm and in the integrity of the capital market system has been shaken. There is some explaining to do. (lines 4–5)

The first sentence is effective rhetorically. It begins with a straightforward, no-nonsense assertion: "I am here today" – not an assistant, not another Andersen senior officer, but "I," the most senior member of the firm, taking personal responsibility and offering personal accountability. Furthermore, the parallel structure of "faith in our firm and in the integrity of the capital market system has been shaken" not only introduces religiosity (through the word "faith") but also partly obscures the unequal treatment of "our firm" and "the integrity of the capital market system": it is only that system in general whose "integrity" has been "shaken." But whoever did the shaking –

person or institution – is unidentifiable. The lack of agency in the explanation "has been shaken" serves as another framing device. If faith in a system's integrity has been shaken, then perhaps a systemic solution is appropriate rather than a solution that draws attention to the responsibility of a person or an organization.

The word "faith" is also important in a framing sense. Although in America there is a constitutional divide between Church and State, religiosity has always been at the core of American society – US currency, for example, bears the motto "In God We Trust." American political leaders routinely evoke religious themes in their speeches.[13] So "faith" might be regarded as a code word with religious overtones, and since it is used in the context of "the capital market system" – a metaphoric institution hallowed by generations of Americans[14] – it has important ideological and framing functions. Berardino's assertion that such "faith ... has been shaken" therefore implies the need for a religious reawakening.

Finally, the metaphor "has been shaken" promotes framing as well. "Faith," an integral part of the American identity, "has been shaken," but not broken, not destroyed. The shaking has already occurred; it is not ongoing, and so the foundation remains sound.

The "shaken" metaphor was likely quite effective due to the timing of Berardino's testimony – three months after 9/11. Americans were in fine jingoistic form, flush with the success of their anti-terrorist campaign against Osama bin Laden and his supporters in Afghanistan. They radiated self-adulation for the heroic resilience in the face of extreme adversity of American society and one of its central ideological icons, the Wall Street capital markets. The Dow Jones index had been "shaken," too, dropping from about 10,300 points on 10 September 2001 to 8,235 points on 21 September 2001. However, by the time Berardino presented his testimony it had rebounded to over 10,000 points. The metaphoric resonance of Berardino's term "shaken" with the financial fallout of the terrorist attacks had subtle framing effects. The metaphor inspired positive thoughts: America had withstood the terrorist assault and had "grown" as a nation; it could certainly withstand the demise of Enron.

The second sentence, "There is some explaining to do," has strong cultural echoes. It is structurally similar to "Lucy, you got some 'splainin' to do!" – Ricky Ricardo's despairing exhortation to his zany wife on the 1950s television show *I Love Lucy*. The show, still in worldwide syndication, and its leading characters and classic situations, are American cultural icons. So, Berardino's use of this stock, almost folkloric expression immediately after his introductory sentence regarding "faith" being "shaken" also serves as part of a rhetorical frame for his testimony. For an expression to work as a framing device, it must elicit widespread and immediate recognition, and this one clearly does – for the baby boomers on the congressional committee and the television-saturated American public it would have prompted fond memories of a simpler, happier era.

What happened at Enron is a tragedy on many levels. We are acutely aware of the impact this has had on investors. We also recognize the pain this business failure has caused for Enron's employees and others. (lines 6–8)

The euphemism "What happened at Enron" is cleverly deployed to refer to the reason for Berardino's physical presence. Berardino could have been more blunt and direct. He could have referred to the Enron collapse as a "financial reporting fiasco," a "litany of accounting oversight and management errors," or a "share price collapse and bankruptcy," among many other possibilities. But his words are much bolder. Indeed, they are even a bit presumptuous and arrogant. He delivered his testimony much too early in the litigation and investigatory cycle for anyone to state accurately "what happened at Enron." This suggests that Berardino framed his testimony as a sort of pre-emptive, knowledgeable, objective, unassailable, fact-based conclusion. In a sense, he is projecting a bold dare; he is setting up a metaphoric straw man for others to either accept or blow apart, if they can. By choosing such an abstract expression and by naming the event "a tragedy on many levels," Berardino frames it as something illusive and multi-faceted – something that exists on an intellectual plane, something that is not easily understandable from the vantage point of everyday experience. Thus, Berardino frames the account he is about to give as bound up in concepts, general principles, and complexity.

The next two sentences ("We are acutely aware ... We also recognize the pain ...") constitute a strikingly disingenuous, yet cathartic, *mea culpa*. While Berardino acknowledges the impact on "investors" and the pain of "Enron employees and others," he does not offer an actual *mea culpa*. Rather, he refers to the "impact" and "pain" these people have borne, and in so doing he privileges the investors. Investors are first mentioned in a sentence devoted to them alone. Employees and others, grouped together, follow as a sort of afterthought. The language starkly highlights this privileging. Though Berardino and his executive colleagues ("We"?) are "acutely aware of the impact ... on investors," when it comes to everyone else (the non-investor rabble?), they merely "recognize the pain ... caused." The asymmetry is pronounced.

Many questions about Enron's failure need to be answered, and some involve accounting and auditing matters. I will do my best today to address those. (lines 9–11)

These sentences continue the framing in two other, interrelated ways. First, although "Many questions ... need to be answered," only "some involve accounting and auditing matters." So such matters are depicted as a relatively minor part of the Enron story. This subtle ploy of exculpation invites the committee to regard Berardino's testimony (and Andersen's implication in Enron's failure) in much the same way. Second, since Berardino will "address" those "accounting and auditing matters," the implication is that they can be hived off from the many other questions and issues relating to Enron. This suggests that these matters are technical and somewhat peripheral to "Enron's failure." Notice, too, that Berardino refers to "Enron's failure" – there is no admission that an "I" or a "we" (that is, Andersen) has failed.

I ask that you keep in mind that the relevant auditing and accounting issues are extraordinarily complex and part of a much bigger picture. None of us here yet knows all the facts. Today's hearing is an important step in enlightening all of us. I am certain that together we will get to the facts. (lines 12–16)

The first sentence is a request, almost a plea, from the personalized "I" (Mr Berardino, who sits as a flesh-and-blood human being before the committee, who has come himself and not sent an underling, who has expressed his concern) to "keep in mind" two things.
   First, "the relevant auditing and accounting issues are extraordinarily complex." This perpetuates the hiving off of the auditing and accounting issues into an arcane, technical domain, understandable

only to the technically literate. Berardino's words could be construed as brave, but they are also patronizing – they serve notice that the vast majority of the audience (those present at the hearings and readers of the testimony) might as well fall asleep, since it is a truism of popular culture that accounting is profoundly boring. Such truisms have fine rhetorical deployment (especially in situations such as Berardino's stressful and unpleasant appearance before the committee). The "auditing and accounting issues," now framed as "extraordinarily complex," have lost presence – they have been rhetorically shifted to the background.[15]

Second, not only are the issues "extraordinarily complex," but they are also "part of a much bigger picture." By this time, the "auditing and accounting issues" have been framed such that, at least for Berardino (and perhaps for many in his various audiences), they have receded into the "ambiguous ground," which "has the inevitable effect of occluding the interpretations not selected."[16]

The three sentences beginning "None of us here yet knows all the facts" are also important in framing the testimony. The language used invokes a sense of community and inclusiveness ("None of us ... all of us ... together we ..."). The testimony thereby styles itself as being a community effort, a community issue; it's not about any particular individual or group. The noun "facts" assists in framing too, especially when considered in context with the "extraordinarily complex" auditing and accounting (which has already been shifted rhetorically to the background). Berardino asserts that there are "facts" to be "know[n]," and by means of a (metaphorical) journey "we will get to the facts." Facts become a destination, but there is some ambiguity surrounding the journey to reach them. Could the journey be a long one in which the hearing is only one of many "step[s]"? Or could there be a touch of hubris in the interpretation – Berardino "knows all" and he will get to the "facts" later in his testimony?

In all of this, the "facts" related to auditing and accounting are depicted as an "extraordinarily complex" part of "facts" as a whole. Thus, Berardino frames his testimony to minimize the connection of accounting and auditing (and thereby Andersen) to Enron's demise.

If there is one thing you take away from my testimony, I hope it is this: Andersen will not hide from its responsibilities. That's why I'm here today.

The public's confidence is of paramount importance. If my firm has made errors in judgment, we will acknowledge them. We will make the changes needed to restore confidence. (lines 17–21)

These five sentences are the final part of the introductory portion of the testimony. Berardino reinforces his earlier assertion that it is he – Andersen's managing partner and CEO – and no one else, who is "here today." His appearance demonstrates that Andersen "will not hide from its responsibilities." Acceptance of responsibility is seemingly personal and unequivocal – both admirable characteristics. There will, apparently, be no blame shifting here. This frames Berardino and his firm very positively. It will be useful to keep this in mind later, when we examine some of the accounting-related parts of Berardino's testimony.

The final three sentences, beginning "The public's confidence is of paramount importance," help the framing function as well. Berardino assigns "paramount importance" to "The public's confidence." But who is "the public"? Consistent with Berardino's earlier privileging of "investors," is it the investing public? Or does it also include employees and consumers? How are we to identify "confidence"? How are we to know what changes Andersen must make to ensure that "confidence" is "restore[d]"? These are empty, feel-good words and phrases, and Berardino can use them to fashion and justify almost any Andersen action plan. Who can argue against them? To do so would be to argue against goodness, against motherhood.

However, it is not just their hollowness that makes these three sentences rhetorically interesting as frames. They also set up the hurdles that Andersen wants to clear so that it can be regarded as rehabilitated. Berardino makes two promises. The first ("If my firm has made errors in judgment, we will acknowledge them") is a contingent one: they will "acknowledge" "errors in judgment" only if they have made them. The second ("We will make the changes needed to restore confidence") is an affirmation that Andersen will take action to have "confidence" (the public's confidence) restored. This frames Andersen as entirely willing to do the right thing.

But the first promise is an egregious one, since the identification of "errors in judgment" in accounting and auditing practice is not as straightforward as it seems. Furthermore, it is a weak promise, since the acknowledgment of error, of whatever sort, is nothing special, at least in a moral society. There is fuzziness to Bernardino's second

promise, too, since accountants and auditors frequently offer different judgments of the same situation. What standard of evidence
would be needed to elicit an acknowledgment of error from Andersen? But more than an acknowledgment is required – those who
have failed must actively redeem themselves. Berardino stacks the
deck rhetorically by creating Andersen's own redemption criterion.
However, as framing devices, these two promises are effective, particularly if the audience does not pay close attention to them.

THE RHETORIC OF ACCOUNTING

Many people still cling to the shopworn and dangerous notion that
accounting is objective,[17] and that it thus reveals some underlying
reality.[18] But the "reality" that accounting reveals is largely socially
constructed.[19] Nonetheless, through the medium of accountants
and managers, accounting has been remarkably successful in maintaining an aura of objectivity. Moore's example captures this nicely,
if surrealistically:

In August 1991, I had the dubious honor of being present in a room full of
two thousand academic accountants ... listening ... to the distinguished
economist Rudiger Dornbusch and his keynote speech to the American Accounting Association on the future of the global economy. Dornbusch ...
felt compelled to address the accounting-economics relationship at the beginning of his talk, and did so by saying, essentially, that the only thing factual that economists talked about was accounting information – everything
past that was mere theory.

A ripple of unease with the speaker's ignorance filtered through the large
audience as, theoretically aware or not, the assembled accountants noted
to themselves how wrong he was, since every accounting number ever produced has been, to say the least, highly contestable. What Dornbusch revealed in his off-the-cuff remark was that accountants had achieved, at
least in the eyes of certain major economists, the ultimate goal of the rhetorician's art: to be perceived as not rhetoric at all.[20]

So, there are potentially two intertwined levels of accounting
rhetoric in Berardino's testimony. First is the English-language rhetoric about accounting (Berardino's rhetorical framing assertion that
"the relevant auditing and accounting issues are extraordinarily

complex"). Second is the intrinsic rhetorical nature of accounting itself. These two levels of rhetoric have the potential to work together to promote certain perspectives over others. For example, Berardino devotes lines 50 to 245 (56 per cent of his 3,510-word testimony) to an explanation of three accounting issues.[21] His extensive and highly technical description of "what we know about ... [these] three particular accounting and reporting issues" (lines 33–4) is guaranteed to make the eyes of anyone but an aficionado of accounting arcana glaze over. But perhaps this is a cunning rhetorical ploy: undermine the resolve of your inquisitors and accusers by inducing ennui.

Berardino's writing style and word choice reinforce this interpretation. His previous framing admonition that the accounting issues are "extraordinarily complex" is apparent even when he makes a gallant attempt to simplify things: "The rules behind what happened are complex, but can be boiled down to this" (lines 74–5). What emerges is a text replete with accounting techno-babble: "The accounting rules dictate, among other things, that unrelated parties must have residual equity equal to at least 3 percent of the fair value of an SPE's assets in order for the SPE to qualify for non-consolidation. However, there is no prohibition against company employees also being involved as investors, provided that various tests were met, including the 3 percent test" (lines 74–80).

Berardino promises to metaphorically "boil down" the "complex" rules "behind what happened." But his audiences can plainly see that the accounting is so extraordinarily complex that even the "managing partner and CEO" of a Big Five accounting (and consultancy) firm cannot make it plain – cannot "boil it down." This is rhetoric at its most structurally effective. Berardino has framed his testimony – especially the accounting part (56 per cent of the total word count) – with his "extraordinarily complex" assertion. He then launches into the accounting testimony by posing the rhetorical question "First, did we do our job?" (line 24). Next, he confides in his audience, stating that he will "start by telling you what we know about three particular accounting and reporting issues" (lines 33–4). Then, despite his admirable efforts to "boil it down," his reading remains "extraordinarily complex." It is an almost incomprehensible mix of technical accounting and descriptions of a maze of transactions and Enron's labyrinthine structure.

The framing of Berardino's testimony is rhetorically effective. It establishes a platform on which Berardino can define the problem at hand, diagnose the causes, make moral judgments, and suggest remedies – all in ways that favour Andersen. The problem, for example, is framed as a systemic one, not one that that can be attributed to a specific organization or accounting firm. Not only that, but the issues are also portrayed as somehow illusive. Any implication that Andersen is part of the problem is marginalized by attempts to demarcate a domain for accounting and auditing that is too complex and technical for the uninitiated to enter. Furthermore, to elicit a positive response to his implied restorative action plan, Berardino uses framing to exploit religiosity, faith, and redemption; a sense of community; and a version of capitalism popular among conservatives.

What emerges in Berardino's testimony is the rhetoric of accounting working hand-in-hand with the rhetoric of framing. Berardino frames the accounting, which, in turn, frames the presence of Berardino and Andersen in this entire affair.

4

The Gates to Microsoft:
Exploiting Web Sites

Corporate Web pages should be recognized as rhetorical sites, for they seek to persuade their readers to buy a product, to form a favourable view of a company, or to adopt a way of thinking. The ultimate author of each Web page, of each Web site exercise in persuasion, is the CEO. Just as captains of ocean liners bear ultimate responsibility for what happens on their ships, captains of industry and commerce – CEOs – bear responsibility for what happens in their corporations. In the Internet age, CEOs are responsible for the words and images posted on their corporations' Web sites. These words and images are, indirectly if not directly, generated by CEOs, as are the major rhetorical themes pursued on Web sites. The content of a corporate Web site constitutes a form of CEO-speak with multiple audiences. It is to an aspect of this discourse that we now turn.

Bill Gates and Microsoft have become icons in the realm of computing and the Internet, but how do they portray themselves via the Internet? This question is important because the Internet is fashioning a new, rapidly growing, and influential corporate communication environment. Corporate Web sites, with their cybertextual trappings, persuasive properties, and technological idiosyncrasies, are the rage. So public interest will be well served by subjecting corporate communication on Web sites to critical scrutiny.[1] In this chapter we explore Web-based corporate communication, especially CEO discourse relating to financial-reporting matters.[2] We focus on the Web site CEO-speak of Microsoft's Bill Gates.

To improve our understanding of the perception-fashioning features of Web-based CEO-speak, we must appreciate the potential for Web site hypertext, metaphor, and rhetorical devices to influence social cognition and readers' perceptions. The conditioning cybertext of the CEO's narrative in a letter to stockholders, prepared especially as a Web document, is particularly relevant. Such narrative on corporate Web sites acts as a sort of cybertextual overture to the following (including financial) disclosures. Accordingly, we analyse CEO discourse on corporate Web sites primarily from a rhetorical perspective. It is important to do this, for Web site rhetoric can create an unobtrusive world view that might seem quite natural to those who visit such sites, and it can thereby affect perception. So, we look at a Web site as "a rhetoric of media forms in which one is persuaded not primarily to a given content, but to see the world with a certain perceptual, social, and cognitive emphasis."[3]

In adopting a rhetorical perspective, we view a corporation's Web-based corporate reporting, including its CEO-speak, as possessing two interrelated characteristics of a dominant discourse: privileged access and social-cognition influence. Privileged access to a communication genre (such as the World Wide Web) contributes to the power of those controlling access to such reporting. But herein lies a common misconception. The allegedly liberating, democratic qualities of the World Wide Web, which are said to arise from the accessibility of Web sites and global interconnectivity, are illusory: access to content control of corporate Web sites is usually limited to company management.[4]

The World Wide Web has strong potential to be a dominant discourse through its capacity to fashion social cognition, including the way we interpret, think, argue, infer, and learn.[5] Privileged access and social-cognition influence work together to affect CEOs' control over discourse. The implication is that Web-based text can be conceived in terms of discourse control. It has potential to be a form of social-action control over people's minds, and it can be engaged in the "management of social representations."[6]

The images used in corporate annual reports, particularly in the Internet versions of such reports (including CEOs' letters to stockholders), can be seen in at least four ways. They can be regarded as reflecting a basic reality; masking and perverting a basic reality; masking the absence of a basic reality; and constituting, rather than merely representing, reality.[7] The fourth way relates closely to the one adopted in this chapter, a perspective that is especially appropriate for Internet-based annual reports embedded in a new, more visual technology. Corporations reporting via the Internet now have a telepresence. The evanescence and interlinking of the World Wide Web seemingly replace the permanence and hierarchy that people are accustomed to with hard-copy financial reporting.[8]

Also, the Internet contributes significantly to "fast, distance-bridging media of communications and large, monopoly-scale developments around them."[9] This leads preparers and users of financial reports to view the world with a particular perceptual, social, and cognitive emphasis that differs markedly from that which characterized the pre-Internet era. Now, for many companies, the Web-based annual report is the primary one; the traditional hard-copy annual report is merely an adjunct. So, the demands of the cyberworld hold primary influence over the fashioning of such reports.

Microsoft's letter to shareholders, written by CEO Bill Gates, contained in its 1999 report is the principal Web-based annual-report text for close reading in this chapter.[10] It was chosen principally because Microsoft and Gates are profoundly influential forces in Web-based technology,[11] and Microsoft has realized and embraced the communication power of the Internet as the major medium for its corporate reporting.[12] Some of the CEO-text that a person seeking financial information about Microsoft might reasonably be expected to encounter when accessing its Web site is analysed to reveal how metaphorical and ideological features of a Web site can influence the way a company's reporting is interpreted. The following account focuses on the hyperlink pathway on Microsoft's Web site (as it existed in 2000) that led to the company's accounting reports.[13]

Microsoft's main Web page is an entrance portal to a bewildering array of information that (consistent with the World Wide Web itself) "contains multiple lines of association; that is organised not only linearly, but laterally; that follows, not a single hierarchical outline, but a labyrinth of continually returning, criss-crossing pathways."[14] We followed hyperlinks to the page designated "Investor Relations" and from there accessed the 1999 annual report.[15]

Our close reading exposes what Internet reporting by CEOs entails in terms of hypertextual rhetoric and perception fashioning. It reveals the persuasive language of the Internet and its potential to be a biased communication medium that is "ethically and politically, as well as perceptually and cognitively, laden."[16] Identifying the effect of rhetoric on communication bias is especially important because the Internet, behind its wholesome facade of electronic evanescence, has powerful but largely implicit persuasory and ideological properties.[17] These deserve to be acknowledged more keenly for the "subtle, hypermedia, seductive, hypertextual way" in which they fashion users' perceptions.[18]

Web-based corporate communication is newly emergent, idiosyncratic, and accessible virtually everywhere at once. Yet, while assessments of the technical nature, content, and quality of Web sites have received considerable attention,[19] there is a critical need for close readings of the sort we conduct here. The urgency of this task has become apparent as the communication relationship between reporting entity and reader has changed due to Web pages. The relationship is now based more on immediacy and hypertextuality; linearity and sequence are no longer so important.[20] Furthermore, Web site communication "has come to resemble advertising: transparent without depth, immediate and forgettable, simplified and consensual."[21] It is almost as if "audiences are commodities that are sold or delivered to advertisers," pawns to be manipulated within a "consumerist ideology."[22] Companies and their CEOs can exploit these Internet properties to change the way that readers interact with almost all corporate Web site information, including CEO text and financial reports.

The formerly staid and somewhat predictable realm of financial reporting and accountability has morphed into a creature of the Internet. Corporations reporting via the Internet can pursue subtle strategic disclosure policies to differentiate powerful audiences from less powerful ones,[23] and those with compatible interests from those with antagonistic ones. Web site reporting broadens and deepens the total available audience for a CEO's letter to stockholders. Stockholders and potential stockholders who previously relied almost exclusively on professional advisors now have far greater access to corporate information.[24] Employees, activists, and legions of others also share in this new access, as do professional analysts and other experts who have always known how to acquire such information. But Internet reporting is not the same as traditional reporting: it offers corporations a unique means of mediating differently with diverse audiences. This technique is illustrated in our close reading of Gates's letter to stockholders.

Hypertext creates a whole new language. For many readers of Web pages, dealing with hyperlinks has become second nature. But these readers are often unaware of the rhetorical properties and the "immense paradigm" that attaches to the Internet and its hypertextuality. The multimedia technology used on Web pages is more engaging and attractive than the technology of traditional hard-copy documents. Multimedia can increase the faith readers have in the factuality of data. Internet technology seduces readers through the phenomenon of telepresence. The Web site itself becomes the entire corporation in the minds of users, but it is actually an "evanescent, digital, electronic shimmer that is in a very real sense hyper-real."[25] Consequently, a danger of telepresence is that viewers of Web pages will base actions on the hyperreality of companies' Web sites "without realising that they are mere abstractions, metaphors and metonymies."[26] Web site telepresence increases the persuasiveness of the rhetoric employed.[27]

The potential for hyperlinks and hypertext to be rhetorical in nature should be acknowledged too. The positioning of hyperlinks and the content of hypertext are considered carefully by Web-page designers. They have incentives to construct corporate Web sites in such a way that the corporation maintains permanent control over the navigation habits of users by forcing them through pre-chosen pathways. This form of rhetoric uses aspects of cognitive mapping to optimize the order in which users are exposed to company information.

A close reading of CEO Web site text that uses any or all of four protocols – identifying metaphor, examining order and hypertextuality, dismantling dichotomies, and identifying significant rhetorical devices – can provide clues to the thinking of CEOs and corporations.

IDENTIFYING METAPHOR

Metaphors can increase comprehension by mapping an unknown term or domain onto a known term or domain. However, such cognitive mapping can be manipulated. It is vital to assess how metaphors are used in Web site disclosures to create an underlying narrative, and how this, in turn, influences users' perceptions and affects their decisions.

The rhetorical use of multimedia, metaphor, and hyperlinks are all strikingly apparent on the opening page of Microsoft's annual report,

which we accessed from the page entitled "1999 Annual Report" by clicking on the hyperlink "Start." This takes us to a photograph of CEO Gates and a moving graphic hyperlink with strong visual impact and important, if unobtrusive, metaphorical properties.[28]

The inscription (in "Bill's" handwriting?) "any time, any place, any device" (a hyperlink) attempts to connect Microsoft to the lives of readers of the annual report. This metaphor attributes to Microsoft a sort of eternal omnipresence, implying that the corporation will exist exogenous of time or place and will always be able to satisfy requirements. Thus, Microsoft indulges in crude self-eulogy, portraying itself as a universal, almost divine, being.

The photo of Gates and the accompanying "Bill's Letter" is a form of metaphor known as metonymy, and it has subtle conditioning effects. The metonymical implication is that "Bill Gates (good guy) *is* Microsoft." The perception-fashioning intent is to condition readers to accept that such a clean-cut, wholesome individual could only have sound and reliable financial information to report. How could anyone not trust such a fellow? But perhaps some didn't – those who saw irony in the juxtaposition of a smiling Gates and the major antitrust suit that Microsoft faced in the 1999 fiscal year. They would not have allowed such an image to distract them from the widespread impact on social and economic practices of Windows and other Microsoft products and their attendant ideologies.

The Microsoft Web site (and, remember, Bill Gates *is* Microsoft) is a form of social discourse. It plays on the human need for a stable grounding – a need that is becoming more pronounced with the accelerating pace of modern life. Ironically, many would attribute this acceleration to the digital disturbance created by the information technology that is Microsoft's lifeblood. In any case, for Microsoft to satisfy users' needs at any time, in any place, and with any device is a practical impossibility. Such an implication constitutes a subliminal reshaping of users' views of the company and is an attempt to influence the social cognition of readers.[29] We are invited to believe that Microsoft, by virtue of the global dispersion of its products, is an inevitable aspect of daily life; is all-powerful and all-conquering; and has the capacity to solve problems whenever and wherever they arise. The metaphoric imputation is that Microsoft is a community-spirited corporation blessed with invincibility, a corporation in which one can have faith.

The metaphor is enhanced by its presentation, in what is apparently Gates's handwriting, and by its mapping, next to a smiling photo of the man who has "achieved the unachievable." Gates's photo is positioned above a menu of eleven languages in which readers can opt to view the annual report. The implication is that Microsoft (Gates) is positioned on top of the world. This is a subtle means of accentuating the power of Microsoft and of inviting readers to have confidence in the corporation and its financial reporting. This visual imagery and handwritten message are softly seductive. They seem intended to influence perception and social cognition. "Bill" looks and dresses like an everyman (tousled hair, glasses); his handwriting is comfortably sloppy; thus, the visual metaphor is that Bill (and through Bill, Microsoft) is human, like you and me.

The metaphor offers an intriguing counterpoint to the array of powerful Internet-based tools at Bill's fingertips. Bill, though an average sort of guy, can nevertheless perform superior feats by taking advantage of the Internet with Microsoft products. Has Bill changed fundamentally? No – he's still good old "Bill" (just look at him!). Will *you* change? Of course not – you'll just be able to use any device, any time, any place to become a more productive (profitable) servant of the corporate economy, whether at work or at leisure. Of course, good old Bill is no average guy. He is widely identified as the world's richest person, with a personal wealth once estimated at about US$60 billion. But is he as benign and cuddly as Microsoft's Web site would lead us to believe? In August 2000, an interviewer described him as "pugnacious"; in the course of the

interview, he had displayed "a side of his personality which is usually kept under wraps: the mad-as-hell-mogul."[30]

Metaphor has been used to the saturation point not only in
Gates's letter to shareholders but also on the Microsoft Web site
generally. This constrains users' views with respect to Microsoft, as
illustrated by the headings in the letter to shareholders.[31]

Microsoft is built around you – making your world a better place.

This phrasing invokes the power of metaphor to bombard the user
with propaganda about Microsoft. Consistent with the general tone
of the Web site, the metaphor rhetorically epitomizes the power of
Microsoft. It does so by grounding the reader within his or her own
world and then rhetorically implying that Microsoft respectfully acknowledges this world and is powerful enough to build around it.

Connecting everywhere – be at the heart of what matters to you.

This claim is hyperbole. Microsoft cannot connect everywhere. On
a material level, Microsoft, no matter how powerful it is, cannot
connect an infinite number of combinations of places in the physical world. The concept of Microsoft being able to make connections within and between the areas of thought, reason, space, time,
or human emotion is also wild exaggeration. The word "heart," an
anatomical metaphor, is used to persuade readers that a charitable,
omnipresent organization (Microsoft) can help them realize a desirable self-image – they, too, can be at the very centre of things. But
perhaps an equally likely scenario is that readers will find themselves in a sort of new, unknown, and dangerous *Heart of* (Internet-
mediated) *Darkness*.

The metaphors saturating Gates's letter and the Microsoft Web
site contain partly hidden ideologies. The metaphoric allusions per-
sonify Microsoft as a kind of friendly uncle offering words of wisdom to reinforce a family-values ideology. The metaphor "your
business has a lot to tell you" (through voices arising from the use
of Microsoft products) has astrological overtones and a psychic-
force mentality. You, the reader, are encouraged to consider yourself
a lesser person who will become more worldly, urbane, and dexter-
ous as Microsoft helps you to extend your reach.[32] But when interpreting these metaphors we should remember that they are part of

the prelude to the hard (number-based accounting) data soon to be given in the annual report and are therefore intended to shape our views on the information the report contains.

EXAMINING ORDER AND HYPERTEXTUALITY

This protocol is beneficial in assessing how Web site presentation marginalizes certain information in readers' minds. The order in which information is exposed needs to be monitored. In analyzing CEO text or financial reports on Web sites, we must determine whether they are marginalized in terms of the overall Web site.[33] The hidden agendas likely to motivate the positioning and content of hyperlinks should be assessed critically. Specific characteristics to be examined include the positioning on the Web page of the menu (left, right, corner), the order of items within the menu, the persuasive properties of defaulted drop-down menus, ambiguous titles of menu items, the role of hyperlinks in disrupting sequential information processing, and the overall navigation technique (ambiguous direction versus a clear-cut path).

The placement of the hyperlink under "any time, any place, any device" at the beginning of the Microsoft annual report is pertinent. It could be construed as one of the initial components of the cognitive map used by Microsoft to prime users' responses to the information that follows. The text called up by clicking on this hyperlink originally contained a moving montage of photographs, although this has since been removed. As we noted earlier, this capacity is in itself a powerful rhetorical option. The photographs portrayed diverse individuals, apparently contented Microsoft stakeholders, whose common bond was Microsoft technology. There were suited men in offices, women with children in household settings, and men playing golf – all reinforcing gender stereotypes.[34] Despite the implication of Microsoft's universal reach, the photos were principally of white American males and some token Afro-Americans. There were seven males depicted and four females. Three of the four females (and none of the men) were depicted in the home.

These photographs, all visual metaphors, were a distraction from the sequentiality of the users' ingestion of the report. They appeared to be a rhetorical tool with a social-cognition purpose: to persuade users to a contrived perception of Microsoft. They were safe, conventional images that attempted to make readers feel an affinity with Microsoft's all-American values. However, an examination of these images helps reveal Microsoft's ideology. By denying the existence of other points of view Microsoft shows its resistance to disrupting existing power relationships.

A key tool for presenting a company in a positive light is the president's or CEO's letter. As is common practice, Microsoft positions its president's letter near the beginning of the annual report. What is unusual is the informal title: "Bill's Letter." The letter, the photo of a smiling Bill, and the handwritten metaphor ("any time, any place, any device") should be recognized as an attempt to personalize Microsoft as a threat-free friend – as a buddy. Readers could be forgiven for feeling comforted and confident that the information to follow is accurate. So, even before encountering the main body of the accounting reports, readers are subjected to a good-news overture – to a positive spin on Microsoft for which the persuasive properties of the Internet (hypertext, multimedia, and visual metaphor) are exploited.

DISMANTLING DICHOTOMIES

A dichotomy needing to be dismantled exists where mutually exclusive opposites are revealed to be linked inextricably. It is particularly important to identify any dichotomy that "is so central to a text's unstated, fundamental assumptions [that its analysis] can serve as fulcrum point for prying open deeply embedded alternative interpretations of the text."[35] An example occurs in the following cybertext statement from "Bill's Letter":

The PC-plus Era – you're free to work, live and play better.

This Microsoft-as-liberator metaphor implies that Microsoft will make readers "free"; it perpetuates the false dichotomy that computers create freedom. This dichotomy should be exposed and dismantled, perhaps through pointing out that computers have created dependence that previously did not exist. Because society's structures are now fully dependent on information technology, individuals are unable to choose the level of their interaction with technology. In a sense, everyone is bound by the rules of the computer age, enslaved rather than liberated.

Furthermore, there is another false dichotomy in Microsoft's silence about its monopoly over technology. Thus, while this metaphor suggests that Microsoft can help users be freer, it fails to acknowledge that users are dependent on Microsoft products to achieve this (apparent but illusory) freedom. Also, when we clicked on the hyperlinks to "Corporate Information" and the subsection "Microsoft Fast Facts" we found a purported overview of Microsoft,[36] and it harboured a dichotomy of fact/fiction that needs to be examined. The heading "Microsoft Fast Facts" implies that the information is factual and objective. However, this subsection actually uses facts to present a fictional view of the company, and so the true mandates of Microsoft are exposed behind their rhetorical disguise.[37]

IDENTIFYING SIGNIFICANT RHETORICAL DEVICES

Alertness to the impact of rhetorical devices on fashioning perception is important. Consider one such device, antanagoge, or the balancing of an unfavourable aspect with a favourable one. In contemporary idiom, it is the act of "putting a positive spin on something that is acknowledged to be negative or difficult."[38] An example is the saying "When life gives you lemons, make lemonade."

The primary entry page of the Web site and the CEO text throughout it contain a biased communication of the antitrust lawsuit, seemingly a deliberate exercise in antanagoge. Bad-news items are displayed among good-news items, in classic antanagoge fashion, to make the bad news appear more favourable. An obvious display of antanagoge is the declaration (found through a hyperlink under the "Antitrust Trial News" section of "Investor Relations") that "Shareholders have asked how they can become involved in Microsoft's defence of the freedom to innovate." Some shareholders have probably done this. But many other Microsoft stakeholders have not. By choosing to tell only part of the story, Microsoft has become a disingenuous purveyor of antanagoge. Not surprisingly, the site's design directs users to information that is favourable to Microsoft's position. This is another reminder that Web site corporate financial reporting, including CEO discourse, is a means of persuasion and a way of telling the version of a story that the company wants heard.

In order to identify rhetorical devices in Web-page disclosures, one should examine silences. One can understand text (including cybertext) better by researching the "blank spaces of the text, the spaces between the lines, the margins, the spaces between words."[39] In essence, one should examine what is not said to better understand the rhetorical features of a text. An important silence in the Microsoft Web pages concerns the effects of the antitrust case on the revenue, income, and viability of the corporation. At the bottom of the investor relations page are fourteen hyperlinks to other pages containing information on the antitrust trial, but none offer forecasted financial information. This omission is clearly inappropriate, considering the profound impact that the ruling to break up Microsoft would have on shareholders.

It is also crucial to identify any (cyber)text on a corporate Web site that fails to make sense. The effects of this void of understanding on users' overall comprehension should then be assessed. Furthermore, the (cyber)text should be examined for contradictions in meaning that disguise a story management is reluctant to disclose. For example, inappropriate visual metaphors could be used to contradict the actual financial position of the company.

The preceding protocols for close reading of CEO text on corporate Web sites demonstrate the idiosyncrasies of an Internet reporting environment and the potential for CEOs to fashion perception and to influence social cognition through rhetoric and metaphor. It is not the apparent surface meaning of accountability communication that should capture our primary interest; "it might be more useful and politically effective for us to concentrate our attention on making visible those practices and realities that are routinely kept out of sight."[40] These include the subtle and hidden rhetoric of Web site corporate reporting.

Internet-based reporting must be recognized more widely as an important medium through which CEOs influence social discourse, fashion perception, propagandize, and become part of the apparatus of manufacturing approbation of corporate activity. CEOs have "considerable power ... [to] command the techniques of representation."[41]

5

AOLTimeWarner:
Claiming the Internet Kingdom

CEO-speak is not necessarily a singular act of a lone CEO. It can be a rhetorical strategy that corporations and their senior executives have learned in order to construct "hyperreal communicative spaces that facilitate top-down control of public discussion and anesthetize the citizenry."[1] In this sense CEO discourse often represents a collective rhetorical pronouncement by an agglomeration of executives constituting a corporate elite. The subject matter, whether authored by a clearly identified individual or by a collective of executives under the guise of "the corporation," has an impact beyond the immediate domain of the issuing corporation. Such discourse can overtly and brazenly influence societal values, human behaviour, and public policy.

In this chapter we analyse the document that an executive elite at AOLTimeWarner proclaimed as its Internet policy. AOLTimeWarner (renamed Time Warner in 2004) is a major media corporation that arose from the 2001 merger of America Online and Time Warner (see table 5–1). Close examination of this policy can reveal a great deal about the corporation and the society in which it operates.

The example of CEO-speak we focus on is a policy document published on AOLTimeWarner's Web site (the document is reproduced in full in appendix 3). It manifests, and is a manifestation of, the corporation's strategic engagement with the Internet. Its content promulgates the corporation's policy governing Internet-based

Table 5–1
AOLTimeWarner's Businesses

Six Strategic Business Groups	Businesses	Operations
Interactive services and properties	America Online	AOL Services ("the world's leading interactive service, with more than 27 million members"); AOL Anywhere; AOL International; AOL@School; CompuServe; Digital City; DMS (Digital Marketing Services); ICQ ("the world's No. 1 – and fastest-growing – communications portal, with more than 85 million registered users"); iPlanet; MapQuest; Moviefone; Netscape; Spinner
Networks	Turner Entertainment Networks	TBS Superstation; Turner Network Television; Cartoon Network; Turner Classic Movies; Turner South; Boomerang; TCM Europe; Cartoon Network Europe; TNT Latin America; Cartoon Network Latin America; TCM and Cartoon Network/Asia Pacific; Cartoonnetwork.com; Atlanta Braves; Atlanta Hawks; Atlanta Thrashers; Goodwill Games; Joint Ventures: Cartoon Network Japan; Court TV (TWE-owned)
	CNN News Group	CNN/US; CNN Headline News; CNN International; CNNfn; CNN/Sports Illustrated; plus various other businesses, including joint ventures and Web sites
	Home Box Office	Several HBO and related businesses, including overseas joint ventures
	WB Television Network	The WB; Kids' WB
Publishing	Time Inc.	*Time; Sports Illustrated; People; Entertainment Weekly; Fortune; Money; Sports Illustrated for Kids; Teen People; Southern Living; Progressive Farmer; Family Life; Popular Science*
	Time Warner Trade Publishing	iPublish; Little, Brown and Company; and others
Filmed entertainment	Warner Bros	Warner Bros Pictures; Warner Bros Television; Castle Rock Entertainment; DC Comics; *MAD Magazine*
	New Line Cinema	New Line Cinema; New Line Television

Table 5–1
AOLTimeWarner's Businesses (*Continued*)

Six Strategic Business Groups	Businesses	Operations
Music	Warner Music Group	Warner Bros Records; Rhino Entertainment; Atlantic Group; London-Sire Records; WEA Inc.; plus several joint ventures
Cable systems	Time Warner Cable	"Time Warner cable is the nation's most technologically advanced cable operator … with over 90% of its more than 12.8 million customers in systems of 100,000 subscribers or more."

Source: Information posted on www.aoltimewarner.com

discourse, but no human author is identified. "We" is used thirty times in the document, so the author is some representation of the AOLTimeWarner entity. To assess the effect of authorial ethos on the document's rhetorical impact, we interpret "we" in two ways: first, as the top leadership of the newly merged entity, Steve Case and Jerry Levin, and their managerial acolytes; second, as something more ethereal and more potent – the new company, an Internet/media cultural juggernaut.

Clearly, setting the public agenda and determining public policy are objectives for which the public interest should be central. But should we rely upon leaders of Internet/media mega-corporations to realize them? They are part of an elite that is prone to defining the public interest in a narrow, self-serving, and perverse way. Consequently, pronouncements of Internet policy by leaders of mega-corporations closely allied with the Internet should be regarded as suspect. They demand vigorous and public challenge.[2] Such CEO-speak should be dissected thoroughly; its underlying assumptions, ideologies, and metaphors should be exposed. We should not allow a mega-corporate elite to hijack the policy debate about a basic public utility such as the Internet.

Our close reading emphasizes a rhetorical perspective in order that we may better appreciate how the AOLTimeWarner policy statement privileges the strategic perspectives of a mega-corporation. We show how the statement operates to influence public policy and social expectations.

THE LANGUAGE OF NEW CAPITALISM AND THE PRIVILEGED POSITION OF CORPORATE LEADERS

In the Internet age we are becoming what every 1950s Madison Avenue marketer dreamed of – a malleable, consuming extension of the corporate producer.³ We have no choice but to consume the product of whichever entity dominates our "new world." This is what makes AOLTimeWarner's policy document crucial: with it, the corporation is simultaneously constructing us and this new world. The AOLTimeWarner corporate elite would be delighted if we would help them achieve this according to their policy blueprint.

The "new world" is not a phenomenon of nature. Rather, it is built, perceptual nut by cognitive bolt, by AOLTimeWarner and many others – including ourselves, the consumers.⁴ "We" are simultaneously being made into suitable citizens of this world, citizens who enthusiastically, even unthinkingly, embrace being mediated by digital Internet and allied devices. This, of course, is a corruption of the word "citizen." AOLTimeWarner did not use the word in its public policy statement, instead referring to "consumer" and "subscriber." Thus, the document is designed to influence, as strongly as possible, the creation of this new world and its inhabitants.

There is a profound difference between the intelligence level and life experience of the executive elite who have authored (or overseen the writing of) the document and the rest of society. The authors are an isolated and "rich and powerful" elite. Korten maintains that "there is good reason to conclude that people who are isolated from the daily reality of those they rule are ill prepared to define the public interest."⁵ Proxy statements filed with the US Securities and Exchange Commission (SEC) by AOLTimeWarner and its predecessor companies in 1999 show the isolation of the corporation's leaders. For example, they disclose the annual compensation for CEO Levin. Stock options aside, Levin's 1999 remuneration exceeded US$10 million, sufficient to isolate him in the way Korten describes. And, since the processes of large corporations and the governments they influence (and with whom they share ideology) "are substantively linguistic processes,"⁶ close scrutiny of the rhetoric and the means of persuasion of AOLTimeWarner's Internet policy document is socially important. A privileged, cognitively isolated elite should not be permitted to construct the master discourse of a new medium.

THE AOLTIMEWARNER INTERNET POLICY STATEMENT

In a news release on 11 January 2001 announcing that the Federal Communications Commission (FCC) had approved the merger of AOL and Time Warner, the FCC's chairman, William Kennard, wrote: "Our conditioned approval of the AOL-Time Warner merger is significant not only for the size of the merger ... but also for its scope. AOL Time Warner is a marriage of old media and new media, content and conduit, 20th century know-how and 21st century vision. In a phrase, it's 'Convergence Illustrated.'"

Thus, sheer size, while awesome, accounts for only part of the merger's significance.[7] The portrayal of it as "Convergence Illustrated" and as a "marriage" strongly suggests that this Internet/economic entity is a whole new phenomenon. Anything AOLTimeWarner has to say about Internet and media policy must be taken seriously. This becomes even more evident when we scrutinize Kennard's description of the merger as a union of "content and conduit." He views the Internet and allied digital phenomena as an information conduit, an ideologically neutral e-channel through which a commodity (information) will flow, much like oil through a pipeline.[8] Although this is consistent with the "Internet is an information highway" metaphor, with all its cognitive entailments,[9] it mistakenly assumes that the Internet has a sole function – conducting information from one location to another – and disregards its immense social importance.

From the perspective of public policy, it is more realistic to think of the Internet and new media as the current manifestation of a dominant communication medium that results in a bias.[10] It therefore makes sense for us to expand our interest in new communications media such as the Internet "into the notion of media of communication as a theory of expressive forms" in which "a medium is not simply a technology, but the social relations within which a technology develops and which are re-arranged around it."[11] The rhetorical context of the AOLTimeWarner Internet policy statement – most particularly the fanciful "conduit" image that apparently structures the federal regulator's cognition – makes critical analysis especially important.

RHETORICAL FEATURES

The following discussion of several of the rhetorical features of the
AOLTimeWarner Internet policy statement (reproduced in appendix
3) is illustrative rather than exhaustive.

The expression "the Internet Century" is used in the title of the
document and at line 32. Like the term "the American Century," it
has echoes of a new beginning, perhaps even a manifest destiny.
Neither the "Democratic Century" nor the "People's Century"
await us – the "Internet Century" does.

"Internet" is spelled with a capital letter throughout (it appears
seventeen times). Capitalizing this term has been common practice
since the mid-1990s, but why? Typically, the names of persons and
geographic locations and revered non-corporeal entities or places
(God, Heaven) begin with a capital letter. We do not capitalize
"computer" (a physical thing), or "air" (which is physical, all
about us, invisible, and essential to life). So, the rapid and almost
universal acceptance of capitalizing "Internet" is a rhetorical and
social coup that is exploited and reinforced in AOLTimeWarner's
policy statement. The capital signifies that this is an entity that de-
serves respect. The difference between "internet" and "Internet" is
no trivial matter, since, as Kenneth Burke has pointed out, the very
act of naming is consequential.[12]

The preference for the word "Internet" rather than a term like
"computer-linked telecommunications system" is a rhetorical and
ideological one. Its lexicological sharpness and artistry obscure the
social implications of the Internet.[13] Indeed, this descriptive naming
has a certain magic to it: "How objects, feelings, and events are
named affects orientation, interests, perspectives, and pieties.
Whether we ... call a foreign movement 'freedom fighters' or
'rebels' has a profound implication for policy formation with respect to that other group in another country; each term, with its historical and ideological baggage, is highly suggestive of a policy.
Naming can be an intentional or unintentional act. Naming something 'our common mission,' for example, suggests, whether intended or not, that those opposed to it in any way are peripheral or
perhaps antagonistic."[14]

Consequently, using "Internet" in the policy statement is far from
an innocent, neutral act. Once AOLTimeWarner's many publics, particularly its consumers, speak conventionally and matter-of-factly

about the Internet, the corporation's policy struggle is almost won: the Internet exists as a social entity, a social fact of life. It is deserving of everyone's respect to the extent that we honour it by beginning its name with a capital letter.

A fundamental change is taking place in the media and communications landscape – a change made possible by the Internet and the advent of new ways to connect, inform and entertain that we only dreamed of even five years ago. (lines 3–6, first paragraph)

This rhetorically fascinating, punchy, and action-orientated first sentence in the policy document leaves no room for debate. The "change" train has left the station, and we had better all be on it. This change is so fundamental that it affects the landscape of media and communications. And what is more fundamental than a changing landscape – the (physical) place in which we live and breathe? Furthermore, this change is depicted as good, because it is "made possible" by the technologically virtuous Internet and "the advent of new ways to connect, inform and entertain that we only dreamed of even five years ago." Because new things are almost always good, at least according to our advertising-saturated culture, we are invited to conclude that connecting, informing, and entertaining are socially virtuous as well.

The word "advent" and revelations of the "fundamental change" made possible by the Internet evoke the powerful rhetoric of religion.[15] This "change" was stuff that "we only dreamed of even five years ago." Since we typically daydream about desirable future states, call an attractive person a "dreamboat," and refer to nice things as "dreamy," all this sounds exceptionally good.

Does the inclusive "we" in line 5 refer to AOLTimeWarner? Or does it refer to every one of us – the potential beneficiaries of the abundant good things bestowed by all this terrific stuff? It is impossible to tell. "We" is used thirty times in the policy statement. Each time, except in line 5, the context clearly indicates that "we" is AOLTimeWarner. The ambiguity in this paragraph is rhetorically slick, because the sense can be either inclusive or exclusive.

The first unambiguous reference to humans outside of AOLTime-Warner is in line 11, where the word "consumers" is used. It occurs twenty-five times in the document, far more often than any other word referring to non-AOLTimeWarner humans. The textual content

Table 5-2
References to "Consumer" in AOLTimeWarner's Internet Policy Statement

1 and 2	"Broadband connections that enrich the quality of online content like digital music and movies and broaden the distribution of news, information and entertainment … wireless services and handheld and household devices that make these products and services available to **consumers** anytime and anywhere – these are just a few of the exciting new opportunities **consumers** can already access and enjoy" (lines 7–12).
3	"In short, a new world is emerging – a more converged world, a more interactive world. At AOL Time Warner, we want to lead this new world, not only by providing our millions of readers, viewers, listeners, members and subscribers with instant access to a breathtaking array of choices in content and ways to connect, but also by spurring the development of innovative products and services that benefit **consumers**" (lines 17–22).
4	"As the Internet has become increasingly central to people's lives, AOL Time Warner has established the strongest **consumer** protection and privacy standards in the industry. Our commitment to ensuring children's online privacy and security is a centerpiece of our public policy agenda: from putting in place special parental controls that help parents guide their children's online experience, to working within our industry to increase public awareness, provide families with valuable new tools and resources for the Information Age, and teach young people what they need to know to have a safe, enriching experience in cyberspace" (lines 88–97).
5	"We are committed to upholding fundamental principles of notice and choice in our business practice and to helping establish industry-wide standards that benefit the development of the online medium and **consumers**" (lines 98–101).
6 and 7	"Ultimately, industry, government, and **consumers** share an interest in building confidence in the online medium through robust, market-driven policies, and we will continue to engage in dialogue with policymakers and **consumer** advocates on these important issues" (lines 102–5).
8 and 9	"AOL Time Warner has a history of recognizing and respecting the privacy of our customers online *and* offline. We have led private sector efforts to build workable mechanisms that address **consumers'** concerns about the safety and security of their personal information, while fostering **consumer**-friendly marketing practices tailored to individual tastes and preferences" (lines 106–11).
10	Efforts such as the Direct Marketing Association's Privacy Promise – which AOL Time Warner adheres to and helped to create – illustrate the successful execution of an industry-led program that offers the **consumer** clear information on how information is used and specific actions they can take to direct its use (lines 112–16).

of each of the first ten uses of "consumers" and "consumer" in the document is reproduced in table 5–2.

Consumers are variously regarded as passive receptacles into which Internet content can be poured, once they make (correct) purchasing decisions. These consumers merely consume what is on offer; they have been constructed to fulfill AOLTimeWarner's economic necessity. They are portrayed as beneficiaries of mega-corporate righteousness and munificence, rewarded for buying more products from AOLTimeWarner; and the corporation is depicted as a kindly uncle who dotes on his nephews and nieces. AOLTimeWarner seems to imply that there is a common good and a single world view. It notes that consumers may have an axe to grind, a point of view, and in this they will require advocacy. But how much of the genuine dialogue envisaged by AOLTimeWarner will actually occur?

In short, a new world is emerging – a more converged world, a more interactive world. At AOL Time Warner, we want to lead this new world, not only by providing our millions of readers, viewers, listeners, members and subscribers with instant access to a breathtaking array of choices in content and ways to connect, but also by spurring the development of innovative products and services that benefit consumers. (lines 17–22, fourth paragraph)

The fourth paragraph reveals the "fundamental change ... in the media and communications landscape," mentioned in lines 3–4, to be something even more fundamental. The change is to bring a "new world" with "entirely new industries" (referring back to lines 14–15). So, it is not just the landscape we inhabit that is changing (and changing fast), but also the very terra firma on which we stand. When our world changes, everything changes. But, again, these changes are portrayed as good, because this new world is "more converged" and "more interactive" than our old one. "Converged" implies that we're all coming together – and this sounds nice. "Interactive" implies that we're going to be active (and "active" is good, both physically and mentally). But, even better, we'll be "*inter*active," and this implies mutual benefits. This naming dovetails nicely with the name "Internet."

More importantly, the fourth paragraph contains rhetorical dynamite. AOLTimeWarner asserts "we want to lead this new world." There is no ambiguity about the "we" here. AOLTimeWarner wants to "lead" everyone else (its billions of readers, viewers, listeners, members, and subscribers?). This is classic rhetoric of hierarchy,[16] albeit a hierarchy of two levels: "leaders" (AOLTimeWarner) and "followers" (everyone else).

AOLTimeWarner claims that it will provide "instant access to a breathtaking array of choices."[17] It indulges in a rhetoric of development, progress, and journey by "spurring the development of innovative products and services that benefit consumers." So, the leader of this new world regards the vast majority of humans as economic caricatures in need of gratification through instant access to a stupendous number of choices. This assertion is again characteristic of the rhetoric of development, progress, and journey. The notion of journey is representative of a very basic and pervasive motif: the event-structure metaphor.[18]

However, the destination of the proposed merged company is hard to discern. It must be reached via a journey into unknown territory, and that journey must be undertaken by organized, self-confident leaders and acquiescent non-leaders. They must move forward towards the greater public good. This notion is nicely captured by the "becoming" metaphor and the illuminating image of a "wagon train" travelling across the hostile, virtually limitless American frontier.[19]

AOL Time Warner believes that a few basic principles should guide the development of a new public policy framework for a new world. (lines 260–2, "Policy Guidelines")

The use of "believes" softens and humanizes AOLTimeWarner. After all, to believe is much softer than to know, to declare, and so on. Only real people believe, and belief evokes the notion of faith, perhaps in a religious sense. Such an evocation is rather subtle, but it is effective in introducing a mild form of evangelical capitalism. Belief in a few basic principles sounds simple enough – nothing too complex or confusing – and it's consistent with the "few basic principles" that "guide" religious people.

Rhetorically, this sentence is astounding in its assertion that "a few basic principles should guide the development of a new public policy framework for a new world." Here, "new" is exciting, but it needs taming. The sentence is spare but deeply evocative; it seems to address core ideographs of American life.[20] It contains a religious metaphor, too: "belief" with a pathway to salvation ("a new world") through the divine guidance of "a few basic principles" (the Ten Commandments?) that are administered by AOLTimeWarner.

The policy statement outlines four such "basic principles":

1. Public policy should foster individual choice and empowerment in the economic and social dimensions and rely on individual decision-making for determining the products, services and content available from media sources and on the Internet. Practices developed in the crucible of the private sector and the marketplace can best direct the development of these creative industries. (lines 263–8, first basic principle)

This principle is far from "basic." Its meaning camouflages a strong ideology. The word "empowerment" conjures images of positive energy and activity, but individuals in the "Internet Age" will not be "empowered" in any free-ranging, unencumbered sense. Their "empowerment" will be restricted to the narrow options laid out for them by "media sources and on the Internet."

The document claims that the practices of the "private sector" (that is, the mega-corporate elite) will "best direct" development of creative industries. Moreover, the "private sector," along with the "marketplace," is likened to a "crucible" – a powerful metaphor that evokes a melting pot from which good things emerge, a receptacle in which a diversity of ingredients is transformed into gold.

2. Public policies should be market-driven and industry-led. Policies should be developed collaboratively, with input from industry leaders, government officials and, perhaps most importantly, consumers and other stakeholders. Public or private gatekeepers should not be allowed to prevent new entry, deny business opportunities or limit the free flow of information. (lines 269–74, second basic principle)

The opening normative assertion that "Public policies should be market-driven and industry-led" slides quickly over complex issues, such as the meaning of "market." Indeed, "market" has a curious status in a world dominated by mega-corporations that seek to destroy competition and convert the "market" into a series of internal administrative mechanisms. This raises the issue of how the word "market" (as well as variations "market-driven" and "marketplace") is employed throughout the document. The word is probably better re-garded as an ideograph.[21] It often bears an at least partly hidden ideological burden.

The sheer size and scope of AOLTimeWarner (table 5–1) indicates that its market is radically different from that described in introduc-tory economics textbooks: the small-producer-facing-a-given-price market. To build rhetorical capital by drawing upon the positive emotive meaning that "market" holds for many people is to pervert the word – but this is naming in full bloom. If we are convinced through benign naming that the powerful machinations of AOL-TimeWarner are merely the operations of a simple firm in a compet-itive market, then an impressive rhetorical turn has been achieved. Far from being a juggernaut, AOLTimeWarner appears to be just an-other economic producer competing in a market, like the greengro-cer who competes in the town-square produce market.

3. Where government involvement is determined to be necessary, policies should be technologically neutral and narrowly tailored, to ensure that the information, entertainment and interactive industries are permitted to re-spond to consumer tastes and preferences for news, entertainment and communications and that the value of the unique, interactive nature of this new converged and networked medium can be fully realized. (lines 275–81, third basic principle)

The essential rhetoric of development, progress, and journey is har-nessed here to argue that the determination of Internet public policy should be left to the private sector rather than governments. The language is telling. There is the grudging concession that govern-ment involvement may be "determined to be necessary" – presum-ably by some misguided soul who is unaware of the virtues of a free-wheeling private sector. We are implored to view government involvement negatively, as "neutral" and "narrowly tailored." The implied corollary is that private-sector involvement will have much more positive outcomes – uniqueness, interactivity, and the capacity for "full realization."

But all this mildly hysterical free-market language emanating from those seeking to dominate economic and social activity and to privatize everything that moves is part of a game laden with ideo-logical and social implications. This can be shown in many ways, but we focus on the "narrowly tailored" metaphor. It expresses a normative ideal on the part of AOLTimeWarner, even in those instances when government "involvement"[22] is "determined to be necessary."[23] A "narrowly tailored" business suit constrains movement; unfettered roaming is prevented, at times to the extent that discomfort or even minor pain results. What a view of government! Keep it under wraps, but if it gets out, dress it in something close to a straightjacket.

4. Policies should be designed to ensure that all segments of society and all countries of the world have access to the potential economic and social benefits of entertainment, information and communications capability – and that this new networked and converged medium becomes as essential to our daily lives as the television and the telephone, and even more valuable. (lines 282–7, fourth, and final, basic principle)

This "principle" is staggering in its faux idealism and hypocrisy. AOLTimeWarner paints itself as a company of compassion, concerned with "all segments of society [labour unions? anti-globalization radicals? the Internet-illiterate? the destitute? bad governments?] and all countries of the world [the dirt-poor ones?]." AOLTimeWarner invokes the rhetoric of religion to portray policy as something akin to the Salvation Army, dispensing charity to all who are in need, without question. But, incredibly, it confesses to wanting the "entertainment, information and communications" dispensed to be essential – that is, it wants everyone to develop dependency on the Internet and related new devices. Disturbingly, this is to be "even more valuable" than current dependencies, indicating that AOLTimeWarner has no qualms about potency.

The use of "our" in this "principle" suggests that the managerial elite at AOLTimeWarner wants to join the rest of us to experience the media becoming "as essential to our daily lives as the television and the telephone, and even more valuable." But how can AOLTimeWarner both join with us as our daily lives are rendered Internet-friendly and (as it insists in lines 17 and 18) lead this new world? Perhaps what appears to be an implausible metaphysical trick is just good bluster, as AOLTimeWarner toggles between an exclusive ("lead") and inclusive ("our," in a universal sense) representation of itself?

In sum, the AOLTimeWarner public policy statement entreats the "public" (portrayed as passive purchasing receptacles of AOLTime-Warner products) to acknowledge a belief in certain basic principles (the rhetoric of religion). The "public" is entreated to follow a "leader," the corporate elite at AOLTimeWarner (the rhetoric of hierarchy), on a journey to find greater fulfillment in some utopia (rhetoric of development, progress, and journey). It is vital to highlight such rhetoric, for it helps us to make sense of the words of CEOs and to expose the critically important, deceptive, and insidiously self-serving nature of AOLTimeWarner's policy statement.

The new communications age is one in which society will have to reconstitute itself: it is the age of the Internet, an age dominated by mega-corporations such as AOLTimeWarner.[24] In that context, the rhetorical devices employed by private, powerful executive elites to construct "us" and the "new communications age" in ways that render us disenfranchised, pliant consumers in an Internet-mediated world are very important. If we are to be citizens committed to democratic values in the twenty-first century, we must take with utmost seriousness the "bias of communication."[25]

6

IBM and the Privileges
of an Internet Soapbox

Especially influential is the explicit and implicit CEO-speak on the Web sites of multinational Internet-gatekeeper corporations – the purveyors of enabling software (Microsoft), enabling hardware (Nortel), and major media companies (AOLTimeWarner). These companies have comparative advantages in terms of technical know-how, global recognition, and financial wherewithal. This permits them to use their corporate Web sites as soapboxes.

Even more importantly, such companies have a privileged capacity to shape knowledge, fashion an Internet culture, and influence social relations through the way that their (often subtle) messages are heard and seen. By virtue of their size, importance, and expertise with computer and Internet technology, they are able to influence the millions of people who access their Web sites. A primary means for them to do this is by "educating" those who visit their corporate Web sites – that is, by using the Internet as a teaching device. There is a naturalness to the corporate Internet taking on the role of educator. But is this function being exercised well and without prejudice by the CEOs who bear ultimate responsibility for it? Is the education undertaken on corporate Web sites (ultimately a form of CEO-speak) being implemented neutrally? Or is it merely propaganda intended to convert the public to a particular ideological, cultural, and social perspective that benefits the company and its CEO?

In this chapter, we examine an instance of Internet teaching by an Internet-savvy corporation, International Business Machines Corporation, better known as IBM. We subject IBM's Web site to close readings in order to understand how the corporation – and, indirectly, then-CEO Louis Gerstner – endeavoured to teach financial accounting via the Internet. The site we examined is IBM's "Guide to Understanding Financials."[1] Our examination revealed that a private, self-interested corporation was engaged in teaching about sensitive public and social phenomena such as costs, financial statements, and annual reports. Here we explore the seductive nature of the hyperreal pedagogy in IBM's guide in two ways: first, by performing a technical critique of the guide; and second, by examining the guide's rhetorical features, especially its use of metaphors as visual rhetoric.

What is IBM (and its CEO) really doing here? It is a company that is held accountable by regulators and society, at least partly based on its financial statements. It reports to shareholders and analysts with those financial statements. But we observe it teaching about financial accounting via its powerful Internet site for free. To teach is an important, belief-forming activity, especially when the teacher (IBM) is a powerful and respected institution and its teaching is done via the Internet free of charge. But, more crucially, what it teaches is how to interpret the language – the accounting language of financial statements – by which it (the teacher: IBM and its CEO) is to be held accountable. This is a monumental conflict of interest.

THE RHETORIC AND BIAS OF THE WEB

The technical and factual deficiencies of the content of the IBM guide, whether deliberate or inadvertent, are rhetorical devices too. One of the guide's most striking features is its failure to mention the existence of controversies over financial accounting and annual reports. Neither is any mention made of vexing, unresolved issues in the field of accounting – of our vain search for "singular and clear concepts of income, wealth, capital, assets [and] liabilities ... that tally with the phenomenon of commercial intercourse."[2] Nor is there is mention of the various debates related to accounting standard setting;[3] or of the fact that there are different ways to account for changing price levels; or of the effects of different ways of reporting the financial affairs of groups of related companies. While these and similar topics cannot be covered fully in a basic introduction, their omission gives neophytes a distorted view: financial accounting and reporting appear unimpeachable, complete, and accurate.

The guide evokes an innocent, simple world, long past, and invites belief that annual financial statements are reports exclusively for shareholders, current and potential. It does not allude to the wider reporting and accountability responsibilities of a company – to employees, governments, consumers, and the environment. IBM's obligations to this extended group of stakeholders, and the resulting liabilities, are not acknowledged. None of the devastating critiques of financial reports published in recent decades are mentioned.[4] It is as if they never existed. The guide presents a sanitized view of financial statements. There is no reference to their lack of timeliness, or of the limited extent to which financial statements drawn up in accordance with generally accepted accounting principles (GAAP) depict financial wealth, operating performance, and the market price of a company's stock. Furthermore, the argument that published annual financial statements are nostalgic, backward-looking documents lacking in relevance for contemporary decision making is not broached. IBM's guide merely reflects the conventional wisdom of the 1960s.

Thus, we are presented with a view of annual financial statements that bolsters IBM's entrenched culture and corporate persona: that is, it leads us to envision a large, imperious, patriarchal, risk-averse leviathan that is ignorant of the outside world and slow to adapt. Two major deficiencies of the guide reflect IBM's "elephantine mass and its insularity."[5] First, the guide is oblivious to the last thirty years of scholarly accounting literature. Second, the lists it provides of other information sources are incomplete to the point of being misleading.

The inadequacies of the guide can be illustrated by highlighting several of its many unjustified sweeping statements. The neophyte reader is encouraged to believe that "Most analysts agree that the financial statements, financial ratios, and other comparative measures offer the best starting points for evaluating a company." This is bad advice. Any analyst who puts much faith in ratios constructed from financial statements prepared in accordance with GAAP is misguided, because such ratios are generally a poor indicator of financial prospects. The numerators and denominators of these ratios are based on information derived from the application of a counterintuitive and bizarre set of rules (GAAP) that produce measures lacking in any reasonable sense of contemporary monetary equivalence.[6]

So, the guide is based on an outdated, largely discredited view of conventionally prepared published financial statements. It does not address the extent to which those statements reflect current market measures; have information content;[7] are the product of earnings-management and discretionary-accounting policy choices;[8] indulge in "foozles," "feral" accounting,[9] and "big bath" accounting;[10] and engage in other dubious and highly idiosyncratic practices. These limitations are captured in the various critiques of accounting published over the years by leading scholars.[11] Thus, reading the guide is like being caught in a time warp. Its reassurances about the relevance of financial information should not go unchallenged, and it certainly should not be offered as pedagogic fare to unsuspecting readers.

The guide states that a balance sheet "shows what the company is worth at that set date." Alas, no. This is incorrect according to any conceivable interpretation of the word "worth." It ignores measurement controversies about such things as tangible and intangible assets, ranging over several decades. Readers' common sense ought to prompt them to reject the view that all assets (for example, "goodwill" and "future tax benefit") on a balance sheet are "worth" the money-of-account amounts listed. Yet readers are encouraged to assume that such assets could be exchanged for an equivalent amount of material money – cold, hard cash. For some assets, there is equivalence between money of account and material money, but in most cases there is not.

Finally, the guide claims that "The auditors make sure that the financial statements are complete." How can auditors be expected to do this? What criteria of "completeness" are used? "Completeness" is a philosophical idea, or perhaps an emotional experience. To portray it so simplistically seems almost pernicious. Further, the guide states that "The audit is an attempt to determine whether a company's financial statements report the company's financial status accurately and reliably." No attempt is made to explain how fraught with assumption and equivocation the terms "accurately" and "reliably" are in this context. Even allowing for the introductory nature of the guide, some mention of this and of the equivocal nature of GAAP is surely warranted.

The guide not only contains misleading statements, but it also misleads by omission. No mention is made of the generic financial-accounting problems related to revenue recognition, or of controversies surrounding some of the revenue-accounting choices that IBM has made.[12] Furthermore, the failure to explain the difference between accrual-accounting models and cash-basis-accounting models is likely to mislead readers, as is the failure to make clear that expenses cannot be equated with cash outflows.[13] The nexus of expense, cash flow, and cost becomes a veritable Bermuda Triangle for those struggling to fathom the basics of financial statements.

The guide creates a deceptive impression of financial accounting's accuracy, completeness, understandability, and relevance. It ignores the plethora of critiques of GAAP-prepared financial statements. But our anxiety about IBM's financial-accounting Internet pedagogy arises only partly from such commissions and omissions. There is also considerable cause for concern about the fate of neophyte readers cast adrift among the guide's metaphors.

A CRITIQUE OF METAPHOR

The guide's metaphors of accounting and business "are coded messages that are used to justify an implicit ideological stance."[14] An examination of these metaphors helps us to understand how an implicit ideological stance affects the teaching of a sensitive subject like financial accounting.

Verbal Metaphors

There are many verbal metaphors used for rhetorical effect in the IBM Web site guide. A recurring one is "a company is a person." According to the guide, a company, like a person, "performs," has a "history," has "strengths and weaknesses," will have "future successes or problems," and has "long-term health." Furthermore, like people, companies have intentions and can own and owe things. Companies can be "healthy and mature," have "growth spurts," "need money to grow," and have cash as their "lifeblood."

Other verbal metaphors are "financial statements are a language" ("the language of financial statements may at first seem mysterious, even intimidating"); "financial statements are containers" ("The statements contain the financial information for a publicly held company"); and "financial statements are pictures" ("the statement is like a snapshot because it shows what the company is worth").

Most of these metaphors have entailments that could influence the perceptions of financial accounting that neophyte visitors to the

Web site develop. The verbal metaphor "a company is a person" suggests that companies have lives of their own; need sustenance; must be at liberty to pursue their destinies; have fundamental rights and freedoms; can mature or wither; and have strengths, weaknesses, foibles, and financial status. Such metaphorical entailments could induce readers to acquiesce unknowingly to the rhetoric of "the market" (Carrier 1997), especially those who have never reflected seriously upon corporations and their impact on society. A concern for neophytes faced with metaphors prompted Postman to ask, "Do I exaggerate in saying that a student cannot understand what a subject is about without some understanding of the metaphors that are its foundation?"[15]

Visual Metaphors

The guide also makes important use of visual metaphors for rhetorical effect.[16] The first page features the well-known IBM logo in the upper-left-hand corner – the natural place for a Western reader to begin a new page. On the right-hand side of the top strip is the word "guide" in a prominent font; and it reappears in an even larger font almost directly below the IBM logo. It is hard to ignore the pictorial metaphor "IBM is a guide." This top strip, with the IBM logo on the left side and the word "guide" on the right, appears on each of the guide's pages. Some of the entailments of this metaphor are that IBM, like a guide, shows the way; is knowledgeable; is understanding, trustworthy, and non-threatening; is able to navigate through all types of terrain and weather to reach a safe haven; and knows where we should go and how best to get there. "IBM is a guide" in a larger sense, as well. It guides readers not only through the uncertainties of financial statements by means of this Web site, but also through the unknown and potentially hostile terrain of new technology.

However, the performance of the guide is inconsistent with the metaphor. The IBM guide does not live up to expectations. Our content-only critique exposed many technical and related shortcomings. The guide points out that it is intended "for people with little experience reading financial statements or annual reports" and that it will "cover only the fundamentals of accounting and financial reporting." Novice readers are reassured that the guide will help them make "sense" of accounting numbers and feel "comfortable"; it will allow them to "get friendly with" financial-statement language, which might otherwise seem "mysterious, even intimidating." But in attempting to do all of this the guide is superficial and misleading. It does a considerable disservice to inexperienced readers by failing to alert them to the dubious numbers, fictions, and solecisms of accounting reports.

The metaphor "IBM is a guide" is an example of a new metaphor, as distinguished from a conventional metaphor. Conventional metaphors structure "the ordinary conceptual system of our culture, which is reflected in our everyday language," while new metaphors "are imaginative and creative ... giving us new understanding of our experience ... new meaning to our pasts, to our daily activity, and to what we know and believe." New metaphors give us "new" meaning "through a coherent network of entailments that highlight some features of reality and hide others. The acceptance of the metaphor ... leads us to view the entailments of the metaphor as being *true*. Such 'truths' may be true, of course, only relative to the reality defined by the metaphor."[17]

And since "people in power [such as CEO Gerstner] get to impose their metaphors,"[18] we can offer some interesting speculations on the metaphor "IBM is a guide." Internet surfers of all ages and levels of sophistication encounter IBM's visual iconic metaphor at the top of each page of the guide. This suggests that in order to survive, thrive, and move towards a goal, we should model ourselves according to the guide; after all, what the guide says or implies is true, and we need its truths to safely navigate perilous waters. Thus, we should follow the guide's hyperlinks by clicking on the "next page" icon at the bottom of each page. But if we follow the guide's hyperlinked footsteps, we will privilege the earnings statement over the balance sheet, which, in turn, we will privilege over the cash flow statement. Rhetorical technique involves carefully selecting the order in which users are exposed to arguments and information.[19] So, if being first to occur denotes being first in importance, then our guide is inconsistent with the increasing emphasis in financial accounting on the balance sheet and on cash flow information.

Importantly, the new metaphor "IBM is a guide" is imposed on the Internet audience by a powerful organization, and it confronts all users who telecommute to the guide. It is consistent with the need for guidance through financial accounting and the technology of the Internet, and it is perhaps pervasive enough to influence acceptance of other visual and verbal metaphors residing in the guide.

The visual metaphor "a company is a sports team" also permeates the guide. It entails perceptions of playing hard but fair; favouring balance, co-operation, and strength; knowing and accepting the rules of the game; frowning upon individualism; eschewing personal goals that are inconsistent with team goals; training to achieve a winning performance; following a game plan devised by a coach; and valuing team members for their performance rather than for their humanity. For example, one page contains a graphic of a football umpire blowing a whistle – often the signal to stop play because of an infraction. Under this graphic the letters "S.E.C." appear, so that the Securities and Exchange Commission metaphorically becomes an umpire. The visual metaphor "the SEC is a football umpire" has these entailments: like an umpire, the SEC is impartial; the rules of business and financial accounting are, like the rules of football, clear and known to both sides; there will always be a winner and a loser, but there is also the possibility of a rematch; business, investing, and perhaps life in general is like a sports match.

If the new metaphor "IBM is a guide" can influence our acceptance of other metaphors on the Web site, then we might readily imagine a company as a sports team. If so, this has some interesting implications for accounting: it is relatively easy to determine who won a sports contest (the team with the highest score); and if an umpire can uphold explicit rules, then perhaps accountants and auditors can also.

The metaphor "financial statements are a lens" is established in the guide as both a verbal metaphor[20] and a visual metaphor.[21] Identifying financial statements as a lens strongly reinforces the inapt idea that an objective financial reality exists and can be represented by financial statements.[22] We have a piling-on of distorting metaphors: a camera, via its lens, gives an objective view of some aspect of reality; and, like a camera and its lens, financial accounting gives an objective view of financial reality. The "financial statements are a lens" metaphor is dependent on the assumption that lenses do not distort and cameras report faithfully. It seems consistent with the two visual metaphors discussed earlier – "IBM is a guide" and "a company is a sports team." A guide will teach neophytes how to bring the financial-accounting lens into focus, interpret the scores revealed, and decide whether the sports team is a winner or a loser. In a sense, we have a coherent, self-contained metaphorical structure, but one that is fragile and forms a poor foundation for understanding financial accounting. Neophytes need to tread carefully through the guide.[23]

WHAT PRICE THIS "FREE GOOD"?

IBM's Web-based financial-accounting guide contains much more than is apparent upon superficial examination. Its Web site paraphernalia (endorsed by IBM's CEO) constructs beliefs and helps shape public discourse. Like all curricula, IBM's "Guide to Understanding Financials" prompts debate. In many ways it "teaches" in many ways a technical subject called "financial accounting," and it does so in a superficially pleasing fashion. However, its impacts are unobtrusive and seductive. The guide teaches a particular kind of financial accounting – one that ignores social dimensions and renders unproblematic the numerous decisions and social structures that give rise to the "financials" for which IBM wishes to provide a "guide to understanding."

The "understanding" that emerges is likely to be superficial and dangerous – it will not admit contention, conflict, or alternative views. In its siren-like way, the IBM Web site calls to us: "Here's some easily digestible, Internet-based (therefore technologically virtuous) help in learning about a purely technical subject: financial statements. And it's free." But this allegedly free corporate financial-accounting pedagogy (and CEO-speak) carries the huge hidden cost of severe misapprehension.

7

Constructing Jack Welch, GE's Corporate Chieftain Incarnate

> Welch issued a stern warning: "I love you, and I know you can do better. But I am going to take you out if you can't get it fixed [achieve earnings targets]." [Jeff] Immelt [GE's current CEO] got it fixed. That's how GE works.[1]

In this chapter we examine the words of Jack Welch. Between 1981 and 2000, Welch served as CEO of the General Electric Company (GE), "a diversified services, technology and manufacturing company ... operat[ing] in more than 100 countries and employ[ing] 313,000 people worldwide." GE's roots can be traced back to a company founded in 1878 by Thomas Edison. In the last year of Welch's tenure, GE reported revenues of US$130 billion and net earnings of US$12.7 billion.[2]

We review Welch's CEO-speak as he inherits power, reaches the zenith of his tenure, and prepares for retirement, focusing on the construction of Welch's "brand name of managerial excellence." Welch is an important figure; he dominated GE and seemed to embody the ethos of corporate America. He constructed brand names for "GE" and "Welch" by managing the interplay between the iconic, historic GE corporation and his symbolic power as CEO. Sociologist Tim Hallett describes this as "the *power to define the situation* in which the interactions that comprise the negotiated order take place."[3] The result of this ongoing interplay was the continuing construction not only of Welch's brand name, but also of "the character of a company."[4] This is a concept very close, if not identical, to what today is often termed "corporate culture" or "organizational culture."[5]

Jack Welch rose from a working class background to become a charismatic corporate icon. Fawning media commentators identified him as the best businessman of his generation. He has been lionized as "the incarnation of a corporate chieftain,"[6] and revered in academic journals.[7] University of Michigan management professor Noel Tichy, a long-time observer of GE, has rated Welch one of "the two greatest corporate leaders" of the twentieth century, along with Alfred Sloan, former CEO of General Motors. But Tichy claims that Welch is "the greater of the two because he set a new, contemporary paradigm for the corporation that is the model for the 21st century."[8] Welch's CEO-speak therefore commands our attention.

In the London-based *Financial Times*/PricewaterhouseCoopers World's Most Respected Companies Survey for 1998–2002, GE was judged number one.[9] Not surprisingly, Welch was voted by his peers "the world's most respected business leader" from 1998 to 2002. Although he retired in 2000, Welch's reputation lingers on. Each year since 1983, *Fortune* magazine has published its America's Most Admired Companies list. From 1998 to 2002, GE topped that list. Its other appearances on that top-ten list during Welch's tenure as CEO were in 1983 (ninth), 1984 (seventh), and 1985 (eighth). The cause of all this admiration has been cited as GE's "long history of training great managers, its straight-talking celebrity CEO [and] its vaunted culture of entrepreneurship and achievement."[10]

Although Welch has been praised widely as an exemplary CEO, he is not regarded universally as an angel. Indeed, he earned the unflattering sobriquet "Neutron Jack" for his ability to eliminate people and their jobs while leaving GE's buildings intact. He has been described variously as ruthless, impatient, and intimidating; as possessing an "unbridled passion for winning"; and as being a "take-no-prisoners tough guy who gets results at any cost."[11] In 2003 the halos of Welch and GE slipped. GE was relegated to fifth place on the *Fortune* list, perhaps due to criticism of its accounting practices, "Wall Street's impatience with opaque financial statements after the Enron scandal," and the disclosure of the details of Welch's "gargantuan retirement package."[12]

As for the first of these factors, GE's accounting practices have been the subject of much critical commentary in the business press. For example, in an article on the Enron crisis published in the *Toronto Star* in 2002, journalist David Olive wrote: "The origins of the current era of fuzzy accounting can be traced to General Electric during the regime of Jack Welch, whose firm began in the 1980s to master the art of 'managing' the income statement to meet Wall Street's demands for predictable results – a tactic that distorts actual performance. Today, hundreds of blue-chip companies in North America succeed in hitting their projected numbers to the penny through the artful use of timely acquisitions or divestitures and abrupt reductions or hikes in R&D and marketing budgets – devices for manipulating earnings per share that win CEOs a reputation for surpassing acumen."[13]

Olive has not been alone in pointing out that Welch's actions contributed to the collapse of companies such as Enron. His unflattering commentary on Welch, while overblown, is nonetheless intriguing. It prompts further reflection on the Welch regime at GE. Was Welch playing a perverse game in which accounting language was both a means of expression and a creator of meaning? Was he "managing by the [fuzzy accounting] numbers"?

EXPLORING WELCH'S "MANAGERIAL EXCELLENCE"

To investigate the (rhetorical) construction of Corporate Chieftain Welch, we have closely read the twenty-one annual report letters of GE bearing Welch's signature as CEO.[14] We focus here on three specific letters to expose Welch's thinking during important phases of his tenure: the 1981 letter, which represents the birth of Welch as CEO; the 1991 letter, which represents the apex of his tenure; and the 2000 letter, which provides insights into his thinking immediately prior to his retirement.

Our principal intent is to explore CEO-speak during the tenure of a CEO and show how it evolves as the experience, track record, and confidence of the CEO develops. Of the three letters we discuss, only the 1991 letter is reproduced in full (in appendix 4); extracts from the other two letters (the 2000 letter is available in full on the GE Web site[15]) are cited and discussed. Our interest in the 1991 letter is based not only on the fact that it was written during the middle years of Welch's reign – a time when he had clearly established his mark on GE, corporate America, and the world – but also on its cultural uniqueness. Research into cultural differences between Japanese and American companies using semantic network analysis of the 1991 CEO letters of Fortune 500 firms demonstrates that

"Among the companies in this study, the location of General Electric is intriguing. It does not belong to either cluster [Japanese or American], rather it is located far away from the center ... Overall, the semantic structure of General Electric is extremely different from the other companies."[16]

We peer into Welch's CEO letters in an attempt to uncover some of his "thinking, values, strategies, and initiatives"[17] and to understand how Welch helped construct the brand "Welch." We regard the CEO letters fashioned during the Welch era as even more important than most such letters. Former GE executive Ian Wilson seems to concur. In his review of Welch's autobiography, *Jack: Straight from the Gut,* he claimed that "those who want a detailed account of the year-by-year evolution of Welch's strategy and leadership in transforming GE will, I am convinced, gain more from his chairman's messages in 20 years of annual reports. These remarkable documents, so different from the sterile numbers-only reports from most CEOs, are enlightening communiqués from the battlefront, documenting the evolution (as it occurred) of Welch's thinking, values, strategies, and initiatives."[18]

And in that autobiography Welch himself (presumably "straight from the gut") explained how important the annual crafting of GE's CEO letter was to him. He acknowledged that he was "especially grateful to Bill Lane, a guy who worked with me on the annual report letters every year. Bill took them as seriously as I did."[19] GE clearly regards them as exemplary, too – it has had the twenty-one letters bound and sends them out on request.

THE CORPUS OF WELCH'S TWENTY-ONE CEO LETTERS

The length of Welch's letters increased considerably during his tenure as CEO, from about 1,000 words in 1980 to just over 4,000 words in 2000 (with an average for the period of 2,620 words). It seems that as the company grew larger and more complex, Welch gained confidence and had much more to say. His CEO letter became a vehicle for conveying his philosophy and ideology.

The corpus of letters reveals much about how Welch conceived of the company and its relationship with shareholders. One way of gaining insight into this conception is to review how Welch used the word "company" year by year (see table 7–1). He deployed it to suggest a

Table 7–1
Some Features of Jack Welch's CEO Letters, 1980–2000

		Number of Case-Independent Occurrences of ...				
Year	Number of words in letter	"your company"	"our company"	"the company"	"GE"	"culture"
1980	1,006	5	0	1	6	0
1981	970	1	0	2	6	2
1982	1,236	0	2	2	14	0
1983	2,044	2	3	2	16	5
1984	2,392	3	3	2	12	6
1985	2,315	0	0	5	16	2
1986	2,192	2	0	5	30	0
1987	1,958	5	0	2	25	2
1988	2,875	0	3	7	22	2
1989	2,976	2	1	8	15	6
1990	2,695	0	4	9	11	1
1991	3,174	0	6	3	18	2
1992	2,978	0	0	2	17	2
1993	3,108	2	4	7	27	1
1994	2,571	0	0	5	19	0
1995	3,254	1	4	9	31	9
1996	2,992	1	0	3	27	16
1997	3,022	2	1	4	22	3
1998	3,155	2	2	4	22	13
1999	3,852	0	1	12	58	2
2000	4,249	0	4	11	37	9
TOTAL	55,014	28	38	104	451	83
MEAN	2,620	1.33	1.81	4.95	21.48	3.95

commonality of interests between shareholders and top management ("our company" occurs thirty-eight times); less frequently, he used it in constructions that suggest the dominance of shareholders ("your company" occurs twenty-eight times). The difference in frequency intensified over the last ten years of his tenure (he used "our company" twenty-two times from 1991 to 2000 inclusively, while he employed "your company" just seven times). And he often used words to suggest that GE was a type of being, a sort of person. Over his entire tenure he used "the company" 104 times and the name "GE" 451 times.

Speculating on the implications of this word usage over the twenty-one years, we suggest a continuum in which, linguistically at least, the agency of shareholders decreases from "your company" to "our company" to "the company."

HERALDING THE NEW CEO: THE 1981 LETTER

On April Fools' Day 1981, Jack Welch became chairman and CEO of GE.[20] The 1981 CEO letter (which appeared in the company's annual report for 1981) was Welch's first, and it was accompanied by a photograph of the new CEO that occupied almost the entire right-hand side of the first page.

We see Welch leaning lightly against a desk, framed by his two vice chairmen, who stand a foot or so behind him. All wear dark business suits, white dress shirts, and ties. Welch dominates the photograph.[21] The visual rhetoric of this photo is strangely revealing. Welch gives the impression that he is spoiling for a fight: his arms are folded, he has a stern look on his face, and his senior executives look like his henchmen. Since this photograph serves to frame the 1981 letter, one wonders why its subjects have assumed such an intimidating pose. Perhaps they were exploiting visual imagery to establish that the tough, no-nonsense Welch era had begun at GE – "We're here and we mean business! Don't mess with us!" The photo complements the letter's opening sentence nicely: "Your company's underlying strength and resiliency were reflected in its 1981 performance and year-end financial position." Indeed, in the photo Welch looks strong and resilient – just the type of CEO to lead the company to better sales and earnings at a time when, as the letter later tells us, there were "weak economic conditions in the United States and most foreign markets."

Metaphors of health and well-being abound in the 1981 letter, with references, for example, to GE's "underlying strength and resiliency" and to its businesses being "revitalized." These metaphors are deployed to help sustain what seems to be Welch's view of the corporate world in which GE operates.[22] In this world GE is a human-like entity; economic success is tantamount to biological health; accounting is a diagnostic tool that can measure good health; and GE, as a human-like entity, has a natural right to health, growth, and privacy. It is easy, yet perilous, to stretch metaphors in such a manner. Of course GE is not actually a biological entity;

neither is there anything particularly human about it. But the pervasive use of metaphors of health and well-being in the 1981 CEO letter, in combination with the reification of GE in the corpus of letters and Welch's later assertions, is intriguing. For example, Welch claims that "Corporations are human" and "easy targets."[23]

Such metaphors prompt several questions. First, if GE can be healthy or sick, can it also have a will of its own? The frequency with which words of reification are used throughout the twenty-one letters suggests as much. Second, how are standards of good health determined – who is the doctor, and what sort of medical philosophy does that doctor espouse (Western or holistic?). Welch writes that GE must have strength and resiliency; it must show sustained growth; it must be vital, lean, high-spirited, adaptable, and agile; and it must have entrepreneurial energy. But are these irrefutable indicators of good health? Third, does accounting, in the form of the financial statements, serve as a neutral reflection of health and well-being? (Keep in mind Welch's opening sentence: "Your company's underlying strength and resiliency were reflected in its 1981 performance and year-end financial position.")

What are the implications of this liberal use of metaphor and the resultant "humanization" of GE? How does determining this help us to understand Welch's notion of leadership as he embarked upon his tenure as CEO? Is Welch a (metaphorical) doctor or a (metaphorical) occupational therapist? Regarding (even subconsciously) a powerful corporation as human and accounting as a diagnostic lens with which to track the health, well-being, and growth of that corporation is fraught with social problems. This is because corporate law has evolved to the degree that corporations have become persons under the law, but the social effects of this legal status vary enormously. Large and powerful corporations, such as GE, that are subject to monolithic control by a small elite headed by a CEO could be regarded productively as psychotic persons or psychopaths.[24]

Furthermore, it can be dangerous to use accounting as an optical mechanism for reporting on the progress of such a "person" and constructing performance incentives. To do this is to ignore the social construction of accounting results and the reductionist nature of accounting numbers. When deployed with the corporation-as-person metaphor, accounting can narrow the world view of even the most esteemed CEO, as evidenced by the opening of the 1981 letter:

Sales of $27.24 billion were up 9% over 1980. Earnings of $1.65 billion – $7.26 a share – were also 9% ahead of 1980. Total assets exceeded $20 billion for the first time: our debt-to-capital ratio was 19.4%; cash and marketable increased 12%, to almost $2.5 billion.

These 1981 earnings were produced in the face of weak economic conditions in the United States and most foreign markets; they also came on top of record levels of expenditures for research and development ($1.7 billion) and Company investments in plant and equipment ($2 billion). A number of electronics and computer software companies were acquired, strengthening General Electric in two areas targeted for high growth.

Such a focus at the very beginning of the letter on "sales" and "earnings" reduces the complex world of GE – with its innumerable social and environmental aspects and its effect on hundreds of thousands of employees and millions of others – to abstractions articulated in accounting language. It recalls the proclamation in Enron's CEO letter that "Enron is laser-focused on earnings per share" (see chapter 2). Thus, large, complex corporate social institutions such as GE and Enron seem to be viewed by their powerful CEOs not only as fictitious legal persons but also (metaphorically) as real ones. Companies such as GE are steered, monitored, and evaluated by their leaders' use of accounting abstractions. This was how Welch's world view was framed as he began his tenure as GE's CEO.[25]

THE APEX OF WELCH'S TENURE AS CEO: THE 1991 LETTER

The 1991 GE CEO letter is a long, self-assured, and self-congratulatory epistle by an entrenched and confident CEO. It uses many rhetorical flourishes and subtle (and not so subtle) metaphors to evoke a company whose leader's vision and strategy has led to incredible financial feats – a company that can increase revenues, earnings, and productivity despite having to endure "one of the most brutal economic years most of us can remember" (appendix 4, lines 301–2).

The letter has three important structural elements. First there is the short, powerful, scene-setting, alliterative opening line: "1991 was a tough, terrific year for GE." Second is the textual highlighting, a sort of visual *aide-mémoire* using four keywords – "layers," "speed," "values," and "leadership" – in GE's management credo.

Third is an affirmation, by means of anecdote or parable in the final
paragraphs, that the commitment of the CEO (and through him, GE)
to "speed" and "boundarylessness" were "put to the test" at a
meeting of "450 men and women who lead our company," and
they "passed with flying colors."

   This is a bold letter written by a CEO firmly in control – one who
is unafraid to boast that he has led the company to an "astonishing
success" (line 106) and managed "a total transformation of a century-old Company culture" (lines 14–15). It is a strongly rhetorical
letter intended to convince readers that the strategic pathway
charted for GE by CEO Welch has been the right one. Welch presents
himself as a heroic corporate warrior who fights successfully for increased revenues and earnings in a tough, recession-affected global
marketplace, a gladiator who relishes the thrill of battle.

   GE, under Welch, is portrayed as capable of major feats – of
bringing down the barriers to enhanced productivity by embracing
the sagacity of its CEO. Welch is a buster of GE's functional boundaries and barnacled bureaucracies. He is capable of "de-layering"
GE, but the letter is silent on the implications of this euphemism for
employees. Presumably, the ethos is that employees are dispensable
in the quest for increased sales, earnings, and productivity. It seems
clear that these people are the ones who do not "deliver on commitments" (line 252), or who deliver on commitments but "do not
share [core GE] values" (line 256), or who do not have "fresh, recently tested ideas and proven team-building skills" that conform to
GE ideals (lines 123–4). Thus, conformity with the ideological values of the CEO (and through him, GE) is compulsory for those who
wish to retain their positions: deviation from core values is unlikely
to be tolerated. As well, GE is presented as a company fixated ideologically on serving the market and satisfying customers – it is prepared to do this even in the face of the challenges posed by its
metaphoric depiction of "global marketplaces" as "brutally Darwinian" (line 60).

   GE is a fast company, too. Speed is depicted as exhilarating, fun,
exciting – and, axiomatically, as leading to greater cash flow,
greater earnings, and higher market share. In Welch's 1991 letter,
speed receives prominent treatment. It is described as a force of nature – it can "propel ideas and drive processes right through functional barriers ... in the rush to get to the marketplace" (lines 125–
7). It is like a powerful genie, one that GE has learned to unleash

through "Boundary-busting" (line 137) and other anti-bureaucratic initiatives. Welch proclaims that "Speed exhilarates and energizes" (line 142); indeed, it "transcends" (line 138). He itemizes vehicles and activities that embody the "fun and excitement" "inject[ed]" by speed: "fast cars, fast boats, downhill skiing or a business process" (lines 142–3). But the first three items on his list are sources of individual pleasure. Indeed, the "speed" described in this letter seems suspiciously similar to the drug of the same name. This extolling of speed seems poorly considered. But perhaps it was well-considered. Speeding up business processes may have pleasing outcomes for the corporation-as-person and its leadership,[26] but not for those outside the corporate elite.

Welch's treatment of bureaucracy takes the form of a full rhetorical onslaught. He avers, "But to increase productivity, you first have to clear away all the impediments that keep you from its achievement – primarily the management layers, functional boundaries and all the other trappings of bureaucracy" (lines 68–71). He thereby frames the ensuing discussion by characterizing bureaucracy as underbrush that must be cleared away before "increase[d] productivity" can be realized.[27]

Some of the non-conventional metaphors that Welch uses in this demonization seem curiously inapt. For example, he writes that "Leaders in highly layered organizations are like people who wear several sweaters outside on a freezing winter day. They remain warm and comfortable but are blissfully ignorant of the realities of their environment. They couldn't be further from what's going on" (lines 72–6). This is silly. "[P]eople who wear several sweaters outside on a freezing winter day" are most certainly not "blissfully ignorant of the realities of their environment."

Welch also writes that "We've been trumpeting the removal of bureaucracy and layers at GE for several years now … Layers insulate. They slow things down. They garble" (lines 77, 87). Thus he associates the word "bureaucracy" with the word "layers." "Layer" is defined as "one thickness, course, or fold laid or lying over or under another" and "a stratum."[28] While such a rhetorical move makes Welch's sweater metaphor understandable (although still inapt), it is a narrow view of bureaucratic structure. There are undoubtedly bureaucracies whose individual units are separated by layers, inhibiting communication and response. But this is only one rather extreme mode of organizing. And if by 1991, about ten years into his tenure as CEO, Welch was still permitting such perverse types of bureaucratic structure to exist at GE, then perhaps he wasn't on top of his job. It seems more plausible that Welch, in his enthusiasm for "productivity growth," deployed whatever extreme metaphors were at hand.

RETIREMENT BECKONS: THE 2000 LETTER

Welch's letter to "Our Customers, Share Owners and Employees" for 2000 is remarkable and unconventional. In clear recognition of his impending retirement, it begins by establishing a theme of "transition to a new team," and it is co-signed by GE's next three most senior executives. Unlike most such CEO letters, it devotes few words to reviewing the actual financial and operating performance of the company. That information is treated as an annoying overture to the real business of the letter. It is dispensed with on the opening page – a series of dot points about revenues, net income, earnings per share, cash generated from operations, acquisitions, and stock price. This is followed by a six-page sermonizing essay on the cherished "values," "beliefs," and "behaviours" that GE has embraced under Welch and that (according to Welch) have made GE such a widely acclaimed and successful company.

The letter might be characterized as a reflective, almost biblical manifesto written by an almost godlike leader and endorsed by his disciples (the three executive co-signatories). Welch lays down his credo of values and beliefs and his formula for success in a valedictory scripture. He is a saviour who will "take us to the even better days that we know lie ahead for our company." He seems to intend his words to be regarded as gospel, as a set of commandments for corporate behaviour. He projects an unremitting self-belief and enormous self-confidence. There are few traces of humility, and those that appear ("We're no better prophets than anyone else") betray the writer's disingenuousness.

Welch begins by outlining his "values and beliefs," the most important of which is "Integrity."[29] He goes on to make the remarkable claim that "employees can take risks and believe us when we say a 'miss' doesn't mean career damage." This might be regarded as highly ironic, if not utterly hypocritical, by the many GE employees who have been dismissed for failing to achieve performance targets. He was called "Neutron Jack" for good reason. Indeed, later in the letter he argues that it is good management to routinely "remove" the bottom-performing 10 per cent of staff: not to do so is "management failure," "false kindness" – a form a "cruelty"!

What emerges is a CEO reflecting rather narcissistically on his leadership of a high-energy "can-do" company, a company capable of achieving anything it sets its mind to, a company that "always has the best people." It is fearless, unstoppable, and hyperactive: it has "leapt" into digitization, it is "energized" by change, it "energize(s) people and inspire(s) them to action." It does not hesitate "to use the awful word 'hate'"; it has sufficient "edge," or self-confidence, "to make the tough calls"; it has a "tradition of always delivering, never disappointing"; and it has withstood and benefited from a "punch in the nose." Furthermore, it hectors other companies for their failings: "one of the biggest mistakes large institutions can make is in indulging in the compulsion to 'manage' their size." Is there anything GE cannot do?

The CEO letters written during Welch's tenure are revealing documents, and we have just touched on a brief sample in this chapter. The words used, the metaphors deployed, and the themes evoked offer tantalizing glimpses of the ideals and ideas of a powerful corporate leader. He was a leader who for two decades exerted significant influence over his own company and a whole generation of corporate leaders in the US and abroad, writers in the popular business and general press, and academics. And his influence extended to government. For example, after announcing that he would step down as premier of Ontario, Mike Harris gave a speech in which he offered the following reflections upon his years "as CEO of the Province of Ontario":

I am reminded of Jack Welch, the former Chairman and CEO of General Electric. Welch's autobiography reviewed his 20 years at the helm of GE And I was especially struck by one comment. Near the end of his book, looking back on his entire GE career and the dozens of deals and changes that he personally oversaw and implemented, Welch writes: "Almost everything should and could have been done faster." Now, here was the man who made sweeping transformations to one of the largest and best-known corporations in the world. Who earned the nickname Neutron Jack for the extent of those changes. And yet one of his parting thoughts was, "Almost everything should and could have been done faster." From my own perspective, I couldn't agree more.[30]

But rapid change in large, complex human institutions – whether in a GE of 300,000 employees and millions of other stakeholders or in a Canadian province of twelve million people – is not something to be sought unreflectively, as a rhetorical end in itself. Our social, organizational, and other anchors could be damaged or destroyed[31] in a blind rush to embrace "the fetish of change."[32]

This close reading indicates the extent of Welch's influence and the risks that flow from it. Rapid change and its ally, speed, are only two of many concepts promoted by Welch as CEO of GE. Over the course of his letter writing, he also puts forward the notions that bureaucracy is distasteful, that competition is Darwinian, that accounting numbers are desirable indicators of success. These notions are ideological, political, and – since they are espoused by a powerful and influential leadership in a socially important medium (the CEO letter) – they help structure how people think about corporate governance, management control, and success. Consequently, their documentation and analysis are important. Such an undertaking contributes to public discourse or helps us to understand its absence.

8

Disney's Narrative as Personality Prism

CEO-speak is not just a contemporary phenomenon, but it also has a rich historical tradition. We demonstrate this by turning to Walt Disney (in his role as CEO of Walt Disney Productions) and examining his letters to stockholders in annual reports for 1940 and 1941. These letters were crafted during a crisis by a charismatic, yet complex business and cultural leader.[1] They reveal themselves to be accountability documents skilfully prepared to address the exigencies of the situation facing Disney. They are a prism through which we can view the world as Disney made sense of it, and – perhaps surprisingly – they demonstrate that he was a skilful rhetorician.

In 1940, Walt Disney's company had a pressing need to raise equity capital from the public for the first time. It wanted to fund a major expansion of facilities during a period of market uncertainty, war, and reported losses. Disney's letter for 1940 was the company's first letter to stockholders; it was a public and permanent document signed, and most likely substantially composed, by Walt Disney as CEO (perhaps with contributions from his brother, Roy).[2] It is a unique source of insight into the public persona of Walt Disney, a man once called "the most significant figure in graphic arts since Leonardo."[3]

THE SETTING

To appreciate the circumstances that gave rise to the letters, we must have some understanding of Disney Company history and the persona of Walt Disney.

Company History

In 1924, Walter Elias Disney, a twenty-three-year-old cartoonist, and his older brother, Roy, opened the Disney Brothers Studio in a Los Angeles storefront. They moved this small animation outfit to downtown LA in 1926, at which point it became the Walt Disney Studio. Although earlier ventures were characterized by the kind of hardships typical of start-up businesses,[4] the company achieved its first major success when its animated cartoon *Steamboat Willie*, featuring a new character called Mickey Mouse, made its debut in New York on 18 November 1928. Although Disney's cartoons achieved rapid popularity, by the early 1930s the company was struggling to contain rising production costs. However, the brothers negotiated some lucrative merchandising agreements, licensing images of Disney characters – such as Mickey – for use on manufactured items,[5] and they thus created "a new dimension in fashion merchandising."[6] The introduction of colour improved cartoon quality and led to an Academy Award and commercial success for the studio's first colour cartoon, *Flowers and Trees*. Other innovations, such as providing cartoon characters with unique, focused personalities (like the Three Little Pigs, Pluto, Donald Duck, and Goofy), appealed to Depression-era audiences.

Walt Disney then expanded into the feature film business.[7] His company's first feature-length animated movie, *Snow White and the Seven Dwarfs*, opened on 21 December 1937 and was a great critical and commercial success.[8] Disney undertook other animated features (*Pinocchio, Fantasia,* and *Bambi*) while continuing to produce cartoon shorts, and the company soon outgrew its facilities. Plans for a new, custom-designed studio were hatched in the summer of 1938, and the company (now with about 1,100 employees[9] and called Walt Disney Productions) moved into its new quarters in May 1940. The decision to concentrate on very expensive but potentially very profitable animated features prompted the company to raise funds through a preferred stock issue in April 1940. It published its first annual report in December 1940.

The Disney Persona

By 1940 Walt Disney was an international success. Indeed, even by the early 1930s he was as famous as the biggest Hollywood stars.[10] Mickey Mouse was "a national figure, an international attraction, and finally a cultural totem."[11] Critics from New York to Leningrad "gravely laud[ed]" Disney.[12] In 1934, his films were exhibited in eighty-eight countries, and he was dubbed "an international hero, better known than Roosevelt or Hitler, a part of the folklore of the world."

Fortune magazine's 1934 profile of Disney and his filmmaking operations portrayed Walt Disney as a mythmaker. His products enthralled audiences throughout the world by bringing them to a "delicate balance between fantasy and fact, poetry and comic reality"; they appealed to the simplest emotions. Nothing in a Disney cartoon was impossible – in them, "courage overcomes wickedness and fear; industry triumphs over dalliance; false ambition gives way to resignation." In sum, they were short morality plays. They epitomized "disneyfication" – "sanitized, safe, entertaining and predictable" entertainment.[13] Disney has been described as a moody, deliberately "ordinary" man who possessed "rural gusto and naïve fancy" and a wonderful imagination. He had high artistic standards; he made daring and innovative use of music, sound, and folk material; and he "mistrust[ed] the shoddiness and hypocrisy of the pseudo-artist." His personality was shaped by "a nostalgic yearning for romance or simple values" and a "frugal, authoritarian and moralistic" father.[14]

But Disney had a "darker side."[15] The *Dictionary of American Biography* claims that Disney became "self-satisfied, intractable, arrogant" and was "probably never quite the generous father of a gifted flock that he seemed on the surface."[16] "The discerning eye" could find in his work "breaches of taste, philistine wisecracks, a milking of the nostalgic mood, slipshod cultural references, a growing dependence on received folklore and other people's classics, and an increasingly slick technical achievement of rather tawdry effects."[17] Mickey Mouse was said to be flawed by a streak of sadism and *Fantasia* was judged by some to be a "pretentious hodgepodge." Disney was described as "both paternalistic and domineering ... he brooked no dissent, rewarding loyalists with favours and punishing dissidents."[18]

The Stock Issue

So, in 1940 Walt Disney Productions was a relatively small film production studio in terms of financial and tangible assets,[19] but not in terms of reputation, expectations, and innovation. It had just gone public by issuing 155,000 shares of preferred stock. As a consequence, the company became publicly accountable. Of particular interest is Disney's CEO-speak in his letter to stockholders included in the company's first annual report, for the fiscal year ending 28 September 1940. The letter was signed by Walt Disney as CEO and presented as the first main component of the annual report.

Disney was prompted to go public because the company needed permanent capital for its huge expansion program, which was nearing completion – a three-million-dollar, fifty-one-acre studio complex in Burbank, California.[20] Although Disney had a long history of reinvesting profits to sustain his operations and to improve the quality of future films,[21] the earnings outlook was bleak. By early 1940, earnings had taken an unexpected battering because of the lukewarm box office response to *Pinocchio*, difficulties in containing costs, and the war in Europe.

While the cinema-going public responded very positively to *Snow White*,[22] there was always a risk that after a brief initial success, such films would fail to sustain people's interest. The fact that *Pinocchio*, released in 1940, fared poorly demonstrated how challenging it was to produce full-length animated films with characters audiences would pay to see. The market for such films was new and unproven. Also, Disney was struggling to maintain profitability and keep pace with rapidly changing animation technology. He was confronted by market uncertainty and the considerable risks posed by *Fantasia*'s special sound equipment requirements. Maintaining control over costs while striving for better quality was a daunting task.[23] The war made it difficult to release pictures in European countries,[24] restricting the market for basic cartoon shorts and new features. Furthermore, currency regulations and fluctuations in foreign exchange rates reduced revenues from pictures already released overseas. And perhaps domestic cinema-goers were less inclined to spend their disposable income at the cinema because of the prospect of US involvement in the war.

So, at the time Disney signed the 1940 letter to stockholders Walt Disney Productions was in a precarious position. It had to master new technology. It had to sell a product with a potentially vast, but largely unproven market. The war in Europe seemed destined to create havoc with film distribution and markets, worldwide and domestically. Disney's tight control over every facet of the business was being strained by these challenges,[25] the rapid expansion of the company, and the need to raise funds through a public stock offering. To exacerbate matters, the company incurred a loss of $1.26 million in 1940. It was an opportune moment for Walt Disney to display the charismatic leadership for which he was famous, and he did so partly through words – the skilful rhetoric he employed in the 1940 letter to stockholders.

RHETORICAL QUALITIES OF THE 1940 LETTER TO STOCKHOLDERS

The Writer

In 1940, Disney was not just another corporate CEO writing a stockholders' letter for the first annual report of a small, new public company. He was a cultural sensation who had been written about extensively in major national publications like *Fortune*, the *New Yorker*, *American Magazine*, *Scribner's*, the *New York Times Magazine*, and *Time*. He zealously guarded his prerogatives to lead and to control the results of his genius,[26] but he had been compelled to issue shares because of his company's debt. How, then, might a cultural icon whose creative genius had long been publicly acknowledged approach the writing of a stockholders' letter, an accountability document required by the public offering that he was apparently reluctant to launch?

The Audience

While it seems reasonable to surmise that Disney's 1940 letter was an important part of the financial reporting intended for diverse constituencies (current and potential stockholders and creditors, financial intermediaries, employees, unions, competitors, and the public), perhaps the first among equals was the new group of preferred stockholders. Disney was in an invidious position. His company had just been thrown a financial lifeline, and he was confronted with crafting a document that would soothe the new preferred stockholders. While remaining alert to the fact that these people could constrain his authority, he had to acknowledge in the letter the various operating and marketing difficulties the company had faced and might face in the future, and he had to convince readers that top management (the Disney brothers) was firmly in control and leading the company towards success. In clear and compelling terms, he needed to analyse the company's performance and prospects and encourage unwavering support for his own leadership. His letter would serve as a tool for sense-making[27] for preferred stockholders and others interested in the company.

The Initial Substantive Section

The 1940 letter to stockholders is reproduced in appendix 5. Its second section, following immediately after the warm but respectful welcome and headed "New Studio," is reproduced here, with each sentence numbered for reference:

[Sentence 1] At the time of the sale of the 6% Cumulative Preferred Stock, the Company was constructing and equipping its new studio. [Sentence 2] This studio was substantially completed and equipped and virtually all of the Company's production operations were transferred thereto by the end of May, 1940. [Sentence 3] As a result of the increased facilities, the Company has been able to augment its production of completed footage by more than 100% and has succeeded in lowering the cost of production per foot substantially. [Sentence 4] Therefore, the Company will be able to carry out its new policy of releasing two or more feature subjects each year as well as a large number of short subjects. [Sentence 5] As a result of the reduction in costs, short subjects are now being produced at a figure which the management believes will result in profitable releases even though sources of income in certain foreign countries now at war are no longer available.

Sentence 1 links the preferred stock issue with the positive, forceful activities of "constructing and equipping." While the "ing" endings are a weak example of the rhetorical use of repetition (homoioteleuton), the effect is strengthened by words describing the fulfillment of a major task ("completed," "transferred," "succeeded") in the next two sentences. This is a very positive section of the letter, and it makes good use of forceful action words and strong direction. Indeed, sentence 4 assures stockholders that promises will be kept and that the company has a logical, rational plan, which is unfolding as it should. The following sequential linkage is established:

New financial resources from preferred stock issue

↓

New, larger studio

↓

Increased capacity and efficiency

↓

Lower unit costs

↓

Increased number of features and short subjects

↓

Expected profits

This piling-up of arguments in support of expected profits, rhetorically a sort of diallage, or a presenting of "several arguments to establish a single point," creates a sense of moving forward under an active, in-control management. And within the piling-up of arguments are other rhetorical devices. Repetition of the phrase "As a result of" at the start of sentences 3 and 5 interlaces two references to cost reduction. Such repetition verges on anaphora, whereby the same words "are repeated at the beginning of successive clauses."[28] Use of action-oriented, decisive words and phrases such as "At the time of the sale," "was constructing," "was substantially completed," "were transferred," "As a result of," "has succeeded," "Therefore," "will be able," "now being produced," and "will result in" is the textual equivalent of epitrochasmus – that is, "a swift movement from one statement to the next; rapid touching on many different points."[29]

There is also an almost completely self-contained five-sentence morality-tale narrative of the American success story in this passage. It seems fitting that Disney-the-storyteller would incorporate narrative into his stockholders' letter. After all, if important external and internal constituencies accept top management's strategic narrative, then such CEO-speak has served its purpose.[30] The uncertainty associated with the business is incorporated subtly, almost unobtrusively, by the words "substantially" and "believes" and the rather soft introduction of the threat to "sources of income in certain foreign countries now at war."

The story narrated in this passage seems almost as fictional as a Disney cartoon, and this makes the rhetorical quality even more interesting. The company had borrowed heavily so it could take advantage of lucrative opportunities by establishing new facilities and expanding its workforce. But cost-control problems, some market resistance, and the war had intervened, forcing the Disney brothers to issue preferred stock to reduce debt and obtain liquid funds. In light of this, Disney's use of rhetoric was adept impression management. He was portraying a mirage – an image of himself as in control of all dimensions of his company's affairs.[31]

"Effect of the War" and "Product"

The contrast between the letter's second and third sections is dramatic. While the second section is upbeat and optimistic, the third contains a series of negative news items about the impact of the war, characteristic of diallage. The first sentence – "The effect of the war in Europe upon the affairs of *your* Company has been serious and the full measure thereof cannot yet be determined" (emphasis added) – contrasts starkly with the final sentence of the previous section, in which, almost as an afterthought, the war is blamed for making "sources of income in certain foreign countries ... no longer available." This sudden shift may have stemmed from the problems Disney was encountering in his roles as leader and entrepreneur in 1940. He had an unpalatable story to tell in his company's first public annual report, especially since $1 million of the $2.6-million cost of producing *Pinocchio* had been written off during the year. Thus, first serving up bad news about the war (the effect of which had already been marginalized by the end of the previous section) could be regarded a deft use of order as a rhetorical device.

But the rhetoric has an even more subtle dimension. Disney refers to "the" company forty-four times in the letter. Only once, and in this section, does he refer to "your" company. In doing so, he brings home the implications of the bad news to shareholders.

His tone is almost accusatory, as if the shareholders themselves are somehow responsible for the bad news.

The letter begins with very good news related to increasing production, reducing costs, and anticipating profits – all due to factors presumably controlled by management. The next section describes the potential impact of the war in very general terms – all beyond the control of management. The following section, "Product," delivers the even more sombre news about *Pinocchio* and possibly *Fantasia*. Bad news about *Pinocchio* is first described as due to "the conditions prevailing throughout the world" – that is, as beyond management's control. Despite this, the letter mentions the company's growth ("the transition period through which the Company passed when it changed its policy of making one feature in two years ... to a policy of producing from two to four features a year") and the "discarded work of untrained personnel," "the schooling and training of personnel," and the "inadequate plant facilities at the old studios." The portion of the third section devoted to *Fantasia* reminds the reader that the company is an innovator, and that innovation sometimes requires changing strategies and revising profit expectations. The remainder of the "Product" section is a barrage of upbeat news about new animated features, cartoons in process, and other sources of revenue.

Disney's Rhetorical Use of Accounting

Disney displayed an innate understanding of the rhetorical capabilities of accounting in his stockholders' letter. Under the heading "General," he attacks the strictures of accounting convention by invoking a statement made in the company's prospectus inviting subscriptions to the preferred stock issue:

[Sentence 1] In considering the profit and loss statement of the Company, it is worth while to repeat the following statement made in the prospectus offering the 6% Convertible Preferred Stock: [Sentence 2] "The Company's principal income accrues according to the rapidity with which its features are exhibited in theatres and, accordingly, the relationship between dates of release and dates of accounting periods has in the past produced and will probably continue in the future to produce wide variations in earnings as they may from time to time be reported. [Sentence 3] This is made more pronounced by a program which contemplates the release of only one or two features per year. [Sentence 4] In connection with SNOW WHITE AND

THE SEVEN DWARFS, the Company adopted a policy of writing off the entire cost of the picture against the first revenues received, and the Company may in the future follow this policy with respect to all of its feature productions. [Sentence 5] Consequently, if any given accounting period closes at a time when revenues have failed to exceed the costs incurred in connection with the production of a feature released during such period, it is possible that a loss may be reported in such period notwithstanding the fact that an actual profit may eventually be realized on such feature."

In sentence 1, Disney appeals to the authority of the prospectus (a state-approved legal document) to add weight to the text. Such a rhetorical move is consistent with the central role that appeal to authority – or apomnemonysis[32] – which is often embodied in generally accepted accounting principles (GAAP), serves in modern accounting. The prospectus excerpt cited in sentences 2, 3, and 4 tells of the company's virtuous and conservative accounting, by which the entire cost of an animated feature is written off against the first revenues received. Sentence 5 suggests strongly that the resulting accounting losses are an artifact of the interplay between this conservative accounting policy and the arbitrary relationship of accounting periods and revenues. In effect, Disney signals the company's sober purpose by using a conservative accounting method,[33] but he then draws upon the prospectus to urge readers not to take the results of this accounting too seriously. Rhetorically, can he have it both ways? Can Disney draw upon the authority of accounting to influence readers and, at almost the same time, plead the arbitrariness of certain accounting conventions? It is not surprising that such a creative storyteller chooses to employ accounting, for it is a serviceable and elastic mode of representation and argument.

However, the conservative method of revenue recognition chosen by Disney had a decidedly non-conservative aspect as well. Feature animated films whose costs had been fully recovered could be taken off the shelf and redistributed; 100 per cent of the producer's revenues for these re-releases would go directly to the company's before-tax profits. This happened in 1940, when the income statement in the annual report included revenues of $103,526 from the reissue of *Snow White* but cited no costs, since they had been recovered in previous years. So, Disney's conservative accounting had a temporal dimension: it was very conservative in the years when feature film production activity was high and non-conservative once features were completed and re-released. The non-conservative dimension was unobtrusive during the crucial year of 1940.

In the 1941 stockholders' letter, Walt Disney again demonstrated his rhetorical ability to use accounting strategically. He constructed (or had his accountants construct) a detailed accounting comparison between the company's 1941 and 1940 results and included it near the beginning of the 1941 letter (see appendix 6). His purpose was to show that in spite of a reported loss of $789,297 in 1941, great progress had been made in that year. Such an unusual accounting schedule, placed near the front of his stockholders' letter, conditioned readers' perceptions of the rest of the letter and perhaps the rest of the 1941 annual report. It was an artful rhetorical move. The authority of the accounting information was conferred by the audited financial statements: in effect, apomnemonysis. When it was combined with "order," the resultant "harmony" was very persuasive.

The "Summary of the Balance Sheet and Income Statement" presented in the 1941 stockholders' letter was also rhetorically adept because it presented a mass of numbers across several rows and columns. Clearly, accounting materiality and rounding had not been embraced by Disney and his accounting advisors, because the financial data were cited to the penny.

Although this may have simply reflected Disney's typical attention to detail, it could equally have been a crafty rhetorical ploy. This so-called summary was a visual onslaught likely to repel all but the most determined of accounting-trained readers. Perhaps Disney created it as a visual metaphor for his frustration with complex accounting practices. As the product of a skilled graphic artist renowned for his beautiful images, the financial summary seems strangely bereft of aesthetic appeal.

It is not surprising that Disney's letters to stockholders are rhetorically well constructed. Walt Disney was a master storyteller, so why wouldn't he use this talent to tell his company's financial story during a period of crisis in a way that would garner a positive reaction from his audience? The author of any accountability document (such as an audited financial statement, a stockholders' letter, a corporate press release) has a vast array of rhetorical choices. Such choices, some of which are made subconsciously, influence the perceptions of the audience. Our analysis of some rhetorical features of Disney's letter merely touches the surface possibilities.[34]

METAPHOR IN THE 1940 LETTER
TO STOCKHOLDERS

The metaphor "the company is a sentient being on a purposeful journey traversing an at-times hostile environment" permeates the 1940 letter. This is evidenced by metaphoric language in the section headed "New Studio": "the Company was constructing and equipping its new studio"; "the Company's production operations"; "the Company has been able to augment its production"; "the Company will be able to carry out its new policy." These are instances of verbal reification, and they also attribute sentience and purposiveness to the company. Such ways of talking and writing about companies are commonplace, and because of this they are important rhetorically.

There are numerous other instances of reification. The company takes action (for example, in the "Product" section, "the Company delivered to RKO Radio Pictures, Inc."); it enjoys benefits (in the "*Pinocchio*" subsection, "there have accrued to the credit of the Company"); it creates saleable names and characters (see the "Short Subjects" section); and it has expectations about the future (in the "General" section, "the Company expects to have three new feature pictures in general release"). Perhaps the most important language manifestation of this metaphor is in the "*Pinocchio*" subsection, where Disney writes, "the transition period through which the Company passed when it changed its policy of making one feature in two years ... to a policy of producing from two to four features a year." Here we have a company that not only engages in the sentient activity of changing policy but also weathers a transition period in the course of its journey.

Calling a company "a sentient being on a purposeful journey traversing an at-times hostile environment" has several implications. The company knows best because it is capable of understanding and making decisions (through its CEO) about its goals; it knows which path to take through a hostile environment; and it knows how to adapt when circumstances change. Therefore, acknowledging the interests of other stakeholders is of limited use, because these stakeholders cannot be part of the being itself (that is, the company) unless they submit to the authority of the company as a sentient being – a strongly managerialist view. Furthermore, any obstacles in the company's path are adversaries, and goals are non-negotiable.[35] To show the consistency of these ideas in Disney's managerial discourse, we briefly re-examine the 1941 stockholders' letter (see appendix 6).

In the section titled "Labor Relations," Disney describes the company's journey as "beset by labor troubles." He ventures that in 1941, this obstacle to purposeful travel has occurred "For the first time in [the company's] history." The section describes Disney's view of the famous 1941 strike, a view that stands in sharp contrast to his hostile, and perhaps illegal, anti-union activity.[36] If we think of a company as a sentient being on a purposeful journey, then what do we think of the people who attempt to unionize and impede the journey? Disney characterizes the 1941 cutbacks that led to union activity and a strike as a "program ... designed to bring output in line with results reasonably to be anticipated from the distribution of the Company's pictures under present world conditions." He portrays it as a technical problem requiring a reasonable technical solution. Thus, the union advocates and strikers, who had several complaints about Disney's treatment of them,[37] were the source of the "labor troubles" that "beset" the company. Readers are given the impression of big labour and its goons ganging up on the company (the American Federation of Labor is mentioned, as are "secondary boycotts" and "'hot cargo' activities"). The arbitration award is described as being "imposed" on the company.

So, the metaphor established in the 1940 stockholders' letter is carried over to the 1941 letter and is consistent in its implications: unreasonable employees joined a union and went on strike, preventing the company from implementing a reasonable program to assist itself on its journey. Then, despite "Repeated efforts by the Company to effect a settlement," government intervened and arbitrated a settlement that imposed several bad things, further impeding the journey. However, "the plant is now operating smoothly."

Nonetheless, Disney was in no mood to see future journeys disrupted by what he regarded as ideologically perverted union behaviour. The 1941 strike is said to have caused him to become "a militant anti-communist" and, in the 1950s, "a [secret] special FBI agent charged with passing on information about supposed communist infiltration" of Hollywood.[38] His embrace of a business structure of vertical integration – in which his company controlled the production of film and television programs, their distribution, and the associated product licensing and retail merchandising – points to the adoption of the metaphor of the uninterrupted journey as a tangible business goal.

Disney's language and ideology are metaphorical: the company pursues its life journey largely by entering into transactions within the ambit of a metaphorical "free market." Anything that interferes with its freedom in this market will be treated with non-metaphorical hostility (as was, for example, the national labour union with which Disney's striking employees allied themselves in 1941). The fiercely independent, self-made Disney probably could not conceive of his company in any way other than metaphorically. His 1940 and 1941 stockholders' letters set out his ideology and philosophy of management and management control, and this discourse represented the way he made sense of the world.

PERSONALITY PRISM

The letters reviewed offer an accounting, a crafted story that portrays the tensions between the company's financial problems and Disney's creative, cult personality. They reveal Disney to be as talented at writing financial reports and accountability narratives as he was at creating animated cartoons and features. His letters to stockholders were designed to inspire the allegiance of new preferred stockholders, despite the fact that he resented having to go public. They reveal aspects of his thinking, especially about key social and economic institutions. Disney the accountant was as complex as Disney the cultural sensation. He was a skilled, yet subtle rhetorician who could strategically manipulate accounting data. He was not only a master storyteller in the context of the cinema, where he could exploit the glitz and glamour of visual and sound imagery, but he was also adept in a grey and glamour-free domain where few would ever imagine him: financial reporting.

A close reading of Disney's CEO-speak uncovers a "darker side" to the wholesome, friendly "Uncle Walt." The Disney who emerges in the CEO letters is an enigma – a cultural icon who was almost as skilled at producing financial narrative in a hard-nosed business world as he was at fashioning animation.

9

Nortel's "Remarkable" Letter

And now we turn to the CEO-speak of a "remarkable" CEO. On 10 March 2001, journalist Michael Den Tandt described a letter to shareholders written by John Roth, CEO of Nortel Networks, as "remarkable."[1] This would not have surprised many, for Roth had been named Canadian CEO of the Year in 2000 and inducted into Canada's Business Hall of Fame. *Time Canada* had designated him Canada's Newsmaker of the Year for 2000.

Many business commentators, media pundits, and investment analysts believed that Roth's company, Nortel Networks, epitomized the New Economy. In what seemed like the twinkling of an eye, it had transformed itself dramatically. No longer was it a staid, century-old telephone equipment manufacturing subsidiary of Canada's giant telephone company, BCE ("Ma Bell"). Nortel had become a vibrant global producer of fibre-optic networks and a high-tech success story in search of a new cyberspace persona.[2] It proclaimed that it would metamorphose from a vertically integrated enterprise into a virtually integrated one;[3] and it did so, very rapidly, between 1998 and 2000. Nortel placed saturation advertisements that asked "What do you want the Internet to be?" The portents were that Nortel was intending to somehow *become* the Internet for corporate North America. To fulfill these intentions, Roth had to create a public profile for Nortel that was consistent with its fresh new image.

In its annual 10-K report filed with the US Securities and Exchange Commission for its halcyon year of 1999, Nortel described itself as:

incorporated under the laws of Canada on January 5, 1914 as the Northern Electric Company, Limited, a successor to ... Northern Electric and Manufacturing Company, Limited, a telephone set manufacturing subsidiary of Bell Canada incorporated in 1895. The Corporation changed its name to Northern Telecom Limited on March 1, 1976 and was amalgamated with two wholly-owned subsidiaries on January 4, 1982 under the Canada Business Corporations Act. On April 29, 1999, the Corporation changed its name to Nortel Networks Corporation in the English language ... Nortel Networks is a leading global supplier of networking solutions and services that support voice, data, and video transmission over wireless and wireline technologies. Nortel Networks is focused on building the infrastructure service enabling solutions and applications for the new, high-performance Internet. Nortel Networks' business consists of the design, development, assembly, manufacture, marketing, sale, financing, installation, servicing and support of networking solutions and services for Service Provider and Carrier customers, and Enterprise customers. Nortel Networks' solutions and services are used by customers to support the Internet and other public and private voice, data, and video networks.[4]

Nortel was a boom business in the emerging dot-com era. Anthropologist Anna Tsing describes the investment climate of that era nicely, drawing on metaphor and simile to convey the climate that surrounds such businesses and motivates their CEOs: "In speculative enterprises, profit must be imagined before it can be extracted; the possibility of economic performance must be conjured like a spirit to draw an audience of potential investors. The more spectacular the conjuring, the more possible an investment frenzy."[5]

In the case of Nortel, a conjured investment frenzy was not a possibility: it was an eventuality. By July 2000, its common shares were trading at about CDN$120 (up from about CDN$20 in early 1999). At certain times, staggering volumes of shares traded daily. Nortel was the toast of international investment funds. But then, after it reported an astounding loss of US$19.9 billion for the second quarter of 2001, Nortel saw its bubble burst, and its share price collapsed to about CDN$10.[6] As it turned out, the investment frenzy had, in fact – to use Tsing's terms – been triggered by a spectacular conjuring of profits.[7] And Roth's CEO-speak was implicated strongly in the profit conjuring. What were Roth's motives?

An important element of the profit conjuring was the seductive interplay and rhetorical power of the language of accounting (hereafter Accounting) and the natural language we use (English).[8] Nortel became the virtually integrated phenomenon that it had wished to become, partly by employing language (Accounting and English) to justify its virtual accounting numbers, such as those it claimed represented "supplementary earnings" measures. The mutually reinforcing and mutually dependent interplay between English and Accounting is subjected to close scrutiny here as we examine CEO Roth's "remarkable" letter to shareholders.

Roth had been constructed by Canadians as a revered businessman. Media outlets, schools, university faculties of business, governments, and individual citizens put him on a pedestal – CEO as hero. Such behaviour is not unusual. Societies throughout the Western world develop personality cults for influential CEOs. We seem eager to beatify high-profile CEOs like Jack Welch.[9] It is as if we think such people are somehow different from the rest of us, but when their glory days are over we recognize that they are human and vulnerable after all. This was the fate of John Roth. When interviewed in early December 2001 (five weeks after he had been replaced as CEO, and several months after his fall from grace had begun), he used some revealing and poignant words and phrases.[10] They suggest someone far removed from the CEO described in media reports as one "who could do no wrong,"[11] and who was "arguably the most influential Canadian business person in a generation."[12] The now-retired Roth was revealed as fallible. He acknowledged that he had not foreseen the business downturn ("I was leaving that to the other guys") and claimed that he now enjoyed simply pottering about his home, in retirement.[13] The transformation was stark. How did Roth-the-person shift so abruptly from CEO icon to pottering retiree? Or did the icon ever really exist, in a corporeal sense?

The CEO-icon was more a metaphoric construction than flesh-and-blood reality. Roth-the-human was like Disney-the-human, but on a culturally and socially smaller scale. Roth-the-human had become a sort of sideshow to Roth-the-CEO-icon. Accounting and English, including Roth's CEO-speak, were instrumental in elevating Roth to icon status, but when the CEO-icon did not perform according to socially constituted desires, Roth-the-human was pilloried, metaphorically. And what triggered this reaction was Roth's open letter to shareholders, dated 8 March 2001. The letter was published as an advertisement in major Canadian newspapers just as Nortel's star entered its full eclipse. The timing is significant. It was three weeks after Nortel issued a news release in which it informed those involved in the stock market of the likely effects of a US economic downturn, and just over a week after Roth's regular letter to shareholders was published in the 2000 Nortel annual report.

NORTEL'S ACCOUNTING AS SOCIAL ENGINE

Accounting, "the language of business," has long been regarded as objective and factual. Accounting numbers, attested to by independent auditors, allegedly portray the results of operations and the cash flows of organizations in accordance with generally accepted accounting principles (GAAP). If this were so, then we could view accounting numbers as establishing the boundaries of truth within which all CEO-speak must operate. But it isn't – this outdated and naive approach ignores the possibility that accounting is actually part and parcel of CEO-speak and should therefore be regarded as rhetorical.

In order to radically remake itself so that it could beat its competitors and establish itself as purveyor of newly emergent networking technologies, Nortel embarked on a corporate buying spree. Its 1999 annual report included disclosure of recent acquisitions (see table 9–1)

The company largely used its common stock as currency to purchase these companies and acquire their technology. The higher Nortel's stock price rose, the higher the "price" Nortel could afford to "pay" and therefore the better able it was to prevent competitors from making acquisitions. But what factors drive up stock prices? One theory is that a company's expected future earnings are the key driver, and that if those expected earnings are greater than what the market would normally require from a company (given the company's risk), then the stock price will increase. Conversely, if expected future earnings are lower, then the stock price will decrease. Another theory is that stock-price movements are the result of "irrational exuberance."[14]

Table 9–1
Nortel's Major Acquisitions, 1998–99

Acquisition	Date	Purchase Price (US$)	Cash or Nortel Shares
Periphonics	12 November 1999	$650 million	shares
Shasta Networks	16 April 1999	$340 million	shares
Cambrian	15 December 1998	$248 million	cash
Bay Networks	31 August 1998	$6,873 million	shares
Aptis	22 April 1998	$286 million	mainly shares
BNI	9 January 1998	$433 million	mainly shares

Source: Nortel Networks Corporation 1999, 4.

Perhaps these theories hold at different times for different companies, or perhaps they are simply wrong. It could be that they hold simultaneously. Or maybe, as we surmise, the stock market is occasionally "irrationally exuberant" about something, such as earnings. If so, and if capital markets had increasingly optimistic expectations about increasingly positive abnormal earnings for Nortel in the form of higher stock prices, then Nortel (and presumably the capital markets) had a problem. Why? Because while Nortel was reporting increasing *revenues* under GAAP (US$15.5 billion in 1997; US$17.6 billion in 1998; and US$22.2 billion in 1999), it was also reporting *losses* (US$569 million in 1998; and US$197 million in 1999).

These reported losses derived principally from the accounting requirement, enshrined in GAAP, to cite significant portions of the costs of the unproven technology and goodwill Nortel had acquired on its corporate buying sprees as expenses against revenue. Thus, the more Nortel paid for high-tech acquisitions with' its ever-increasing stock-cum-currency, the higher these costs rose and the lower its reported earnings were. So, if the capital markets used current reported earnings as an input when predicting future earnings, then these low reported earnings could hinder the growth engine. Consequently, the bountiful "currency" that Nortel was using to bankroll its strategic corporate acquisitions could collapse, taking the company (and the value of executive stock options) down with it. In these circumstances, Nortel had good reason to redirect the capital market's attention away from bottom-line GAAP "earnings" towards something it could control more easily. In other words,

Nortel and Roth had a rhetorical problem, and they dealt with it in two interrelated ways.

First, they engaged in the tactic of denial. They denied that bottom-line earnings were relevant – even earnings sanctified by GAAP and an unqualified audit opinion. They did this principally by including the following note in the 1999 audited financial statements:

3. Supplementary measures of net earnings and earnings per share [in US$ millions]
As a measure to assess financial performance, management utilizes supplementary measures of net earnings and earnings per common share which exclude the impact of Acquisition Related Costs and one-time gains and charges. The supplementary measures of net earnings and earnings per common share are as follows:

	1999	1998	1997
Net earnings (loss) applicable to common shares	$(197)	$(569)	$812
Add back:			
Acquisition-related amortization			
Purchased IPR&D	722	1,241	–
Acquired technology	686	228	–
Goodwill*	553	161	–
One-time gains	(264)	(441)	(102)
One-time charges	209	447	95
Net tax impact	16	(2)	(1)
Supplementary measure of net earnings	$1,725	$1,065	$804
Supplementary measure of earnings per common share	$1.28	$.93	$.77

* Amortization for Bay Networks and all acquisitions subsequent to the acquisition of Bay Networks.

By means of this note, Nortel and its Business Hall of Fame inductee, Roth, contended that the better measure of Nortel's financial performance was its "supplementary measure of net earnings" of US$1.725 billion in 1999, and not the GAAP-computed loss of US$197 million. They also contended that real earnings had increased to (then) present levels from US$804 million in 1997, a spectacular growth rate averaging 47 per cent annually.

The irony is delicious. Note 3 is an integral part of the audited GAAP-compliant financial statements. Yet in those statements

Nortel and Roth proclaim the irrelevance of the GAAP-computed and audited earnings number (a loss of US$197 million for 1999). Instead, they offer a newly conjured earnings number (a profit of US$1.725 billion for 1999) – and they do so despite the fact that the auditors had attested to the "fairness" of the financial statements (and the GAAP-based net loss of US$197 million) in their unqualified audit opinion covering all of the audited financial statements, including the notes. This behaviour is consistent with Tsing's "conjuring." In effect, Nortel and Roth were saying that what you see (a loss of US$197 million) is not what you really get (a profit of US$1.725 billion).

Nortel and Roth also dealt with their rhetorical problem by emphasizing revenue growth rather than current earnings as the driver of the firm's value. There was nothing unusual about this during the heady Internet stock boom of 1997–2000. The stock market rhetoric of the time extolled revenues and downplayed earnings as the harbinger of stock value and corporate financial success.

But Roth was involved in a contest. He was competing to acquire Internet technology, the so-called dot-com companies, market share, and revenues. To succeed he needed to buttress Nortel's share price, and to do that he had to portray significant revenue growth. Of course, when to formally recognize revenue and how much revenue to recognize in any accounting period are delicate and contentious issues within the accounting fraternity. But the equivocation of accountants made it easier for Roth to stretch the flimsy accounting rules governing revenue recognition – at least, that's what lawsuits against Nortel contended. A *Toronto Star* headline summarized it thus: "Nortel Inflated Sales, Suit Claims: 'Pulled Forward' $500 Million US, Documents Say."[15] This is tantamount to an accusation of revenue conjuring.

Roth and Nortel present us with two very rich examples of "the rhetorical dimensions of accounting practices."[16] First is the redirecting of interest away from GAAP earnings towards Nortel's version of earnings. Second is the exclusive focus on revenues and revenue growth. But it doesn't much matter, after the event, whether the revenues were "true" or "real." What matters is that the appearance of financial success was created in one way or another. Accounting assisted in a narrative conspiracy of sorts. But the final attempt to sustain persuasive rhetoric was Roth's "remarkable letter," which we now examine.

ROTH'S OPEN LETTER TO SHAREHOLDERS[17]

We analyse this letter, dated 8 March 2001, paragraph by paragraph. It was published as a full-page advertisement in Canadian newspapers,[18] and it was also featured prominently on Nortel's Web site.

It is a short letter, comprising 465 words (as compared to Roth's shareholders' letters in Nortel annual reports from 1997 to 2000, which averaged 1,970 words). It is addressed to "Nortel Networks Shareholders" and thereby ignores thousands of Nortel employees (including those who were "downsized"), customers, suppliers, and creditors. This address was controversial, because it failed to acknowledge the harm done to a broad spectrum of Nortel stakeholders. Indeed, if the job of the CEO was to help "the organization to see itself as a broader community that shares core values"[19] through important strategic choices such as the development of "optimal trust in relationships with stakeholders,"[20] then the exclusive selection of shareholders as the letter's audience was quite bizarre. Rhetorically, it makes very little sense, particularly since it was inconsistent with Roth's 2000 annual report shareholders' letter, published a week earlier. The following two excerpts from the 2000 annual report letter to shareholders help illustrate important aspects of this rhetorical inconsistency:

[Excerpt 1] The high-performance Internet is the backbone of the networked global economy and the foundation of a new era in global communications that's touching the lives of people in all regions of the world.

[Excerpt 2] A Source of Pride

Throughout the past year, we continued our efforts to be a company valued by our customers, employees, shareholders, and the communities where our people live and work.

We worked to attract and retain the most talented people in the business by offering exciting career opportunities at the forefront of the Internet revolution.

We maintained our long-standing tradition of social responsibility and corporate citizenship, with an emphasis on expanding educational opportunities in the regions where we operate.

It's a source of pride to all of us that our efforts have been widely recognized.

These excerpts show that the Internet, the essence of what Nortel Networks wants to be, is "the foundation of a new era ... that's touching the lives of people in all regions of the world." So, Nortel conceives itself as affecting everyone profoundly. Furthermore, it takes pride in being valued by its customers and employees, and for being socially responsible and a good corporate citizen. Yet, curiously, about a week later, none of this found its way into the open letter. Its first paragraph reads:

[Paragraph 1] Much has been said and written about Nortel Networks in recent weeks. I recognize that this has been of concern to our shareholders. It has also been a concern to me and all those associated with the company. That is why I want to review and update you on what has transpired since we issued a press release on February 15 revising our guidance for the first quarter and year 2001.

Roth contends that "all those associated with the company" join him in his "concern." This group necessarily includes Nortel employees (including those fearful of further downsizings, and perhaps also recently downsized employees). His use of the word "I" twice in this paragraph ("I recognize" and "I want to review and update you") is intended to forge a direct connection with readers. It signals that this is Roth's personal narrative, an account directly from the leader. However, the paragraph contains an interesting shift between "I" and "we." It is CEO Roth who recognizes that the shareholders are concerned; he acknowledges his own concern and announces his intention to provide shareholders with a review and an update. But it is "we" (Nortel, collectively?) who issued the press release on 15 February. Here we begin to see the positioning of CEO Roth as an empathetic human. He is sensitive to that which is "of concern to our shareholders," and it is apparently he who will perform the review and update. By positioning himself in this way, Roth seems to be starting, ever so slightly, to distance himself (his persona, at least) from the "we" of the company.

The passive construction of the opening sentence creates an almost conspiratorial air, but the conspirators – those who have "said" and "written" – are not identified. The phrase "in recent weeks" suggests that all this saying and writing has just happened. But this is not so. Much of it was done inside Nortel, initially at least, and not so recently. For example, the 2000 annual report shareholders' letter, published several weeks *after* the revised guidance of 15 February (and therefore well after it is reasonable to conclude that the company and its CEO knew about the "much" that had "been said and written"), discloses nothing about any "concern." Indeed, the letter to shareholders in the annual report issued the previous week is positively glowing in its description of Nortel's recent accomplishments and the company's future. So, the open letter, CEO Roth's personal communication to Nortel shareholders (published one week after the 2000 annual report shareholders' letter) establishes a rhetorical disconnect between itself and the 2000 shareholders' letter largely because of this glaring inconsistency. We now turn to the second paragraph of the open letter.

[Paragraph 2] When issuing that release, we stated that Nortel Networks was not immune to the current economic downturn in the United States. Based on previous experience, we had anticipated a longer lead-time for the effects of a downturn to be felt by our sector and by our company. The current downturn occurred with unprecedented suddenness and severity. Our decision to revise guidance on February 15 occurred as soon as the effects of this downturn were clear to us.

Rhetorically, the second paragraph is the work of a virtuoso: it socializes any potential blame away from Roth; it provides a seemingly plausible, coherent narrative to explain Nortel's actions in the face of a virulent and fast-moving pandemic; and it obscures inconsistencies between the narrative and external "facts."

The paragraph seeks to justify behaviour during circumstances that resulted in adverse outcomes for members of Roth's (actual and intended) audiences. Roth, as narrator, seems to be attempting to make sense of experience,[21] to "impose order on otherwise disconnected events,"[22] and to help others "understand the ways in which individuals experience and identify with [the meaning thus created] and their social world." The passage may be interpreted as a "social explanation of events" or as a "construction of accounts to justify unexpected or disrupted social interaction." But it has been constructed as an organizational explanation rather than CEO Roth's personal explanation, with the rhetorical effect of deflecting or diffusing blame. No "I"s appear in this paragraph, just "we"s. This makes Roth's use of the "I"s in paragraph 1, as empathetic positioning and distancing from Nortel (the "we"s), even more striking. The narrative of paragraph 2, a story explaining bad news, is not CEO Roth's personal story – it is a collective story. CEO Roth, it seems, cannot be held solely, or personally, accountable.

Another interesting rhetorical feature is the use of the word "immune." Since only living beings can be immune or not immune, Nortel is casting itself as a living being. It is also evoking entailments of communicable disease. (Nortel, a living being, could not avoid catching the disease. People catch diseases when, despite their best intentions, they are caught off guard by, say, an influenza epidemic. And is this really anyone's fault?) Also, the word "current" reinforces the contention that Nortel was, like everyone else, caught unaware by a sudden change in the financial climate. This belies the idea that Nortel management knew well in advance of 15 February about the downturn (as alleged in various class action lawsuits). It also ignores serious questions about the construction of the financial-accounting numbers, revenue, and earnings, discussed earlier. Furthermore, Roth claims that Nortel applied prudence "Based on previous experience," regardless of the fact that the economic downturn "occurred with unprecedented suddenness and severity." But how can this be, especially since Nortel had just reinvented itself to partake in a brand new industry of which no one had "previous experience"?

[Paragraph 3] We were among the first to recognize the severity of the downturn occurring in the U.S., our largest market. Since February 15, a growing number of technology companies with heavy dependence on the U.S. market have also revised their forecasts. This is clearly a broad market/economic slowdown that has affected companies in our sector with unprecedented speed.

The first two sentences are self-eulogy. In the first sentence, CEO Roth asserts that "We" (presumably the collective leadership of Nortel) "were among the first to recognize the severity of the downturn." But notice that he says "*among* the first," and not "*the* first." Precisely when did this realization occur? Not by 1 March 2001, the date of the cheery 2000 annual report shareholders' letter. And what does the word "recognize" mean here? Was "the severity of the downturn" known inside the virtual corporation that Nortel was becoming? Was it known, but in only a fuzzy, inchoate way, at the very summit of Nortel's leadership?

The second sentence continues the self-eulogy by presenting the date of 15 February as a milestone; this is the date that Nortel released its revised "guidance." Since then, according to the open letter, "a growing number of technology companies ... have also revised their forecasts." Being "among the first," Nortel then issued a clarion call (the 15 February announcement), which prompted "a growing number" of others to follow suit. But this is not unusual, since, according to Nortel's 2000 annual report shareholders' letter, Nortel is "delivering an industry-leading portfolio" and "is already leading the way." This verges on arrogance and apologia.

[Paragraph 4] At the same time, I want you to know that our position as an industry leader and innovator remains strong, despite the unfavorable economic and market conditions we are facing. Our fundamentals remain sound and we offer an industry-leading portfolio of end-to-end communications solutions. We have a diverse and strong base of customers throughout the world. And we have some of the most talented and committed people in the world working to provide those customers with breakthrough technologies that create value and competitive advantage for our customers around the world.

The language used here strives to position Nortel in the minds of readers. Nortel is portrayed as a resilient company, impervious to unfavourable economic conditions. The language is positive and conducive to an image of strength and financial well-being. We are twice informed that Nortel is "an industry leader" (not a follower or an also-ran), and that it is "strong," with a "strong base of customers." Nortel is portrayed as "an innovator," as "offering solutions," as "providing breakthrough technologies," and as "creating value." The company's global reach is emphasized with three mentions of Nortel operations throughout/in/around the world. The implication is that global reach is reliable testimony to Nortel's strength and virtue. This paragraph is powerful, reassuring, feel-good rhetorical bluster, rounded off with hyperbole – Nortel staff "are some of the most talented and committed ... in the world."

But the positive features of Nortel asserted in this paragraph – its "fundamentals," its "industry-leading portfolio," its "diverse and strong base of customers," its "talented and committed people," and its "breakthrough technologies that create value and competitive advantage for our customers around the world" – would be characterized by communications scholar George Cheney as "slogans that simultaneously command emotional allegiance and are devoid of precise meaning."[23]

[Paragraph 5] Where the class action lawsuits resulting from our February 15 announcement are concerned, our shareholders, customers and employees should also know that we will defend ourselves vigorously. Quite simply, we believe the allegations in the lawsuits against your company in Canada and the United States are without merit. I can assure you that your company is committed to maintaining the highest integrity and credibility of business practices. The way in which we conduct our business is as important as the business we conduct.

This paragraph announces a resolute intention to contest the class action lawsuits against the company. An interesting feature is the distancing of Roth and the senior management team from culpability. And there is a fascinating transformation in tone, pitch, and intended audience. The paragraph heralds a shift in the manner of reference to Nortel – it is now referred to as "your company." The lawsuits (the bad news) are portrayed not as allegations arising from poor management decisions or corporate governance; instead, the use of "your" (and a specific identification of shareholders, customers, and employees) directs responsibility to a wide group of Nortel stakeholders. The "open letter to shareholders" is now something broader. Nonetheless, we can all breathe easy. Roth soothes us with powerful rhetoric: "I can assure you." He tells those who have been subjected to legal process that they have been falsely accused and have nothing to worry about.

[Paragraph 6] On behalf of everyone at Nortel Networks, I want to thank our shareholders, customers, suppliers and friends for their expressions of support and encouragement. We greatly value our hard-earned reputation for integrity, ethical behavior and corporate citizenship. I want to assure you that the senior executives of Nortel Networks and myself, as significant shareholders in the company, are fully committed to delivering the long-term performance and results you have come to expect of your company.

Sincerely,
John Roth
President and Chief Executive Officer

The inclusiveness of "On behalf of everyone at Nortel" is amazingly presumptious. CEOs of large companies rarely speak for all employees. We are encouraged to believe that Nortel is one big happy family – including those employees who have, or will be, laid off. The company is portrayed as a corporate angel. It has integrity, it behaves ethically, and it is a good corporate citizen. Many are thanked for their "support and encouragement," but there is no acknowledgment of critical voices.

There is a hollowness to Roth's "we're all in this together" assurances, to his insistence that his interest as a "significant" shareholder is to "deliver long-term performance and results" and that this is also the interest of people associated with "your" company (those specifically mentioned are "shareholders, customers, suppliers and friends").

This hollowness becomes even more pronounced when we regard paragraphs 4, 5, and 6 as working rhetorically together. The "slogans" of paragraph 4, those New Economy buzzwords, are a poor entree to paragraph 5, in which CEO Roth reminds us that Nortel is facing several lawsuits. This bad-news paragraph is staid and formulaic, using such stock phrases as "we will defend ourselves vigorously," "we believe the allegations … are without merit," "The way in which we conduct business is as important as the business we conduct." Such phrases seem to have been fashioned by lawyers to avoid a legal backlash; they do not appear to reflect a desire for honest and open communication. Indeed, it is the combination of paragraphs 4 and 5, with their cold, off-the-shelf quality, that dooms an already rhetorically feeble open letter to failure. Paragraph 6, a formulaic thank-you, only reinforces the strong impression that the writer, an engineer by qualification, is heartless.

This is an essential point. The CEO, as chief rhetor of a corporation, must be a master of the communication art and its varying demands. Techno-icon CEO Roth failed in his most important effort to exercise the language of leadership. He wrote a letter that was short, formulaic, cold, and obscure – and decidedly not "open." He did so when there was a clear need for a letter from an inspirational, trusted leader. But perhaps the letter CEO Roth wrote was the only one he could possibly write, because the bare facts precluded anything but platitudes and formulas.

Roth's "special letter" seemingly is a rhetorical betrayal of what the media and the market expected from the iconic CEO they helped to construct. There is nothing valiant about the letter. A true hero might have fallen on his sword, admitting personal responsibility. For many, Roth *was* Nortel, yet suddenly, with this letter, he destroyed that impression. He claimed collective responsibility for the company's woes, thereby making Nortel a collective. His words flounder in a sea of mediocrity. When times were good, Roth let the cult of CEO personality prevail; he basked in the plaudits for his personal skill and eminence. But when times were tough, he distanced himself from personal liability.

Three Tenors in Perfect Harmony

CEO-speak can have multiple authors, as evidenced on 11 August 1999, when the CEOs of three major aluminium companies – Jacques Bougie of Alcan (headquartered in Canada), Jean-Pierre Rodier of Pechiney (France), and Sergio Marchionne of Alusuisse (Switzerland) – issued a joint letter announcing that their companies would merge to create the "world's largest aluminium company."[1] The three CEOs were on song, three tenors in perfect harmony.

The joint letter was addressed to audiences outside and inside the three merging companies. It was released through the usual public relations media and appeared on the Web sites of the three companies. The text of the joint letter is an important example of CEO-speak because it announces a multi-corporate, multinational, strategic change, and it sets the thematic framework for the then-imagined-but-soon-to-be-constructed entity.[2] Our close reading of the letter focuses on its metaphorical features; and reveals the cognitive world of the three CEOs and the way in which they used CEO-speak to shape the world according to their vision.

We tease out the letter's principal underlying metaphors, beginning with the title – "A Compelling New Future Together" – and paragraph 1.

[Paragraph 1] We are announcing today the exciting proposal to create the world's largest aluminium company and the global leader in flexible and specialty packaging. In what will be the world's first international three-way merger, we are combining the resources of Alcan, Pechiney and Algroup, three successful companies in their own right.

The "new future" envisioned by the three leaders evokes positive attributes (freshness, unencumbered opportunity) rather than negative ones (being unknown, untried, untested). The title brings to mind Aldous Huxley's *Brave New World*, published in 1932, and the estranged, programmed society it imagined for the future.[3] It also suggests a future of social compulsion in which ordinary people lack self-awareness. And in case this metaphoric allusion is insufficient, the "new future" is described as "compelling." But it is unclear whether it is compelling due to some naturally occurring, unstoppable force or to the three leaders, who will make it so. Also unclear is the matter of who will be "together" and who will be excluded – although obviously excluded are the 11,000 employees who will be retrenched as a consequence of the merger. We wonder whether the "compelling new future" will be so attractive that no rational human being could possibly want to be excluded from it. The title is evidently laden with coercive ideological overtones.

The three CEOs are adamant: they will create an even better company ("the world's largest" and "the global leader"). The agents of this creation are not the companies themselves, but "we" – the three CEOs. The direct and forceful cadence of the first paragraph is riveting, and it reinforces our metaphoric interpretation of the joint letter's title.

[Paragraph 2] The combination will establish the new world leader in aluminium, with complementary operations and technologies, the most sustainable low-cost primary aluminium position, superior aluminium fabricating on a global scale and excellent positioning for growth and expansion.
[Paragraph 3] The combination will also create the world's leading flexible and specialty packaging business, with leading global positions in areas such as pharmaceuticals, personal care, food, and cosmetics.

The use of "combination" and "we are combining" in these paragraphs suggests that the three companies are in mutually advantageous harmony – this is not a hostile takeover. More practically, such terminology signals an intention to account for the merger using the pooling method of accounting rather than its alternative, the purchase method. Indeed, a press release describing the proposed merger confirmed that the merged company would employ the pooling method of accounting. This method, permitted for use by merged companies, ignores the current values of assets, reports relatively low expenses, and inflates net income and calculations of return on investment.[4]

The multiple uses of "we" emphasize jointness. The repetition, almost an incantation, of words having "combine" as a root reinforces, at the highest corporate level, the case for the pooling method. By adopting this method, the three leaders have a better chance of ensuring that the results reported in future balance sheets and income statements will represent seemingly objective accounting evidence of good performance and thus verify their "vision."

[Paragraph 4] The international scale and capabilities of these businesses will enable the new company, which will temporarily be referred to as A.P.A., to better serve our customers and enable our employees to be part of a stronger, more dynamic company that is uniquely positioned to grow in the future, while it creates substantial value for our shareholders. The combination will also benefit from a geographically balanced portfolio between two major economic areas.

The wording of paragraph 4 stresses size, global scope, strength, and dynamism – attributes that will result in a stronger company and generate growth and value. Bolstered by similar wording in paragraph 2 ("the new world leader in aluminium, with ... excellent positioning for growth and expansion"), this invites belief that a big global company is stronger and more dynamic, that it will grow even larger and thus "create" even greater value. The following metaphors arise: "a company is a sentient being having strength and dynamism but needing to grow and expand," and "company growth and expansion creates value."

COMPELLING FOR CUSTOMERS
[Paragraph 5] Our customers want to work with companies who can serve their needs around the world and meet their requirements for efficient and effective manufacturing and marketing solutions. Our aluminium customers will benefit from working with a company that has a sustainable low-cost position, superior R&D and technical capabilities, and the capacity

and reach to address aluminium fabrication needs in any region. In particular, A.P.A. will be the world's largest aluminium rolling company with world class facilities in each of the world's key markets. The merger will enable us to pool our manufacturing expertise, research, technology, and customer knowledge to become a leader in serving customers in industries such as aerospace, transport, automotive and beverage cans, among others. [Paragraph 6] Flexible and specialty packaging customers will benefit from working with a company that will have leading positions in each of its chosen areas of business as well as 159 manufacturing facilities serving them throughout the world. Again, through our combined expertise and resources we will be able to meet the demands of this dynamic and growing market.

The three CEOs purport to know their customers' wants and needs and how to meet them – customer metaphors are rife. This "knowledge," when considered in light of their vision of "a compelling new future" for customers, employees, and shareholders, gives rise to an intriguing metaphor: "the three leaders are an omniscient being." The metaphor – which might be even better expressed as "the three leaders are the company's brain" – is further supported by the leaders' decision, announced at the same time as the joint letter, to make the merged enterprise "an EVA©-driven company,"5 with all that this entails ideologically.

COMPELLING FOR EMPLOYEES

[Paragraph 7] A.P.A. will be a broadly based aluminium and specialty packaging company with 91,000 employees in 59 countries.

[Paragraph 8] The scale and financial strength of the new company will put us in a strong position to take advantage of growth and expansion opportunities in both industries. The combination of complementary businesses, management expertise, skilled employees and strong professional cultures will enable employees of all three companies to be part of a more dynamic global enterprise and to benefit from significant opportunities for growth and development.

COMPELLING FOR SHAREHOLDERS

[Paragraph 9] The management of all three companies is committed to this three-way merger and to quickly capturing the value it creates for our shareholders. The financial strength of the new company, the ability to achieve a variety of synergy benefits and the platform it provides for future growth mean that the merger should be a compelling prospect for investors.

THE PATH FORWARD

[Paragraph 10] It will take several months to put all the building blocks in place and our target is to launch our new company early next year. We are committed to keeping our employees, shareholders, customers, and stakeholders fully informed as we progress towards realizing this vision.

[Paragraph 11] We understand that such a major change sometimes fosters uncertainty and concern for the future. However, we encourage our employees, customers, shareholders and other stakeholders to embrace this opportunity to help us create a new global leader in the aluminium and packaging industries. We fundamentally believe this proposed three-way merger is the best opportunity for our respective companies to grow and prosper in the future.

Paragraph 9 refers to management being "committed" to "capturing" value "quickly." This language is like that used to describe a military campaign, and the impression is reinforced by the references in paragraph 10 to the "launch" of the new company, to "our target," and to keeping those outside the inner circle "fully informed." Such top-down communication is characteristic of the military, and it suggests the following metaphor: "business is war." To win a war, one must have superior strength and size. Winners are lean and mean (they hold a "sustainable low-cost position"; they are "efficient" and "effective"). They must also be able to acknowledge leadership and follow orders – all qualities evoked in the joint letter.

Like leaders in war, leaders in business have superior strategic understanding and must be obeyed. Although there will inevitably be casualties, they are unlikely to occur among those with expertise and a strong professional culture. This reading, which reveals the fundamental metaphor "business is war," suggests that the joint letter is a call to arms by a supreme general staff.

Another basic underlying metaphor is "the company is a sentient being on a purposeful journey towards success." Other companies will threaten the merged company and attempt to block it, but all parts of the company must submit to the brain ("the three leaders are the company's brain") if the company is to move ahead in such a hostile environment. Identifying the company as "a sentient being on a purposeful journey towards success" implies that the company's brain best understands the company's goals and how to achieve them; it knows which path to take, how to adapt to changing circumstances, and how to wage business war. Stakeholders' interests are of marginal importance, for stakeholders are obliged to accept the authority of the sentient company. When regarded this way, the joint letter is a chilling piece of discourse: anyone who impedes the company in its forward movement is the enemy.[6]

Three other important metaphors emerge. First, "the organization is a physical structure." This basic metaphor is suggested in paragraph 10 ("It will take several months to put all the building blocks in place") and emerges more subtly when the three leaders write that the company they propose to create will have "international scale." References to the physical size and scope of the company are instances of this metaphor: "capacity and reach" (paragraph 5); "159 manufacturing facilities" (paragraph 6); "growth and expansion" (paragraph 8); "platform" (paragraph 9). The metaphor becomes especially interesting when we consider that the proposed company is described as: "the world's largest ... the global leader" (paragraph 1); "sustainable" and "superior" (paragraph 2); holding "leading global positions" (paragraph 3); "stronger, more dynamic" and "geographically balanced" (paragraph 4); "efficient," "effective" (paragraph 5); and possessing "financial strength" (paragraph 9).

These characteristics are tantalizingly close to the notion of gestalt – that is, of "rightness, beauty, and natural order" and of "inner coherence."[7] Metaphorically, we have "the proposed organization of the three leaders is a structural gestalt." This suggests a natural, unified whole whose need to maintain inner coherence will require sacrifice, dedication to a common goal, and strong leadership.

The proposed organization is going somewhere; it's on a journey (as suggested by the heading of paragraph 10 – "The Path Forward"). The three leaders intend to "launch" the new company, and they wish to "progress towards" their goal (paragraph 10). However, the destination of the soon-to-be-merged company, although hard to discern, is described as a "vision" that the leaders wish to realize. Elsewhere, goals are characterized in terms of "growth" (paragraph 8), "growth and expansion" (paragraph 2), and other "slogans that simultaneously command emotional allegiance and are devoid of precise meaning."[8] The leaders' proposed merged company, or "structural gestalt," is on a metaphorical journey without end through hostile territory. It requires the company to be "stronger, more dynamic" (paragraph 4); to be "efficient and effective" (paragraph 5); to have "expertise, research, technology and customer knowledge" (paragraph 5); to possess "scale" and "strength" (paragraph 8); to be beset by "uncertainty" (paragraph 11). It also requires non-leaders to "embrace" the "opportunity" inherent in the leaders' "vision" (paragraphs 11 and 10).

The notion of a journey through dangerous unknown territory in which visionary leaders guide submissive followers is well characterized by the metaphor of the wagon train traversing the vast American frontier. The analogy for firms is

> precisely that of the pioneer, leaving first a Europe stifled by bureaucracy, class and hierarchy and then the similarly restrictive eastern USA to strike out into a wilderness where ... there is no safe path and everything is risked in pursuit of a vision ... Leadership, in the person of the wagon boss and the scout, is inspirational and expert. Under its guidance the pioneers learn the wisdom to survive. They also learn to be flexible, acquiring skills as teamsters, soldiers, wheelwrights and veterinarians. But above all, they learn the importance of commitment. Dissent, or mere lack of enthusiasm, jeopardizes the whole enterprise ... [and furthermore] the arrival itself is irrelevant. There is no arrival. To travel hopefully is the crux of the metaphor. Arrival suggests the end of change ... [but the metaphor] is about perpetual change. The challenge is to "thrive" ... on the chaos of disorganized capitalism, the chaos of the unfettered market.[9]

The three CEOs' metaphorical notion of the company as "structural gestalt-cum-wagon train" seems so natural as to be beyond question, as are their wisdom and their decision-making prowess. While "employees, customers, shareholders and other stakeholders" (paragraph 11) are along for the wagon train ride, they have to toe the line and rely on the CEO trail bosses to keep them "fully informed." The trail bosses don't want any advice from such greenhorns, and they won't tolerate dissent. What emerges is a frighteningly complex metaphoric construct that cries out for resistance, because it is quite plausible that such a construct would become the ideological foundation for the proposed mega-firm's management control system.

The three CEOs, as authors of the joint letter, are shown to be decisive, knowledgeable, visionary, entrepreneurial, aggressively capitalistic, and single-minded. Yet they also present themselves as understanding and compassionate when they reassure readers that they "understand that such a major change sometimes fosters uncertainty and concern for the future." They expect benefits for customers, employees, and shareholders, but they aren't explicit about who will bear the brunt of the downsizing.[10] They reinforce their ethos with hyperlinks to flattering biographies of themselves and with small portrait photos displayed at the top of the Web site version of the joint letter. This prompts the visual metaphor "the three executives are the three wise men," with its echoes of religious rebirth.

The Web site biographies demonstrate the educational and business virtuosity of the CEOs – something akin to wisdom in our culture. Their use of key words validates this, so much so that it all seems rather far-fetched. The implication is that they are the only ones who can announce the "vision" of the "exciting" merger and the wonderful things that it will bring. They are the only ones who can (wisely divine?) "the path forward." They even possess another attribute of wisdom – understanding – since they "understand that such a major change sometimes fosters uncertainty and concern for the future." The tone suggests that the new merged entity is a leader with a vision who will take us, messiah-like, into a new world. Like the prophets of old, these three wise men "fundamentally believe" in their "vision," which they regard as "compelling." They resemble religious extremists with their apparent intolerance. Although some individuals must be sacrificed on "the path forward" (the unmentioned 11,000 employees who will be retrenched), this is portrayed as an inevitable cost of creating an entity that will "meet the demands of a dynamic and growing market." Thus, the market is depicted as a beast who demands sacrifices: the market is natural, its demands are natural, the three wise men's vision of meeting and satisfying the demands of the market is the only one that will succeed.

The three CEOs emerge as corporate heroes from this complex of reinforcing metaphors. The CEO-speak of the joint letter reveals important connections between financial reporting (using the pooling method of accounting) and the management control methods (EVA©) that the merging companies adopt. The letter skilfully allays fears, encourages commitment to the merger, energizes a wide variety of audiences, and announces an ideology of business and a management control strategy. The metaphor "the three leaders are an omniscient being" does not seem far-fetched. The three CEOs sing the same song in a style influenced by a framework of mutually agreed-upon, exclusionary, and elitist world views.

11

Creating "North America's Railroad"

> Privatization is a language game, sometimes played
> sincerely, sometimes disingenuously. And sometimes it
> generates excitement as it circulates through the polity,
> phonier than a counterfeit $20 bill.[1]

In previous chapters we concentrated mainly on the rhetoric of CEOs in their communications with shareholders, the media, governments, and the general public. Here we extend our examination of CEO-speak by reviewing accounting-related CEO rhetoric directed specifically at employees. And rather than continuing to focus on the discourse of CEOs in the private sector, we concentrate on the words of a public sector CEO in a setting unique to that sector: privatization.

We explore the ways in which accounting language, concepts, and information were deployed by Paul Tellier, CEO of Canadian National Railway (CN) in the two and a half years prior to the February 1995 announcement that the Canadian government intended to privatize CN. We give a close reading to the articles that Tellier contributed to CN's monthly employee newspaper during the prelude to privatization. They reveal how accounting was used to construct a privatization mentality to persuade employees to accept a change in CN's orientation and culture, and to help sustain the economic wisdom of the privatization decision.

The privatization of CN,[2] a Crown corporation, in mid-November 1995 was a significant event in the commercial history of Canada.[3] A Canadian financial journalist described it as "at least in Canadian terms, a seminal example of how to sell state-owned assets."[4] The term "seminal" prompts us to scrutinize the role of CEO-speak in bringing the privatization to fruition.

The principal architect of the privatization and force behind it was Paul Tellier, CN's CEO as of 1 October 1992. Such was Tellier's influence that in December 1995 the *Financial Post* named him "Newsmaker of the Year," recognizing him for making CN "smaller, leaner and more profitable" and for then "taking [CN] to the stock market" in Canada's largest and most successful public stock offering. The paper also praised Tellier for overseeing "a massive corporate restructuring and downsizing program" and for turning a chronically under-performing and loss-producing railway into a profitable one less encumbered by debt.[5] The *Financial Post*'s plaudits reflected the feelings of many Canadians.

There are strong anecdotal and circumstantial grounds for believing that Tellier was appointed in 1992 with at least a partial privatization agenda in his kit of instructions from the Canadian government (CN's owner in its incarnation as a Crown corporation). In opinion pieces published after the (allegedly) wildly successful initial public offering (IPO), in November 1995, most commentators agreed that the government "should be given a vast amount of credit" for "properly positioning" CN as a "North American company operating in a competitive environment"; for undertaking "a major restructuring prior to the IPO"; and for taking costs out of the company "largely by reducing staff and closing some unprofitable lines."[6] The Canadian government's amanuensis in effecting the "proper positioning" was its former Cabinet secretary – the politically savvy "chameleon" Paul Tellier.[7]

We examine Tellier's CEO-speak published in CN's monthly employee newspaper, *Keeping Track*, during the three years prior to privatization. We direct particular attention to the way accounting language, concepts, and generally accepted accounting principles (GAAP) were implicated in Tellier's construction of knowledge and employee outlook. Some of the influential metaphors, rhetorical devices, and ideological stances framed by accounting are highlighted. Our general finding is that Tellier used accounting rhetoric very effectively to condition employees to accept his ideological values and privatization agenda.

The evisceration of the public sector has been a central feature of social and economic life in recent decades.[8] Despite promises that privatized organizations will have better financial and operating systems, the result of privatization has often been a "transfer of wealth from the public at large to a relatively few individuals and corporate entities." The accompanying language is an "efficiency rhetoric" employed as "a device to legitimise privatisation."[9] Therefore, it is important to understand how the rhetorical process of privatization unfolds and how language is employed by CEOs and others to implement a privatization agenda. The "seminal example" of how to effect privatization, provided by the CN case, is ideal for promoting such understanding of an important instance of CEO-speak.[10]

The process of privatizing an organization involves three campaign stages. First, there is the before-privatization stage (in which prominence is given to successful privatizations and to the virtues of downsizing). Second is the during-privatization stage (in which a specific campaign to pursue privatization is launched and enabling legislation is introduced and passed). Third is the post-privatization stage (in which the focus is on dealing with "winners" and "losers" of the privatization and ensuring that the "vision" of the promoters is shown to have been achieved). Accounting language is integral to each stage; for example, a discourse on poor profits and the need for cost-cutting is often used as an ideological frame in the first two stages. A laudatory language of improved return on investment might be used to prove the sagacity of the privatization project in the third stage while at the same time obscuring any social dislocation and any underlying transfer of wealth.

To understand the three campaign stages in the privatization of CN, we must first be aware of the chronology. What follows is a list of important events in the privatization of CN.

July 1992: Tellier's appointment as CEO is announced.

1 October 1992: Tellier formally commences duties at CN.

July-August 1993: First "Dialogue with the President" appears in *Keeping Track*.

30 September 1994: Transport Minister Doug Young forms a task force to investigate the possibility of "commercializing" CN.

27 February 1995: Government announces its intention to privatize CN.

5 May 1995: CN *Commercialization Act*, Bill C-89, is introduced to Parliament.

May 1995: First issue of *On a New Course for the Future*, CN's newsletter on privatization for employees and pensioners, appears.

13 July 1995: CN *Commercialization Act* takes effect.

17 November 1995: CN IPO is issued.

Our focus here is on the before-privatization stage, which we identify as extending from July 1992, when Tellier's appointment as
CEO was announced, to 27 February 1995, when the Canadian
government announced its intention to privatize CN.[11]

KEEPING TRACK OF A RHETORICAL AGENDA

We read closely twenty-five issues of CN's monthly sixteen-page tab-
loid employee newspaper, Keeping Track, which was published in
the before-privatization period.[12] Of particular interest were articles
or columns whose authorship is attributed to Tellier or that prominently feature interviews with him. Our reading revealed that CN
(through Tellier) used accounting arguments to condition employees to behave in a way that would "properly position" the company
for privatization. Keeping Track had a circulation of about 50,000
– all of CN's employees (approximately 34,000) and CN pensioners
and their survivors. Of particular interest were the fifteen monthly
columns, titled "Dialogue with the President," that appeared during this period.

Paul Tellier's appointment as president and CEO of CN was reported to employees in the July-August 1992 issue of Keeping
Track. Basic biographical details were provided: Tellier was a
Queen's Counsel who had been Canada's most senior federal public
servant (clerk of the Privy Council and secretary to the Cabinet of
the Government of Canada) since 1985. From other sources we
learn that he was also a workaholic, fifty-three-year-old, cranberry-
juice-sipping, self-confessed "fitness nut" who did not "suffer fools
gladly" and could be "as blunt as a bulldozer" and "as tough as
saddle leather."[13] Tellier had had some exposure to privatization
when he was on the board of directors of Petro Canada, a government entity whose partial privatization had been botched.

Shortly after he took up his duties as CEO, Tellier was featured
prominently and at length in Keeping Track. In the December 1992
issue – in "An Interview with Paul Tellier," subheaded "CN's New
Agent of Change" – he presented his views on CN, its performance,
and its future. It is striking that early in this interview, in offering
his first substantive comment on CN, Tellier uses accounting language to explain his motivations. He uses the metaphor of "the bottom line" to explain how important profit is to him,[14] and how it
ought to be uppermost in the minds of CN employees as they go

about their work: "At CN ... not only every month, but several times a month, we look at the bottom line and see how well we're doing, moving grain, potash, sulphur and so on. It's very stimulating, and it makes you realize that everything you do has a direct impact on that bottom line."[15]

Here Tellier is beginning to sketch for employees the ideology that they and CN must follow. Financial performance, and not matters of social equity or environmental behaviour, will be paramount. A sense of social obligation (for example, for CN to provide services to remote Canadian communities) will be a thing of the past, it seems.

Tellier draws attention to CN's reported loss of $14 million in 1991 and to the likelihood that losses in 1992 and 1993 will be even worse. He indicates that he has "little trouble" defining the main task ahead: "to turn a first-class railway into a first-class, viable, profitable, business concern." He uses the metaphor of the "big black cloud" to acknowledge the uncertainty he imagines is hanging over employees; and he expresses the need for CN not only to "downsize" and realize surplus assets but also to aggressively develop new business, increase market share, and ensure that all employees give "optimum performance." This is a rallying cry to the troops to adopt, unashamedly, a market rules ideology. It is a call to arms. If market indicators are improved through the toil of employees operating at 100 per cent efficiency, all will be sweetness and light in the garden of CN.

The conclusion of the interview is revealing. When asked whether he sees CN being privatized in the future, Tellier replies, "I would say that the policy rationale for CN being a Crown corporation does not exist any longer. Therefore when the balance sheet is ready for CN to be privatized, the CEO has a responsibility to raise this question with the shareholder [the Canadian government], and ask what to do. We're not there yet, though." Clearly, privatization was on Tellier's mind. His reply raises several puzzling questions. Just when does an entity's balance sheet reflect readiness for privatization? What are the characteristics of such readiness? Is there an obligation for Crown corporations to engineer balance sheets to appeal to prospective private investors? Does this mean that the values of assets are understated so that the IPO float price can be depressed artificially, or that the corporation must engineer a rising trend in "real" profits and net cash flows? Should privatization be contemplated in the case of an entity that is debilitated by high debt levels?

However, Tellier's reference to "when the balance sheet is ready for CN to be privatized" is both literal and metaphoric. It is literal since the underwriters, financial analysts, and others in the IPO community have quantitative evaluation criteria based on the balance sheet (and other financial statements). But it is metaphoric since it seems to stand for CN *in toto* – an organization of human beings whose humanity is obscured by a linguistic emphasis on the balance sheet. In this metaphoric sense the privatization is portrayed as non-threatening. Because it is the balance sheet that must be "ready," the lives of real people will not be dislocated by the privatization. There is also a suggestion that those CN employees who join productively in helping to "ready" the balance sheet will remain employed.

Two months later, in the February-March *Keeping Track*, Tellier announced plans to substantially reduce CN's rail-track network and workforce.[16] Its Canadian workforce was to be reduced by 10,000 (or about one-third) over the next three years, and a further 1,100 would be cut from its US operations. There would be a reduction of about 3,300 in 1993, 3,900 in 1994, and another 3,900 in 1995. The need for change was described as "urgent." CN comptroller Ronan McGrath had no doubts about what was driving this initiative: "This was all part of a highly focused effort to make the company privatizable."[17]

What is interesting about Tellier's language here is that he uses it to assign a central role to accounting in motivating the privatization-positioning changes at CN. Tellier employs metaphor to explain that one objective of his plan is to address "a need to return to financial health." A recurring metaphor, sprinkled liberally throughout Tellier's communications to CN's employees, is "profit is a diagnostic barometer of well-being," or "profit is a stethoscope." He portrays financial health as CN achieving "a competitive operating ratio of 85.0" through reducing "its annual expenses by $650 million per year by 1997, while seeking to generate new revenues."[18] According to Bruce, CN's operating ratio was a "crucial gauge of efficiency," widely used in the railroad industry, showing "how many cents a railway spends to earn a dollar": "in 1992, when CN was still putting out 97.5 cents for every dollar it collected, the operating ratios of U.S. Class I railways were driving towards the low 80s."[19] Tellier reinforces his views by providing a comprehensive corporate plan requiring significant cost reductions, revenue growth performance, and "quick change" by "everyone" in order to achieve "financial and competitive success."

Soon afterwards, following the release of annual financial statements for the year ending 31 December 1992, Tellier conducted a series of meetings with CN employees throughout Canada. His purpose was to "dialogue on anything and everything [that] might help him turn CN around," and the proceedings were duly reported in *Keeping Track* in May 1993 under the headline "Hard Times ... Hard Questions ... Hard Answers ... Hard Solutions." Tellier noted that "CN has broken all possible records in corporate history – with the largest corporate loss ever recorded in Canada." He wanted to "communicate the urgency of CN's [financial] situation" to employees, to present them with "the company's plan of action, and to generate increased awareness and understanding." The report of his meetings was juxtaposed, on the front page, with a news item titled "CN Records Billion Dollar Loss for 1992."[20]

Tellier seemed to relish highlighting the reported 1992 loss of $1,005 million. He had good reason. It suited his privatization-positioning rhetorical agenda. He appeared to enjoy drawing attention to the developing trend in reported profits: a profit of $8 million in 1990, a $14 million loss in 1991, and the record 1992 loss of $1,005 million. But Tellier was being mischievous. Most of the reported "bottom line loss" of $1,005 million was taken up with one-off "special charges" and a substantial extraordinary item, thereby vitiating comparison with 1991 results. The reported loss in 1992 arose after $887 million of "workforce reduction charges," which were expended principally in the following three years, were charged entirely against 1992 revenues. A one-time charge of $64 million for "post-retirement benefits other than pensions" was also written off against 1992 revenues, despite the strong likelihood that such costs would be borne well into the future.

In choosing to include these charges in the reported loss figure he highlighted, Tellier was being consistent with his rhetorical agenda. He would have had strong incentive to show that under his management, CN could be resuscitated financially, generate profits, and pay dividends. But he had to be careful not to raise profit expectations too high, because this would give critics of privatization the ammunition they needed to argue that CN could succeed without privatization. So, Tellier was faced with the task of turning CN's financial situation around and actually earning some profits; but he had to convey the idea that he could make this change and sustain it without overstating his case. His rhetorical agenda would benefit if he managed the reported accounting numbers so as to win support for converting CN into an entity that revered the primacy of private sector commercial values (including accounting expressions of achievement).

What Tellier did was compare apples and oranges. He persisted in comparing bottom line profits that had been calculated and reported from year to year using different accounting methods. He acted as a conjurer – Paul the Prestidigitator. His comparisons used profit figures that had not been adjusted for the effects of intervening changes in accounting policy or for the effects of one-off special charges. Such behaviour is anathema to accountants who have worked to attain and maintain comparability, consistency, and freedom from bias in accounting measurements. Furthermore, Tellier was comparing the actual CN (a Crown corporation with public-transportation and other government-imposed social-obligation policy mandates) with an imagined profit-seeking, privatized CN. So, we observe two instances of Tellier using accounting to create a discourse and sustain a rhetorical agenda: one, he employs unadjusted profits; and two, he presents the actual CN-cum-Crown corporation as a benchmark for an imagined CN-cum-free market financial success.

The "workforce reduction costs," tallying approximately $900 million, were, according to CN comptroller Ronan McGrath "front-loaded … into the financials right away."[21] If the objective had been to measure CN's operating performance by matching costs and revenues or consigning operating expenses to the period in which they were incurred, then these atypical and material costs should not have been dumped in such a way.[22] This seems a classic example of "big bath accounting."[23] The net income "bottom line" was confounded by attention-grabbing charges, most of which were under the control of CN management when it came to timing and magnitude. The workforce reduction charges of $887 million, and the $64 million arising from a change in accounting policy with respect to the accrual of post-retirement benefits, when added back to the reported 1992 loss of $1,005 million, converted that loss to only $54 million – nowhere near as dire as that portrayed by Tellier. His emphasis was on "the bottom line," but he failed to compare losses constructed on a consistent basis of calculation. He failed to make adjustments for

Table 11–1

	As per Tellier	As adjusted
1992	*($1,005)	($54)
1993	($79)	($362)
1994	$245	($89)

*All figures in Canadian millions

"costs" that were not fully attributable to CN's operations in 1992. And, the cyclical effects of the recession, fluctuations in the US dollar, and higher interest rates, all of which helped explain CN's overall performance in 1992, are conveniently overlooked. The negatives are emphasized and the positives are downplayed.

Furthermore, the accounting involved is curious. The workforce reduction charges were related to staff shedding programmed to occur and to be largely paid for in 1993 (3,300 employees would be laid off), in 1994 (3,900 employees), and in 1995 (3,900 employees). A better, though still imperfect, accounting treatment might have been to apportion the workforce reduction charges over these three years according to the number of displaced employees.[24] This would have resulted in the workforce reduction costs of $951 million being apportioned as charges against revenue of $283 million in 1993, and $334 million in 1994 and again in 1995. When this adjustment is made, the "bottom line" picture is somewhat different (see table 11–1).

The July-August 1993 Keeping Track featured a new column titled "Dialogue with the President," written (ostensibly) by Tellier. As one might expect, in his first column he emphasizes his commitment to "open lines of communication with employees." He also stresses that CN's "number one priority must be customer satisfaction. That's really the bottom line." The ideology of the market is elevated to prominence. This issue of Keeping Track also contained an article on Tellier titled "This Guy Means Business!" It is laden with metaphor, rhetoric, and cliché. Tellier is characterized as "a CEO who pulls no punches" and "talks straight" about his "vision and plans" to "tur[n] the company around," about "stiff competition," about CN being "at the crossroads," and about "the tail [slack employees?] wagging the dog."

In the next issue of Keeping Track, Tellier continues his barrage, again invoking a health-related metaphor. His "Dialogue with the President" is headed "Strong Medicine." He begins immodestly: "I have a vision for CN." This echoes Martin Luther King's famous "I have a dream," but what Tellier offers is another example of the hackneyed "CEO as seer" metaphor. He strongly enunciates his "vision" in terms of accounting-related variables: "I want CN to be financially sound and I want CN to deliver quality customer service. To become profitable, we have to bring our operating ratio down and increase revenues. I want us to be well on our way to accomplishing all this by 1997. A strong recovery requires strong medicine."[25]

Tellier relentlessly uses profit and financial measures to spur CN employees to achieve "healthier" financial outcomes. In the following month's "Dialogue with the President," he fires more accounting-laced rhetoric at his audience: "Our basic challenge is to take a first-class railway and turn it into a first-class, viable, profitable business concern. And we have to do it fast … we have too much track which generates too little return … there has to be more effective use of our assets … we have to face the fact that no matter how hard we try, some rail lines cannot run at a profit. Lines that swallow scarce financial resources and offer no payback must go."[26]

Clearly, Tellier was not deterred by compassion for the many Canadian communities that would lose their rail service because the track that ran their way generated "too little return." Here we observe reductive accounting language running rampant; the lifeworld of the CEO is articulated in terms of "profitable business concern," "too little return," "profit," "scarce financial resources," and "payback." Such language cannot encompass those who will lose their jobs and see their lives utterly disrupted, or communities that will lose their railways. We may ask whether CEO Tellier really thinks within the confines of this language or whether he simply sees it as a powerful rhetorical device. What is of ultimate importance is that he chose to use this language in the first place.

In his next column, which appeared in November 1993, Tellier refers to CN's "projected year-end results" as "nothing to be proud of" and makes the hyperbolic claim that "we're in a do or die situation." This has strong religious overtones. The way to salvation – the way to "do" rather than "die" – is to follow the Gospel According to Saint Paul (Tellier). Thus we have the metaphor of "the CEO as messiah." Tellier then encourages employees to "become partners" with management to create success in the same way that "co-owners of a small business would work together to make their business a success."[27] One wonders how many employees were gobsmacked by this exhortation. Tellier was certainly not contemplating that employees and management would share equally in any ensuing success. And it is only the survivors of the downsizings that have occurred (and that will occur) who will be around to partner up with the CEO.

The health metaphor, established earlier, continues. It is the "root metaphor" in Tellier's campaign to secure his "vision." For example, his December 1993 *Keeping Track* column is titled "The Long Road to Recovery."[28] In it, he reports some "progress" in restoring "financial health," due, in part, to CN striking "a healthy balance between revenue and costs." This mingling of accounting and health metaphors is rhetorically astute. It employs the ideograph-like word "balance,"[29] which is essential to good health ("a balanced diet") and good accounting ("balanced books").[30]

Tellier uses accounting measures as a sort of mantra to justify his "vision." In his *Keeping Track* column published in January/February 1994, he refers to "the tough situation CN faces," to "the overriding financial and competitive threats which face us," and to "our costs" being "too high for the business we are able to attract."[31] In a column he wrote later that year, he speaks of the "shedding process we have to undergo of our unprofitable lines" and the ongoing need for "large-scale and widespread cost reductions." He credits accounting measures with helping to improve CN's financial health: "Our second quarter profits of $98 million are an encouraging sign that the company is on the mend financially. But, as you know, it's still not enough to make us profitable. We need average annual profits of $400 to $500 million to fund the investments necessary to meet customers' needs, and to maintain the price competitiveness of their products on world markets. To attain that level of profit demands our continued attention to lowering costs and improving service quality."[32] This statement implies a peculiar interpretation of profitability. For Tellier (and CN), "profitability" is not simply the excess of accrued revenues over accrued expenses; it is something that emerges after one has made the investments necessary to satisfy customers' needs. It is a sort of EVA© (economic value added) notion. Again, it reinforces the importance of market ideology in the privatization-positioning of CN.

In his 1997 book *The Pig That Flew: The Battle to Privatize Canadian National*, Harry Bruce praises the "tough decisions" taken by Tellier to make CN a "stock market winner." Indeed, Tellier's accounting-related rhetoric is consistent with the view that he was driven by a hardline, economic-rationalist, free market ideology – that he was unencumbered by concerns about human needs or social justice. Tellier's tenure as CEO in the before-privatization stage was characterized by a privatization ideology created partly through the accounting language and images he used in his discourse directed at CN employees. Profit, achieved principally by serving the market well, was to be the dominating concern. The root metaphor was "profit is a diagnostic barometer of well-being."

People throughout the world hold Canada and Canadians of all walks of life in high esteem for their compassion and social conscience. Why, then, was such a dispassionate, economic-rationalist, social-obligation-free rhetoric uncritically accepted by the government of the day? One explanation is that some powerful members of the government were ideologically predisposed to privatization. One can imagine them drooling at the thought of the huge cash injection to government from the sale of CN. They would also have been dazzled by the prospect of the political benefits that would result when CN was removed from government accounts. And, of course, top management of the new market-driven entity would have been happy that their commercially refashioned compensation packages would be topped up with bonuses "earned" by achieving accounting targets.

The accounting treatments in the before-privatization stage helped create a new accounting income stream that would better please clients of the consortium underwriting the IPO. But employees, their families, and the small towns and industries abandoned by the new "lean and mean" CN weren't part of the equation. The language and rhetoric directed at them (by Tellier and others) was merely placatory. It was intended to disarm threats to the tremendous money bonanza the IPO would bring for the underwriters, the new CN management, and other privatization players.

Tellier's bombardment of employees with accounting-related rhetoric was skilful, effective, misleading, and misplaced. The interests of employees, CN, and the public were conflated with "market efficiency," "financial efficiency," and the "need" for CN to "compete" with "the more efficient" US railway companies. The rhetorical agenda of CEO Tellier, amanuensis of the government of the day, privileged right-wing economic values, language, and ideology. Tellier was aided and abetted by accounting and the language of accounting. Competing views and the voices of many CN stakeholders (here employees, but many others as well) were marginalized. Accounting-related rhetoric was deployed as an instrument of power elites. And, most frighteningly in a democratic society, accounting language became the exclusive means of expressing CN's privatization. In effect, the only language acknowledged was the language of the market,[33] providing further evidence that "the trouble with our civilization is that it has stopped questioning itself."[34] Perhaps we are losing the language(s) with which to do so.

Sociologist Kevin Delaney's poignant *cri de coeur* regarding accounting provides an apposite coda: "But if we continue to treat financial figures as objective reflections of firm health ... we will miss the crucial role that power and strategy play in creating the financial portrait of the firm."[35] Such "power and strategy" seem especially egregious in instances of extreme resource asymmetry, such as the before-privatization campaign at CN.

12

Towards Greater Accountability for CEO-Speak

So, there we have it: an examination of a sampling of the written words and hypertext deployed by CEOs to fashion our view of corporations and their leaders. We have highlighted how CEO-speak (especially that which invokes accounting language in the context of corporate financial accountability) operates in a diverse array of settings. This has revealed, among other things, ways in which CEO-speak has been targeted at multiple and singular audiences; and how it has been a framer of rhetorical objectives, a fashioner of perceptions, a shaper of knowledge, and an influencer of social cognition and cultural relations. We have shown, too, that CEO-speak can have multiple authors constituting an executive elite; that it is not a recent phenomenon; that it can operate in the public sector; and that it has the capacity to exploit hypertextuality for rhetorical effect.

Close readings of CEO-speak have helped us to understand CEOs as individuals, to appreciate how they make sense of the world, and to be more aware of the reasons corporations behave as they do. We have revealed CEO-speak to be a seductive, placatory, variegated, socially constructed language of accountability. But, as well (and confoundingly), we have shown how it can permit CEOs to be *un*accountable. Our exposé leads us to reflect upon some of the fundamental implications of CEO-speak for contemporary society.

CEOs live in a rarefied world. They are often cosseted and insulated from the daily experiences of the average person by a bevy of

sycophantic minders. A tally of the CEOs of the world's largest corporations indicates that there are only a few thousand of them. Yet,
at least for a brief moment in time, each wields immense power
over us, and over the management control systems that structure
the working lives of countless employees. Some CEOs, like Jack
Welch and Bill Gates, hold the reins of power for extended periods.
Some, like Walt Disney, exert a social and cultural influence long after they die. Their CEO-speak influences the world around us and
how we view it. It is certainly worthwhile to subject CEOs and all
that they say and do in the public arena to greater surveillance. This
is an especially urgent necessity in the case of CEOs of large corporations, for the legal institution of these corporations – as critics Bakan and Estes both argue[1] – is most perverse. Bakan uses vivid
imagery to promote closer scrutiny and monitoring of corporations:
"oddly, we are asked to believe that corporate persons – institutionalized psychopaths who lack any sense of moral conviction and
who [have] the power and motivation to cause harm and devasta-
tion in the world – should be left free to govern themselves."[2]

The servings of written CEO-speak we have reviewed here have
been compiled serendipitously and opportunistically. They cover a
wide variety of CEO discourse by mode, time, and context. The
source texts we chose are loosely representative of the wide range of
CEO-speak that warrants close reading. The analysis we provide
merely scratches the surface of a rich vein of discourse by influential
leaders of powerful corporations (or, to use Bakan's term, "institutionalized psychopaths"). What we have analysed is not exhaustive,
but indicative. The selected cases feature male CEOs of very large US
and Canadian companies (the Disney company, small in 1940, is
the sole exception). And although these cases are culturally specific
to the US and Canada, we believe that they reflect attitudes and behaviours in other countries as well. There is, we submit, a global
genre of CEO-speak.

The examples of CEO-speak explored have a key feature in common: to varying degrees, all are public narratives that influence our
outlook and the way we behave in public life. As public narratives authored by powerful CEOs and drawing upon the rugged individualism
of the North American entrepreneurial ethos, their intention is to persuade and influence behaviour. Even more importantly, as we have
highlighted in our chosen examples, they rely heavily on the language
of business, accounting, and the market.[3] The accounting-language

aspect of CEO-speak is vital because it gives particular rhetorical effects to the quest by CEOs for desired outcomes. Accounting language was instrumental, for example, in winning the acceptance of CN employees for a privatization agenda (chapter 11); in fashioning an understanding of accounting and financial reporting amenable to IBM (chapter 6); and in winning the hearts and minds of preferred Disney stockholders when the company was under stress (chapter 8).

In addition to accounting language, we have also analysed CEO-speak in terms of ordinary language – particularly that pervasive feature of the language arts, metaphor. The portrait of the CEO that emerges from our palette of accounting language, ordinary language, and metaphor is far from flattering. CEOs present themselves as visionaries, as messiahs, and as ruthless but effective "trail bosses." And whereas many of them are charismatic and socially revered, they also display hubris, greed, contempt, and deceit. As individuals, CEOs seem adept at suppressing their compassion for the less fortunate, their social conscience, and their concern for the environment. Many are accomplished rhetoricians capable of fashioning a view of financial affairs that serves their ends. They spare little thought for those less well served by the invisible hand of the market.

If there is any truth in Weick's contention that "writing is a tool for comprehension,"[4] then just what is it that our CEOs comprehend? Corporate capitalism and market ideology seem to reign supreme, as if they emitted some sort of irrefutable truth or intoxicating pheromone. CEOs conceive of the public good as the inevitable outcome of a ruthless maximization of profit by individual entities and corporations – an objective towards which they, as CEOs, are guided by the language and measures of accounting ("profit," "rate of return on investment," "economic value added," "cost," and "operating ratio").

Many CEOs revel in their depiction as corporate heroes. They seem convinced that they are latter-day Midases; that their prescience, impeccable leadership, and judgment will produce riches for shareholders; that they themselves will be rewarded with pots of gold in the form of stock options and other types of compensation. CEOs also view themselves as warrior chiefs. They project an image, often constructed for them by pubic relations apparatchiks, of rugged heroism – they are the fierce protectors of throngs of adoring shareholders. They have a strong belief in their innate wisdom, in their intellectual ability to outflank the forces of harm in a ruthless marketplace. They entertain no doubts about their ability to lead their followers to a rosy financial future; and they are eager to exploit a human need to place a mystic, all-powerful, often religious figure on a pedestal. Perhaps, in a society flirting with agnosticism, atheism, and hedonism, the CEO warrior chief has become a surrogate religious icon.

During their tenures, CEOs of large corporations wield enormous power over the day-to-day lives of all citizens. But how effective are we, as a society, in ensuring that they do not abuse that power? How can we make CEOs more accountable for their words and actions? The answers to these questions are complex, but one general imperative is clear. We must somehow engender a new awareness of CEO power and the life-altering consequences of CEO-speak. With this in mind, we now summarize some of the important issues that must be addressed.

As a community, we ought to recognize the power of accounting language and the ways in which we can benefit from employing close readings of accounting-related CEO-speak to identify corporate excesses. The Enron fiasco should act as a catalyst to the new consciousness we envisage. We can no longer afford to be blasé about the use of CEO-speak to inflate expectations, to distort reported profits, and to abet CEOs in amassing obscene fortunes through the exercise of stock options. In recent years, as gleeful voyeurs, we have witnessed the "deranged limitlessness of the greed" of CEOs as their stock options have engendered "quickie fortunes" and "the nearest equivalent that exists to a free lunch."[5] It is heartening that public policy-makers have instituted actions (such as the 2002 *Sarbanes-Oxley Act* in the US) to remove the incentives for CEOs to manipulate their accounts or to "speak up" the financial performances of their companies, thus bolstering their stock options. But the power of big corporations remains largely unbridled, and the potency of new financial accounting and auditing reforms is unproven. This makes ongoing critical scrutiny of CEO-speak a necessary task that should be undertaken widely, including in our schools of business.

The broader question of CEO compensation has even prompted pro-business members of the media to express concern. Lou Dobbs, in a column published on the CNN Web site in 2002, wrote that "overall CEO pay is now 500 times that of the average employee he or she manages. Do you think it's time to think about business reforming business? Or do you believe any of this makes sense?"[6] Like Dobbs, we do not believe that current arrangements for CEO compensation are appropriate. Driving this compensation machine is a complex rhetorical interplay of accounting and other CEO-speak designed to create a social world in which the CEO-as-hero sets corporate goals to which the rest of us acquiesce. CEO-speak is used both overtly and subtly (as in the case of IBM) to manufacture the measures of performance according to which those goals are determined to have been met. But CEO-speak is also very versatile and utilitarian. It is a convenient vehicle for making excuses when things don't turn out as intended (as in the case of Nortel). And sometimes CEO-speak is used to ensure that meaningful societal goals are not achieved (as in the case of CN).

Broadly conceived, CEO-speak is a phenomenon that needs prompt public policy attention. We could brush this task aside on the spurious grounds that "words are just words." Or we could endorse through action the ideas of people like Weick and Searle and advocate making public policy reflect an awareness of CEO-speak and its extraordinary relationship to power and the powerful.[7]

Auditors, too, need a wake-up call, as the spate of corporate collapses in the Western world in the 1990s and early 2000s vividly demonstrates. They need to be conscious that words matter and that executives and company directors exercise accountability through multiple channels, including CEO-speak – especially in its more formal manifestations, such as the annual report shareholders' letter. Of course, audits have to be consistent with these formal manifestations of CEO-speak, but we must remember that there is often a hidden script beneath the apparent meaning. Deciphering this script could well remain beyond the capacity of the auditing fraternity unless there is a major reform of the educational curricula leading to auditor certification. Auditors have a vested interest in upholding the tedious mystique of their craft and of the somewhat perverse "presents fairly" and "true and fair" language in the auditor's report. Enron is an object lesson in the need to take with the utmost seriousness the fundamental concept of accountability. We propose that accountability for CEO-speak should figure prominently in corporate reform endeavours.

We need to ask hard questions to determine whether accountability structures and institutions, enshrined in corporation law and the

disclosure rules of regulatory agencies, have become archaic, ritual-
ized, and ineffective. For example, is the annual general meeting of
a corporation functionally meaningless? Does it serve any accountability purpose? Does it merely provide an occasion for the shareholder tribe and their CEO chieftain to bond? Are the opportunities
for critiquing CEO-speak, for questioning CEOs, and for engaging in
a meaningful accountability dialogue inadequate? And what is the
point of having a rules-based structure for corporate regulation if
we expect our regulatory bodies to function on skimpy budgets? All
the rules, regulations, and accounting standards under the sun will
not ensure good corporate behaviour in the absence of effective
monitoring. We must somehow infuse greater ethicality into the
way we conduct business and into the way CEOs speak about it.
And, of course, our professions (the accounting profession included) must renew their commitment to traditional values of ethicality, integrity, and public service.

So, at the very least, CEO-speak, in all its forms, requires a good
dose of accountability. Perhaps what is needed is a formal commitment on the part of CEOs to broaden their annual shareholders' letters to include reports to all stakeholder constituencies (including
employees, customers, governments). Since incorporation is still a
privilege in many jurisdictions, a new, broader version of CEO-
speak-as-accountability-conversation to a diverse set of stakeholders might be a commendable first step in public policy reform. But it
would only be a tiny first step, since identifying stakeholders to
whom CEOs must be accountable through a grander version of
CEO-speak might prove quite challenging.

Somewhat surprisingly, US president George W. Bush's Plan to
Improve Corporate Responsibility and Protect America's Shareholders – ill-named, because it restricted its purview to shareholders
– contained some good starting points. For example, point 3 of the
ten-point plan is that "CEOs should personally vouch for the veracity, timeliness, and fairness of their companies' public disclosures,
including their financial statements."[8] One hopes that such personal vouching will be extended to include the CEO's public disclosures in the form of CEO-speak.

Educators, employers, politicians – almost everyone, it seems –
have strong views about what should be taught in our schools and
institutions of higher learning. We must confront basic pedagogical
questions. As citizens, do we want to be mindful of the discourse of

the most powerful people in our society? Do we want to be full participants in the democratic process? Do we want to stop being naive and hypocritical when it comes to constructing curricula?

In chapter 1, we quoted Boje (a seasoned observer of the corporate scene) as saying that "corporate writing has been imitated and celebrated by academic writers without much critical reflection on the kinds of issues it raises."[9] We concur, and we hope that the issues we have drawn attention to here create greater impetus to analyse the written words of CEOs. We also hope that such discussion inspires curriculum reform in business, accounting, and management education. In the Internet age, education has become a commodity, and we (and many other critics) believe that this is not a universally good thing for our society.[10] If we are to develop a critical awareness of our social and physical environment and a sense of community, then we must make sure that the curricula of our schools, colleges, and universities allow students to learn about the thoughts and words of the most powerful people in their world – such as corporate CEOs. We need to rethink what we teach. We need to educate students to have a functional civic knowledge, a consciousness of power structures, an understanding of CEO-speak and its hidden assumptions and metaphors. We need to generate an awareness of the need for formal scrutiny of what CEOs say.

University business schools should introduce courses that focus on critical textual analysis (especially of metaphor, rhetoric, and ideology) to equip graduates to understand the language of accountability – a language that now pervades our society.[11] Also, we should vigorously promote the study of the sociology of organizations in a way that emphasizes the importance of critical analysis and multiple perspectives. The accounting curricula, known for its fixation with tedious procedure, needs to devote far more attention to the power structures of organizations and the way in which CEO-speak affects, and is affected by, accounting. Courses on financial reporting should include analysis of words, metaphors, and rhetorical devices and develop a broader sensitivity to the ideological frames within which corporations and society operate. In short, we need to reassess how we educate students about corporations and their leaders.

One wonders how CEOs and their CEO-speak could have had such a charmed run without eliciting more scrutiny and criticism from the financial press, the academic community, public intellectuals, and the accounting and auditing fraternity. The explanation seems to be that many of our opinion formers were making too much money from the current system to want to express even mild indignation. Of course, the disturbing effect of the concentration of media ownership in the hands of a few individuals – Rupert Murdoch, Ted Turner, Conrad Black – all of them CEOs commanding global corporations, explains why the media tend to back off from the fight.

As for academics, their views are often dismissed as out-of-touch rantings from an ivory tower. Critical essays about prominent CEOs generally appear only in academic journals. They are read by few, and the important ideas they contain rarely find their way to a larger audience.

We could subject CEO-speak to an audit or independent review, but we are reluctant to do so. One reason for this may be that we are besotted with CEO superheroes and all they write; another may be that we disregard the power and importance of words. As a society, we are losing our critical faculties. We are so obsessed with the financial and accounting numbers that we ignore the accompanying text. But we must change our ways, for, as we have shown, corporate writing by the most senior of corporate officers, CEOs, can be wicked stuff – it can reveal aspects of CEO psychology that would keep followers of Freud entertained for years.

APPENDICES

Skilling and Lay's Last Letter
to Shareholders of Enron

1 LETTER TO SHAREHOLDERS

2 Enron's performance in 2000 was a success by any measure, as we
3 continued to outdistance the competition and solidify our leadership
4 in each of our major businesses. In our largest business, wholesale
5 services, we experienced an enormous increase of 59 percent in phys-
6 ical energy deliveries. Our retail energy business achieved its highest
7 level ever of total contract value. Our newest business, broadband
8 services, significantly accelerated transaction activity, and our oldest
9 business, the interstate pipelines, registered increased earnings. The
10 company's net income reached a record $1.3 billion in 2000.

11 Enron has built unique and strong businesses that have tremendous
12 opportunities for growth. These businesses – wholesale services, re-
13 tail energy services, broadband services and transportation services –
14 can be significantly expanded within their very large existing mar-
15 kets and extended to new markets with enormous growth potential.
16 At a minimum, we see our market opportunities company-wide tri-
17 pling over the next five years.

18 Enron is laser-focused on earnings per share, and we expect to continue
19 strong earnings performance. We will leverage our extensive business
20 networks, market knowledge and logistical expertise to produce high-
21 value bundled products for an increasing number of global customers.

22 COMPETITIVE ADVANTAGES

23 Our targeted markets are very large and are undergoing fundamental
24 changes. Energy deregulation and liberalization continue, and cus-
25 tomers are driving demand for reliable delivery of energy at predict-
26 able prices. Many markets are experiencing tighter supply, higher
27 prices and increased volatility, and there is increasing interdepen-
28 dence within regions and across commodities. Similarly, the broad-
29 band industry faces issues of overcapacity and capital constraint
30 even as demand increases for faster, flexible and more reliable con-
31 nectivity. Enron is in a unique position to provide the products and
32 services needed in these environments. Our size, experience and skills
33 give us enormous competitive advantages. We have:

34 Robust networks of strategic assets that we own or have contractual
35 access to, which give us greater flexibility and speed to reliably de-
36 liver widespread logistical solutions.

37 Unparalleled liquidity and market-making abilities that result in
38 price and service advantages.

39 Risk management skills that enable us to offer reliable prices as well
40 as reliable delivery.

41 Innovative technology such as EnronOnline to deliver products and
42 services easily at the lowest possible cost.

43 These capabilities enable us to provide high-value products and ser-
44 vices other wholesale service providers cannot. We can take the phys-
45 ical components and repackage them to suit the specific needs of
46 customers. We treat term, price and delivery as variables that are
47 blended into a single, comprehensive solution. Our technology and
48 fulfilment systems ensure execution. In current market environ-
49 ments, these abilities make Enron the right company with the right
50 model at the right time.

51 THE ASTONISHING SUCCESS OF ENRONONLINE

52 In late 1999 we extended our successful business model to a web-based
53 system, EnronOnline. EnronOnline has broadened our market reach,

54 accelerated our business activity and enabled us to scale our business
55 beyond our own expectations. By the end of 2000, EnronOnline had
56 executed 548,000 transactions with a notional value of $336 billion,
57 and it is now the world's largest web-based eCommerce system.

58 With EnronOnline, we are reaching a greater number of customers
59 more quickly and at a lower cost than ever. It's a great new business
60 generator, attracting users who are drawn by the site's ease of use,
61 transparent, firm prices and the fact that they are transacting directly
62 with Enron. In 2000 our total physical volumes increased signifi-
63 cantly as a direct result of EnronOnline.

64 EnronOnline has enabled us to scale quickly, soundly and economi-
65 cally. Since its introduction, EnronOnline has expanded to include
66 more than 1,200 of our products. It also has streamlined our back-of-
67 fice processes, making our entire operation more efficient. It has re-
68 duced our overall transaction costs by 75 percent and increased the
69 productivity of our commercial team by five-fold on average. We are
70 not sitting still with this important new business tool – in September
71 2000 we released EnronOnline 2.0, which added even more customer
72 functionality and customization features and attracted more customers.

73 ENRON WHOLESALE SERVICES

74 The wholesale services business delivered record physical volumes of
75 51.7 trillion British thermal units equivalent per day (TBtue/d) in
76 2000, compared to 32.4 TBtue/d in 1999. As a result, wholesale ser-
77 vices income before interest, minority interests and taxes (IBIT) in-
78 creased 72 percent to $2.3 billion. Over the past five years, as
79 physical volumes have increased, wholesale IBIT has grown at a
80 compounded average annual rate of 48 percent, and we have had 20
81 consecutive quarters of year-over-year growth. We have established
82 core wholesale businesses in both natural gas and power in North
83 America and Europe, where we are market leaders.

84 In North America, we deliver almost double the amount of natural
85 gas and electricity than the second tier of competitors. Our network
86 of 2,500 delivery points provides price advantages, flexibility and
87 speed-to-market in both natural gas and power. Natural gas, our
88 most developed business, has seen substantial volume growth

89 throughout the United States and Canada. In 2000 our physical nat-
90 ural gas volumes were up 77 percent to 24.7 billion cubic feet per
91 day (Bcf/d). Physical power volumes were up 52 percent to 579 mil-
92 lion megawatt-hours (MWh).

93 We are building a similar, large network in Europe. In 2000 we mar-
94 keted 3.6 Bcf/d of natural gas and 53 million MWh in this market, a
95 vast increase over 1999. As markets open, we tenaciously pursue the
96 difficult, early deals that break ground for subsequent business. We
97 are the only pan-European player, and we are optimizing our advan-
98 tage to conduct cross-border transactions.

99 We are extending Enron's proven business approach to other mar-
100 kets, and integrating EnronOnline into all our businesses as an accel-
101 erator. Our growth rates are rising in areas such as metals, forest
102 products, weather derivatives and coal. We expect these businesses
103 to contribute to earnings even more significantly in 2001.

104 ENRON ENERGY SERVICES

105 Our retail unit is a tremendous business that experienced a break-out
106 year in 2000. We signed contracts with a total value of $16.1 billion
107 of customers' future energy expenditures, almost double the $8.5 bil-
108 lion signed in 1999. We recorded increasing positive earnings in all
109 four quarters in 2000, and the business generated $103 million of re-
110 curring IBIT. Energy and facilities management outsourcing is now a
111 proven concept, and we've established a profitable deal flow, which
112 includes extensions of contracts by many existing customers. Price
113 volatility in energy markets has drawn fresh attention to our capabil-
114 ities, increasing demand for our services. No other provider has the
115 skill, experience, depth and versatility to offer both energy commod-
116 ity and price risk management services, as well as energy asset man-
117 agement and capital solutions. In 2001 we expect to close
118 approximately $30 billion in new total contract value, including busi-
119 ness from our newest market, Europe.

120 ENRON BROADBAND SERVICES

121 We have created a new market for bandwidth intermediation with
122 Enron Broadband Services. In 2000 we completed 321 transactions
123 with 45 counterparties. We are expanding our broadband intermedi-

124 ation capabilities to include a broad range of network services, such
125 as dark fiber, circuits, Internet Protocol service and data storage. Our
126 opportunities are increasing commensurately.

127 Part of the value we bring to the broadband field is network connectiv-
128 ity – providing the switches, the network intelligence and the inter-me-
129 diation skills to enable the efficient exchange of capacity between
130 independent networks. We operate 25 pooling points to connect inde-
131 pendent third-parties – 18 in the United States, six in Europe and one in
132 Japan. At least 10 more are scheduled to be completed in 2001.

133 Enron also has developed a compelling commerical [sic] model to de-
134 liver premium content-on-demand services via the Enron Intelligent
135 Network. Content providers want to extend their established busi-
136 nesses and offer viewers at home an additional convenient way to
137 choose and receive entertainment. Enron provides the wholesale lo-
138 gistical services that bridge the gap between content providers and
139 last-mile distributors. Full-length movies-on-demand service has
140 been successfully tested in four U.S. metropolitan markets.

141 ENRON TRANSPORTATION SERVICES

142 The new name for our gas pipeline group accurately reflects a cul-
143 tural shift to add more innovative customer services to our efficient
144 pipeline operation. To serve our customers more effectively, we are
145 increasingly incorporating the web into those relationships. Custom-
146 ers can go online to schedule nominations and handle inquiries, and
147 they can transact for available capacity on EnronOnline. The pipe-
148 lines continued to provide strong earnings and cash flow in 2000.
149 Demand for natural gas is at a high in the United States, and we're
150 adding capacity to take advantage of expansion opportunities in all
151 markets. New capacity is supported by long-term contracts.

152 STRONG RETURNS

153 Enron is increasing earnings per share and continuing our strong returns
154 to shareholders. Recurring earnings per share have increased steadily
155 since 1997 and were up 25 percent in 2000. The company's total return
156 to shareholders was 89 percent in 2000, compared with a negative
157 9 percent returned by the s&p 500. The 10-year return to Enron share-
158 holders was 1,415 percent compared with 383 percent for the s&p 500.

159   Enron hardly resembles the company we were in the early days. Dur-
160   ing our 15-year history, we have stretched ourselves beyond our own
161   expectations. We have metamorphosed from an asset-based pipeline
162   and power generating company to a marketing and logistics com-
163   pany whose biggest assets are its well-established business approach
164   and its innovative people.

165   Our performance and capabilities cannot be compared to a tradi-
166   tional energy peer group. Our results put us in the top tier of the
167   world's corporations. We have a proven business concept that is em-
168   inently scalable in our existing businesses and adaptable enough to
169   extend to new markets.

170   As energy markets continue their transformation, and non-energy
171   markets develop, we are poised to capture a good share of the enor-
172   mous opportunities they represent. We believe wholesale gas and
173   power in North America, Europe and Japan will grow from a $660
174   billion market today to a $1.7 trillion market over the next several
175   years. Retail energy services in the United States and Europe have the
176   potential to grow from $180 billion today to $765 billion in the not-
177   so-distant future. Broadband's prospective global growth is huge – it
178   should increase from just $17 billion today to $1.4 trillion within
179   five years.

180   Taken together, these markets present a $3.9 trillion opportunity for
181   Enron, and we have just scratched the surface. Add to that the other
182   big markets we are pursuing – forest products, metals, steel, coal and
183   air-emissions credits – and the opportunity rises by $830 billion to
184   reach nearly $4.7 trillion.

185   Our talented people, global presence, financial strength and massive
186   market knowledge have created our sustainable and unique busi-
187   nesses. EnronOnline will accelerate their growth. We plan to lever-
188   age all of these competitive advantages to create significant value for
189   our shareholders.

190   Kenneth L. Lay
191   Chairman

192   Jeffrey K. Skilling
193   President and Chief Executive Officer

Remarks of Joseph F. Berardino, Managing Partner/CEO of Andersen, to the US House of Representatives Committee on Financial Services, 12 December 2001

1 Chairman Oxley, Congressman LaFalce, Chairman Baker, Congress-
2 man Kanjorski, Chairwoman Kelly, Congressman Gutierrez, Mem-
3 bers of the Committee.

4 I am here today because faith in our firm and in the integrity of the cap-
5 ital market system has been shaken. There is some explaining to do.

6 What happened at Enron is a tragedy on many levels. We are acutely
7 aware of the impact this has had on investors. We also recognize the
8 pain this business failure has caused for Enron's employees and others.

9 Many questions about Enron's failure need to be answered, and
10 some involve accounting and auditing matters. I will do my best to-
11 day to address those.

12 I ask that you keep in mind that the relevant auditing and accounting
13 issues are extraordinarily complex and part of a much bigger picture.
14 None of us here yet knows all the facts. Today's hearing is an impor-
15 tant step in enlightening all of us. I am certain that together we will
16 get to the facts.

17 If there is one thing you take away from my testimony, I hope it is
18 this: Andersen will not hide from its responsibilities. That's why I'm

19 here today. The public's confidence is of paramount importance. If
20 my firm has made errors in judgment, we will acknowledge them.
21 We will make the changes needed to restore confidence.

22 Today, I want to address two issues that go to the heart of concerns
23 about our role as Enron's auditor.

24 First, did we do our job? I want to explain what we knew and when
25 we knew it on several key issues, keeping in mind that our own re-
26 view – like yours – is still under way.

27 Second, did we act with integrity? I want to discuss the $52 million
28 in fees we received and respond to concerns that have been raised.

29 I also want to talk about what I believe are some of the lessons we
30 can already learn from Enron
31 – for our firm, for the accounting profession, and for all participants
32 in the financial reporting system.

33 Let me start by telling you what we know about three particular ac-
34 counting and reporting issues:

35 the restatements caused by the consolidation of two Special Purpose
36 Entities, known as SPEs, and the recording of previously "passed"
37 adjustments as a required byproduct of the restatement;
38 a $1.2 billion reclassification in the presentation of shareholders' eq-
39 uity during 2001 – of which $172 million was misclassified in the
40 audited 2000 financial statement, and;
41 the company's disclosures about its off-balance-sheet transactions
42 and related financial activities.

43 I want to emphasize that my remarks are based on the information
44 that is currently available. We have made our best efforts to be com-
45 plete and accurate in describing what we know. But our review, like
46 the work of the SEC, this Committee, Enron's board, and others, is
47 not yet complete. It is always possible that new information could be
48 developed that would change current understanding of events or un-
49 cover new events.

50 *Consolidation of Special Purpose Entities*

51 Let me begin with the Special Purpose Entities. SPEs are financing ve-
52 hicles that permit companies, like Enron, to, among other things, ac-
53 cess capital or to increase leverage without adding debt to their
54 balance sheet. Wall Street has helped companies raise billions of dol-
55 lars with these structured financings, which are well known to ana-
56 lysts and sophisticated investors.

57 Two SPEs were involved in Enron's recent restatement announce-
58 ment. On one, the smaller of them, we made a professional judgment
59 about the appropriate accounting treatment that turned out to be
60 wrong. On the one with the larger impact, it would appear that our
61 audit team was not provided critical information. We are trying to
62 determine what happened and why.

63 Let's begin with the larger SPE, an entity called Chewco. What hap-
64 pened with Chewco accounted for about 80 percent of the SPE-
65 related restatement.

66 In 1993, Enron and the California Pubic Employees Retirement System
67 (Calpers) formed a 50/50 partnership they called Joint Energy Devel-
68 opment Investments Limited, or JEDI for short. Among other factors,
69 the fact that Enron did not control more than 50 percent of JEDI
70 meant that that partnership's financial statements could not be consoli-
71 dated with Enron's financial statements under the accounting rules. In
72 1997, Chewco bought out Calpers' interest in JEDI. Enron sponsored
73 Chewco's creation as an SPE and had investments in Chewco.

74 The rules behind what happened are complex, but can be boiled
75 down to this. The accounting rules dictate, among other things, that
76 unrelated parties must have residual equity equal to at least 3 percent
77 of the fair value of an SPE's assets in order for the SPE to qualify for
78 non- consolidation. However, there is no prohibition against com-
79 pany employees also being involved as investors, provided that vari-
80 ous tests were met, including the 3 percent test.

81 In 1997, we performed audit procedures on the Chewco transaction.
82 The information provided to our auditors showed that approximately

83 $11.4 million in Chewco had come from a large international financial
84 institution unrelated to Enron. That equity met the 3 percent residual
85 equity test. However, we recently learned that Enron had arranged a
86 separate agreement with that institution under which cash collateral
87 was provided for half of the residual equity. What happened?

88 Very significantly, at the time of our 1997 procedures, the company
89 did not reveal that it had this agreement with the financial institu-
90 tion. With this separate agreement, the bank had only one-half of
91 the necessary equity at risk. As a result, Chewco's financial state-
92 ments since 1997 were required to be consolidated with JEDI's
93 which, in a domino effect, then had to be consolidated in Enron's fi-
94 nancial statements.

95 It is not clear why the relevant information was not provided to us.
96 We are still looking into that. On November 2, 2001, we notified En-
97 ron's audit committee of possible illegal acts within the company, as
98 required under Section 10A of the Securities and Exchange Act.

99 Now, about the second SPE structure; specifically, a subsidiary of the en-
100 tity known as LJM1. This transaction was responsible for about 20 per-
101 cent – or $100 million – of Enron's recent SPE-related restatement.

102 In retrospect, we believe LJM1's subsidiary should have been consol-
103 idated. I am here today to tell you candidly that this was the result of
104 an error in judgment. Essentially, this is what happened:

105 After our initial review of LJM1 in 1999, Enron decided to create a
106 subsidiary within LJM1, informally referred to as Swap Sub. As a re-
107 sult of this change, the 3 percent test for residual equity had to be
108 met not only by LJM1, but also by LJM1's subsidiary, Swap Sub.

109 In evaluating the 3 percent residual equity level required to qualify
110 for non-consolidation, there were some complex issues concerning
111 the valuation of various assets and liabilities. When we reviewed this
112 transaction again in October 2001, we determined that our team's
113 initial judgment that the 3 percent test was met was in error. We
114 promptly told Enron to correct it.

115 We are still looking into the facts. But given what we know now, this
116 appears to have been the result of a reasonable effort, made in good
117 faith.

118 *Adjustments previously not made to Enron's 1997 financial statement*

119 As a result of the restatement for the SPEs, Enron was required to ad-
120 dress proposed adjustments to its financial statements that were not
121 made during the periods subject to restatement. Questions have been
122 raised about certain of these "passed adjustments." Let me address
123 that issue next.

124 As part of the audit process, the auditor proposes adjustments to the
125 company's financial statements based on its interpretation of Gener-
126 ally Accepted Accounting Principles (GAAP). A company's decision
127 to decline to make proposed adjustments does not mean that there
128 has been an intentional effort to misstate. If the auditor believes that
129 the company's actions result in either an intentional error or a mate-
130 rial misstatement, it may not sign the audit opinion.

131 Often, there is a timing issue to consider. These adjustments typically
132 are proposed by the auditor at the conclusion of the audit work –
133 usually one or two months after the close of the year-end. Some com-
134 panies, like Enron, choose to book those adjustments in the year af-
135 ter the auditor identifies them, when they are immaterial.

136 Questions have been raised about $51 million in adjustments not
137 made in 1997 when Enron reported net income totaling $105 mil-
138 lion. Some have asked how adjustments representing almost half of
139 reported net income could have been deemed to be immaterial.

140 Auditing standards and SEC guidance say both qualitative and quan-
141 titative factors need to be considered in determining whether some-
142 thing is material. The Supreme Court has described this approach as
143 the "total mix" of information that auditors must consider.

144 In 1997, Enron had taken large nonrecurring charges. When the com-
145 pany decided to pass these proposed adjustments, our audit team had
146 to determine whether the company's decision had a material impact

147 on the financial statements. The question was whether the team
148 should only use reported income of $105 million, or should it also
149 consider adjusted earnings before items that affect comparability –
150 what accountants call "normalized" income?

151 We looked at "the total mix" and, in our judgment, on a quantita-
152 tive basis, the passed adjustments were deemed not to be material,
153 amounting to less than 8 percent of normalized earnings. Normal-
154 ized income was deemed appropriate in light of the fact that the
155 company had reported net income of $584 million one year earlier,
156 in 1996, $520 million in 1995 and $453 million in 1994.

157 It is also important to remind you that the restatement analysis pre-
158 sented in Enron's recent 8-K filing was not audited. When Enron's
159 audited restatement is issued, the $51 million in adjustments pre-
160 sented in 1997 will be reduced for the effect of adjustments proposed
161 in 1996, which were recorded in 1997.

162 *Reclassification of $1.2 billion of shareholders' equity*

163 Now let me turn to the issue of shareholders' equity. Shareholders'
164 equity was incorrectly presented on Enron's balance sheet last year
165 and in two unaudited quarters this year.

166 Auditors do not test every transaction and they are not expected to.
167 To do so would be impractical and would be prohibitively expensive.
168 EnronOnline alone handled over 500,000 transactions last year.

169 Auditing standards require an audit scope sufficient to provide rea-
170 sonable – not absolute – assurance that any material errors will be
171 identified. This testing is based on a cost-effective and proven tech-
172 nique known as sampling. If appropriate accounting is found in a
173 properly chosen sample, this generally provides reasonable assurance
174 that the accounting for the whole population of transactions has been
175 done in accordance with GAAP and is free of material misstatement.

176 Shareholders' equity was initially overstated last year for a transaction
177 with a balance sheet effect of $172 million. This amount was recorded
178 as an asset, but should have been presented as a reduction in share-
179 holders' equity. That amount, $172 million, was less than one third of

180 one percent of Enron's total assets and approximately 1.5 percent of
181 shareholders' equity of $11.5 billion. It was a very small item relative
182 to total assets and equity and had no impact on earnings or cash flow.
183 Accordingly, the transaction fell below the scope of our audit.

184 In the first quarter of this year, Enron accounted for several more
185 transactions in a similar way, increasing the size of the incorrect pre-
186 sentation of shareholders' equity by about $828 million.

187 The quarterly financial statements of public companies are not subject
188 to an audit, and we did not conduct an audit of Enron's quarterly re-
189 ports. Consistent with the applicable standards, our work primarily
190 was a limited review of the company's unaudited financial statements.

191 In the third quarter, Enron closed out the transactions that included
192 the $172 million and the $828 million equity amounts, and we and
193 Enron reviewed the associated accounting. This review included
194 third-quarter impacts on the profit and loss statement and on the
195 balance sheet. This is when the erroneous presentation of sharehold-
196 ers' equity came into focus.

197 We had discussed the proper accounting treatment for similar types
198 of transactions with Enron's accounting staff, and therefore, the
199 scope of our work on the year 2000 audit and this year's quarterly
200 reviews did not anticipate this sort of error. When we informed the
201 company of the error, the company made the necessary changes in its
202 financial statements.

203 *Questions about disclosure*

204 Questions have been raised about the sufficiency of Enron's disclo-
205 sures, especially about unconsolidated entities. I ask you to keep in
206 mind that the company disclosed in its financial statements that it
207 was using a number of unconsolidated structured financing vehicles.
208 Unconsolidated means, by definition, that the assets and liabilities of
209 these entities were not recorded in Enron's financial statements.
210 However, in certain circumstances, footnote disclosures are required.

211 With that disclaimer, let me offer one man's view of what investors
212 were told. Enron had hundreds of structured finance transactions.

213 Some were simple; others, very complex. The company did not dis-
214 close the details of every transaction, which is acceptable under
215 GAAP, but it did disclose those involving related parties and uncon-
216 solidated equity affiliates.

217 JEDI and other entities are listed in footnote nine of Enron's 2000
218 annual report.

219 LJM1 and LJM2, involving the company's former CFO, both were de-
220 scribed in the 1999 and 2000 annual reports and described more
221 fully in its annual proxy statements.

222 In footnote 11 to the 2000 annual report, Enron also disclosed under
223 the heading "Derivative Instruments" that it had derivative instru-
224 ments on 12 million shares of its common stock with JEDI and 22.5
225 million with related parties.

226 Some people say we should have required the company to make
227 more disclosures about contingencies, such as accelerated debt pay-
228 ments, associated with a possible decline in the value of Enron's
229 stock or changes in the company's credit rating.

230 I ask you to keep in mind that the company's shares were coming off
231 near record levels when we completed our audit for 2000. No one
232 could have anticipated the sudden, rapid decline we witnessed in this
233 stock and its credit ratings, and accounting rules don't require a
234 company to disclose remote contingencies.

235 That said, we continue to believe investors would be better served if
236 our accounting rules were changed to reflect the risks and rewards of
237 transactions such as SPEs, not just who controls them. Putting more
238 of the assets and liabilities that are at risk on the balance sheet would
239 do more than additional disclosure ever could. We have advocated
240 changes in these accounting rules since 1982.

241 I offer an additional observation about Enron's disclosures. Press re-
242 ports indicate that some who analyzed the company's public disclo-
243 sures came to the conclusion that perceptions about the company –
244 and thus the market's valuation of Enron – were not supported by
245 what was in the company's public filings.

246 *Fees paid to Andersen*

247 Some are questioning whether the size of our fees, $52 million, and
248 the fact that we were paid $27 million for services other than the En-
249 ron audit, may have compromised our independence at Enron. I un-
250 derstand that the size of fees might raise questions, and I think our
251 profession must be sensitive to that perception.

252 With that in mind, I think it would be helpful for the Committee to
253 have a deeper understanding of the nature of the work we did for
254 Enron, and how the fees for that work were reported.

255 As a starting point, it is important to recognize that Enron was a big,
256 complex company. Enron had $100 billion in sales last year. It oper-
257 ated 25,000 miles of interstate pipeline and an 18,000-mile global fi-
258 ber optic network. Enron did business in many countries. Its
259 EnronOnline trading system was the world's largest web-based
260 eCommerce system and handled more than half a million transac-
261 tions last year – for 1,200 products. Enron was the seventh largest
262 company on the Fortune 500.

263 This was not a simple company. It was not a simple company to au-
264 dit. In addition to its operations and trading, Enron, as we know, en-
265 gaged in sophisticated financial transactions. Not a few, but
266 hundreds. Assets worldwide totaled $65 billion, both before and af-
267 ter Enron adjusted for the restatements

268 Given this complexity, it should not surprise anyone that the fees paid
269 to our firm for Enron's audit were substantial. The $25 million we
270 were paid for Enron's audit last year is comparable to the amounts
271 that General Electric and Citigroup, two sophisticated financial ser-
272 vices providers, paid for their audits. It is slightly more than the audit
273 fees paid by two others – JPMorgan Chase and Merrill Lynch.

274 Because of the way the fee categories for new proxy statement disclo-
275 sures on auditor fees were defined, many services traditionally pro-
276 vided by auditors – and in many cases *only* provided by auditors –
277 now are classified as "Other." Regrettably, without knowledge of
278 the underlying facts, this leads some to believe that such fees are for
279 "consulting" services.

280 In fact, $2.4 million of the $27 million in "Other" fees reported by
281 Enron last year related to work we did on registration statements and
282 comfort letters. This is work only a company's audit firm can do.

283 Another $3.5 million was for tax work, which has never even been
284 mentioned as a conflict with audit work. Audit firms almost always
285 do tax work for clients.

286 Another $3.2 million of the "Other" fees Enron paid us last year re-
287 lated to a review of the controls associated with a new accounting
288 system – a service highly relevant to the auditor's understanding of
289 the company's financial reporting system. Another Big Five firm in-
290 stalled that financial accounting system – for about $30 million.

291 Finally, $4 million of the fees listed as having been paid to Andersen
292 were, in fact, paid to Andersen Consulting, now known as Accen-
293 ture. As most of you know, our firms formally separated last August
294 and had been operating as independent businesses for some time.
295 Nevertheless, the rules said Enron had to report any fees it paid to
296 Andersen Consulting as having been paid to its audit firm.

297 If you take all these factors into account, the total fees that Arthur
298 Andersen received from Enron last year amounted to $47.5 million.
299 And of this, about $34.2 million, or 72 percent, was audit-related
300 and tax work. Total fees for other services paid to our firm
301 amounted to $13.3 million. This was for several projects, none of
302 which was for systems implementation or for more than $3 million.

303 Some may still assert that even $13 million of consulting work is too
304 much – that it weakens the backbone of the auditor. There is a fun-
305 damental issue here. Whether it's consulting work or audit work, the
306 reality is that auditors are paid by their clients. For our system to
307 work, you and the investing public must have confidence that the
308 fees we are paid, regardless of the nature of our work, will not
309 weaken our willingness to do what is right and in the best interest of
310 the investors as represented by the audit committee and the board.

311 I do not believe the fees we received compromised our independence.
312 Obviously, some will disagree. And I have to deal with the reality of

313 that perception. I am acutely aware that our firm must restore the
314 public's trust. I do not have all the answers today. But I can assure
315 you that we are carefully assessing this issue and will take the steps
316 necessary to reassure you and the public that our backbone is firm
317 and our judgment is clear.

318 *Lessons for the Future*

319 When a calamity happens, it is absolutely appropriate to ask what
320 everyone involved could have done to prevent it. By asking the other
321 witnesses and me to testify today, the committee is working hard, in
322 good faith, to understand the issues involved and to help prevent a
323 recurrence with another company.

324 I believe that there is a crisis of confidence in my profession. This is
325 deeply troubling to me, as I believe it is a concern for all of the pro-
326 fession's leaders and, indeed, all of our professionals. Real change
327 will be required to regain the public's trust.

328 Andersen will have to change, and we are working hard to identify
329 the changes that we should make.

330 The accounting profession will have to reform itself. Our system of
331 regulation and discipline will have to be improved. I discussed some
332 of the issues that the profession faces in an op-ed in the *Wall Street
333 Journal* last week, which is attached to my testimony.

334 Other participants in the financial reporting system will have to do
335 things differently as well – companies, boards, audit committees, an-
336 alysts, investment bankers, credit analysts, and others.

337 We all must work together to give investors more meaningful, rele-
338 vant and timely, information.

339 But our work starts with our firm. We are committed to making the
340 changes needed to restore confidence.

341 A day does not go by without new information being made avail-
342 able, and I would observe that all of us here today – and many others

343 who are not here – have a responsibility to seek out and evaluate the
344 facts and take needed action. My firm, and I personally as its CEO,
345 will continue to do our part. I hope that my participation today has
346 been helpful to your efforts.

347 Thank you.

AOLTimeWarner's Internet
Policy Statement

 1 DEVELOPING MEDIA AND COMMUNICATIONS POLICY IN THE IN-
 2 TERNET CENTURY

 3 A fundamental change is taking place in the media and communica-
 4 tions landscape – a change made possible by the Internet and the ad-
 5 vent of new ways to connect, inform and entertain that we only
 6 dreamed of even five years ago.

 7 Broadband connections that enrich the quality of online content like
 8 digital music and movies and broaden the distribution of news, in-
 9 formation and entertainment ... wireless services and handheld and
10 household devices that make these products and services available to
11 consumers anytime and anywhere – these are just a few of the excit-
12 ing new opportunities consumers can already access and enjoy.

13 These changes are energizing existing businesses and transforming
14 traditional media, even as they create new businesses and entirely
15 new industries. And we are really only scratching the surface of what
16 can be achieved.

17 In short, a new world is emerging – a more converged world, a more
18 interactive world. At AOL Time Warner, we want to lead this new

19 world, not only by providing our millions of readers, viewers, listeners,
20 members and subscribers with instant access to a breathtaking array of
21 choices in content and ways to connect, but also by spurring the devel-
22 opment of innovative products and services that benefit consumers.

23 We believe that creating value on this scale requires the right public
24 policy structure. AOL Time Warner will vigorously address the is-
25 sues and opportunities that affect our existing businesses, both on-
26 line and off. At the same time, we will work together with all
27 stakeholders – in both the public and private sectors – to establish a
28 public policy framework for the converging networked world. We
29 believe that such a framework is essential to encourage the continued
30 innovation and dynamism that will drive the next media and com-
31 munications revolution – and benefit communities around the world
32 – in the Internet Century.

33 **Policy Guidelines**
34 AOL Time Warner believes that a few basic principles should guide
35 the development of a new public policy framework for a new world.

36 **AOL Time Warner's position on specific issues of public policy:**
37 **Education and 21st Century Literacy**
38 **Closing the Digital Divide**
39 **Privacy, Security and Consumer Protection**
40 **Consumer Choice of ISPs**
41 **The First Amendment**
42 **Responsible Guidance on Entertainment**
43 **Intellectual Property**
44 **International Telecommunications Issues**
45 **Trade and E-Commerce**
46 **Taxation and E-Commerce**
47 **Postal Rates**

48 **Education and 21st Century Literacy**
49 In the Digital Age, education and literacy matter more than ever be-
50 fore, and media, communications and information technology have
51 an unlimited potential to improve the quality of our educational sys-
52 tems at every level. AOL Time Warner believes that public policy
53 must reflect the changing landscape of education and the changing
54 needs of young people entering today's job market.

55 Together with the AOL Time Warner Foundation, we are committed
56 to making technology, education and 21st century literacy public
57 policy priorities at the federal, state and local level. We support a va-
58 riety of programs and efforts to connect schools, libraries and com-
59 munity centers, incorporate new technology into curricula, improve
60 teacher training, provide young people with the tools and guidance
61 they need to succeed and help people of all ages to improve their
62 skills throughout their lives.

63 **Closing the Digital Divide**
64 Information and communication technologies can be a powerful force
65 for good, offering greater economic, political and social participation
66 to communities that have traditionally been underserved. In the United
67 States and around the world, the online medium holds enormous po-
68 tential to empower communities to meet their economic and social
69 needs. Developing nations have a particularly strong interest in taking
70 advantage of the unprecedented opportunity offered by the online me-
71 dium to meet vital development goals such as poverty reduction, basic
72 healthcare and education far more effectively than ever before.

73 Together with the AOL Time Warner Foundation, AOL Time
74 Warner supports a wide range of initiatives designed to develop the
75 information infrastructure, provide better education and awareness,
76 and bolster community-based projects around the world. We are
77 committed to working with lawmakers and advocates to encourage a
78 policy and regulatory environment that fosters widespread access to
79 information and communications technology in the U.S. and abroad.

80 To us, bridging the Digital Divide is a strategic imperative – the more
81 people come online, the more valuable the global network becomes
82 to everyone. To realize the full economic and social potential of this
83 technology, we must ensure digital opportunity for all.

84 **Privacy, Security and Consumer Protection**
85 Earning our customers' trust by protecting their privacy and ensur-
86 ing their security is essential to the growth of all of our businesses –
87 and the growth of the online medium.

88 As the Internet has become increasingly central to people's lives,
89 AOL Time Warner has established the strongest consumer protection

90 and privacy standards in the industry. Our commitment to ensuring
91 children's online privacy and security is a centerpiece of our public
92 policy agenda: from putting in place special parental controls that
93 help parents guide their children's online experience, to working
94 within our industry to increase public awareness, provide families
95 with valuable new tools and resources for the Information Age, and
96 teach young people what they need to know to have a safe, enriching
97 experience in cyberspace.

98 We are committed to upholding fundamental principles of notice and
99 choice in our business practice and to helping establish industry-wide
100 standards that benefit the development of the online medium and
101 consumers.

102 Ultimately, industry, government, and consumers share an interest in
103 building confidence in the online medium through robust, market-
104 driven policies, and we will continue to engage in dialogue with poli-
105 cymakers and consumer advocates on these important issues.

106 AOL Time Warner has a history of recognizing and respecting the
107 privacy of our customers online <u>and</u> offline. We have led private sec-
108 tor efforts to build workable mechanisms that address consumers'
109 concerns about the safety and security of their personal information,
110 while fostering consumer-friendly marketing practices tailored to in-
111 dividual tastes and preferences.

112 Efforts such as the Direct Marketing Association's Privacy Promise –
113 which AOL Time Warner adheres to and helped to create – illustrate
114 the successful execution of an industry-led program that offers the
115 consumer clear information on how information is used and specific
116 actions they can take to direct its use.

117 **Consumer Choice of ISPs**
118 AOL Time Warner is committed to providing consumers with a
119 choice among multiple ISPs on its cable systems. We have taken the
120 lead in the cable industry in responding to consumer demand for
121 choice and innovation in high-speed Internet services. And we are
122 proud that our actions have helped to create a marketplace impetus
123 for building the architecture and business models needed to make ca-
124 ble an open, competitive platform for advanced entertainment, Inter-

125 net and communications services. In so doing, AOL Time Warner
126 has changed the terms of the "open access" debate – and expanded
127 consumer choice.

128 The coming of broadband technology is turbo-charging media and
129 communications – and benefiting consumers in innovative new ways.
130 AOL Time Warner's multi-year investment in fiber optic and digital
131 technology already enables more than 12 million consumers around
132 the country to receive more and better video programming, enhanced
133 picture and sound quality, improved signal reliability and advanced
134 communications products and services. We are committed to working
135 within our industry and with lawmakers to promote market-driven
136 policies that encourage the continuation of this robust and innovative
137 environment for new digital services and expanded consumer choice.

138 **The First Amendment**
139 AOL Time Warner has been and will continue to be a vigilant sup-
140 porter of the First Amendment and the liberties it protects. In part,
141 this is because we have a rich heritage of the world's finest journalism
142 and an unparalleled record of innovation in the delivery of news and
143 information. From the founding of the world's first news magazine,
144 TIME, in 1923, to the launch of the world's first 24-hour televised
145 news service, cnn, in 1980, to local 24-hour news service and instan-
146 taneous, "anytime" online news, our company has changed the way
147 people around the world seek and receive news and information.

148 The First Amendment also protects freedom of expression – and
149 AOL Time Warner is committed to fostering human imagination and
150 creativity. And we will continue to oppose efforts to censor, intimi-
151 date or chill the freedom to express what is in our hearts and minds.

152 Since the first Internet content debate in 1995 concerning the Com-
153 munications Decency Act, efforts to regulate Internet content – from
154 sex to gambling to advertising and other content – have continued
155 apace. AOL Time Warner has long been an advocate of putting those
156 decisions – through technology – in the hands of consumers.

157 **Responsible Guidance on Entertainment**
158 AOL Time Warner is dedicated to providing world-class entertain-
159 ment, both online and off. Across all of our businesses, our company

160 takes our responsibility to consumers seriously – providing them
161 with the guidance they need to make informed decisions for them-
162 selves and their families.

163 For example, AOL Time Warner supports and participates in film
164 and television rating systems, as well as parental advisory labels for
165 music lyrics. Our subsidiary hbo pioneered a ratings system for pay
166 cable offerings. To ensure that we target our advertising and market-
167 ing of movies appropriately, we support the 12 initiatives of the Mo-
168 tion Picture Association of America. We also refrain from marketing
169 our R-rated films in a format or venue where the audience is 35% or
170 greater children under 17, and we provide additional guidance ex-
171 plaining the reasons for all films rated for violence.

172 AOL Time Warner believes that industry-led initiatives such as these
173 provide responsive, responsible entertainment guidance for parents –
174 and foster the freedom of expression and creative endeavor our com-
175 pany stands for.

176 **Intellectual Property**
177 At the heart of AOL Time Warner beats the creative energies of thou-
178 sands of filmmakers, songwriters, artists and authors, whose work
179 and passions enrich people's lives every day. Protecting the copy-
180 rights and trademarks that safeguard the rights and ensure royalties
181 for these works is essential.

182 Our company supports strong protection of intellectual property
183 rights, both online and off. We have a long history of supporting ef-
184 forts to combat piracy of videocassettes, cds, books and more. We
185 are being just as vigilant in the electronic world.

186 Enforcement of existing law, development of protective technology
187 and new business plans to make these works available to everyone in
188 every format, on every device, and over every medium, regardless of
189 ownership, are the hallmarks of our strategy on intellectual property
190 protection.

191 At the same time, AOL Time Warner believes that liability rules for
192 infringing material and other illegal content should never unneces-
193 sarily impede innovation. A recent U.S. law, the Digital Millennium

194 Copyright Act, provides a model approach – preserving the rights of
195 artists, authors and other creators in a digital world, while appropri-
196 ately limiting the liability of ISPs and other carriers, thereby ensuring
197 that intellectual property can continue to be our nation's leading ex-
198 port and a major driver of e-commerce growth.

199 **International Telecommunications Issues**
200 Information technology and the interactive medium have the poten-
201 tial to greatly expand economic opportunity and strengthen commu-
202 nities around the world. To realize that potential, however,
203 companies, countries and communities must work together in new
204 ways to ensure that people around the world have convenient, af-
205 fordable access to the goods, services and information the Internet
206 makes possible. This is especially true in a world where traditionally
207 distinct media are rapidly converging, offering an even richer range
208 of opportunities.

209 To that end, AOL Time Warner is working to eliminate outmoded
210 barriers to trade and impediments to the free flow of information
211 caused by legacy telecommunications systems, while respecting exist-
212 ing frameworks and cultural differences, and strengthening our glo-
213 bal commitment to protect consumers and children. We are also
214 working toward privatization and liberalization of national telecom-
215 munications and communications marketplaces, so the Internet is af-
216 fordable for the greatest number of people.

217 **Trade and E-Commerce**
218 The Internet and related technologies are advancing at a rapid rate,
219 presenting new issues and challenges – both domestically and inter-
220 nationally – for the Internet to be used to deliver goods and services.
221 The World Trade Organization (WTO) services negotiations offer an
222 important opportunity to address such issues and to expand the ben-
223 efits of e-commerce globally.

224 AOL Time Warner is actively working to persuade WTO members to
225 commit to opening their markets in sectors critical to initiating and
226 completing an e-commerce transaction. We believe that, within such
227 an e-commerce trade package, WTO members should commit to pro-
228 viding national treatment and expanded market access in each sub-
229 sector of the e-commerce "value chain." In addition, AOL Time

230 Warner believes that Internet-based electronic transmissions should
231 not be subject to tariffs or any customs duties, and that national reg-
232 ulations affecting e-commerce should be non-discriminatory, trans-
233 parent and the least restrictive of trade as possible.

234 **Taxation and E-Commerce**
235 AOL Time Warner supports the creation of a neutral taxation system
236 that neither favors nor impedes Internet-based commerce. The Inter-
237 net must not be burdened by discriminatory taxes or ones that create
238 special burdens for electronic sellers. Any tax rules that are imposed
239 should be clear, fair and simple to comply with for large, medium
240 and small companies doing business on the Internet. We will con-
241 tinue to promote pro-growth tax policies for e-commerce, and we
242 are committed to working with governments to develop internation-
243 ally compatible tax regimes through existing forums, such as the Or-
244 ganization for Economic Co-operation and Development.

245 **Postal Rates**
246 In an age of online communications and e-commerce, the United
247 States Postal System remains indispensable to commerce and com-
248 munity. Serving more than 100 million physical addresses daily,
249 moving about 200 billion pieces of mail per year, this system remains
250 a prime medium for business. For AOL Time Warner's magazines,
251 books, promotions, bills and more, USPS is vital.

252 We are committed to a robust and healthy postal system, with rates
253 that are reasonable and affordable, and with service that remains top
254 notch. In an environment where USPS volume – especially in First
255 Class, which serves so many businesses – could decline from elec-
256 tronic competition, we will work with all other stakeholders in the
257 system to develop innovative and forward-looking policies that help
258 to maintain a Postal Service that the public expects and business
259 needs to thrive in the 21st Century.

260 **Policy Guidelines**
261 AOL Time Warner believes that a few basic principles should guide
262 the development of a new public policy framework for a new world.

263 1. Public policy should foster individual choice and empowerment in
264 the economic and social dimensions and rely on individual decision-

265 making for determining the products, services and content available
266 from media sources and on the Internet. Practices developed in the
267 crucible of the private sector and the marketplace can best direct the
268 development of these creative industries.
269 2. Public policies should be market-driven and industry-led. Policies
270 should be developed collaboratively, with input from industry lead-
271 ers, government officials and, perhaps most importantly, consumers
272 and other stakeholders. Public or private gatekeepers should not be
273 allowed to prevent new entry, deny business opportunities or limit
274 the free flow of information.
275 3. Where government involvement is determined to be necessary,
276 policies should be technologically neutral and narrowly tailored, to
277 ensure that the information, entertainment and interactive industries
278 are permitted to respond to consumer tastes and preferences for
279 news, entertainment and communications and that the value of the
280 unique, interactive nature of this new converged and networked me-
281 dium can be fully realized.
282 4. Policies should be designed to ensure that all segments of society
283 and all countries of the world have access to the potential economic
284 and social benefits of entertainment, information and communica-
285 tions capability – and that this new networked and converged me-
286 dium becomes as essential to our daily lives as the television and the
287 telephone, and even more valuable.

288 In sum, AOL Time Warner seeks to maximize the economic and so-
289 cial benefits of media, communications and information technology
290 with industry-led, market-driven policies that allow these dynamic
291 industries to reach their full potential to improve people's.

General Electric's 1991 CEO Letter to Shareholders

1 TO OUR SHARE OWNERS 1991

2 1991 was a tough, terrific year for GE.

3 For the past few years, those of you who invest in our Company, and
4 share our interest in and affection for it, have patiently read letters
5 from us that dealt only minimally with traditional business data and
6 focused instead on soft concepts and values. We wrote of our belief
7 in simplicity as a critical component of business plans and communi-
8 cations. We defined self-confidence in our people as the catalyst that
9 would release the ideas and energy we craved. We spoke endlessly
10 about what we believe to be the ultimate virtue of a company –
11 speed. We used a big, clumsy word like "boundarylessness" to de-
12 scribe a mindset that breaks bureaucratic barriers and draws teams
13 closer. And, finally, we described, in largely promissory terms, a con-
14 cept called Work-Out – our vehicle for pursuing a total transforma-
15 tion of a century-old Company culture, in pursuit of a future of
16 virtually unlimited productivity.

17 This emphasis on the **software** of our Company followed the **hard-**
18 **ware** changes – the restructuring we had undertaken during the early
19 1980s – that produced excellent results – a 22% average annual re-

20 turn on share owner investment during the decade. But those were
21 good times, and we, like our contemporaries, were helped substan-
22 tially by the prosperity that characterized much of the 1980s.

23 But in 1991, all our rhetoric, our 1980s restructuring and our cul-
24 tural changes were put to their first **real** test when much of the global
25 economy settled into a full year of steady decline.

26 So how did we do?

27 • Our revenues grew 3% to over $60.2 billion.
28 • Our earnings grew 3% to $4.435 billion, and our earnings per
29 share grew 5%.
30 • We adopted a new accounting rule for retiree health and life insur-
31 ance benefits, which reduced earnings by $1.8 million but used no
32 cash.
33 • We repurchased a billion dollars worth of our stock while keeping
34 a solid Triple-A debt rating.
35 • Total cost productivity grew 4%, more than twice the rate it did
36 during the comparable recession of 1981–82. Return on equity
37 was close to 20%.
38 • GE Financial Services had another terrific year, with a 17% in-
39 crease in earnings. Seventeen of its 22 businesses grew earnings –
40 11 of them with strong double-digit growth.
41 • Industrial and Power Systems, Lighting, Medical Systems and In-
42 formation Services compiled powerful double-digit sales increases,
43 much of it offshore. GE exports increased 21% to $8.6 billion,
44 making a strong positive contribution to the U.S. balance of trade.
45 • And our share owners were rewarded with a 38% total return in
46 '91, including an 8% increase in the dividend.

47 There were other significant achievements. Most of our businesses
48 overcame much of the negative effect of weak markets with strong
49 productivity, but we did have a few misses as well.

50 NBC saw a decline in ratings, and that, in combination with a soft ad-
51 vertising market, made for a significant decline in earnings. Motors
52 and Plastics, because of weak markets and poor productivity, also
53 had a very difficult year. And, finally, two of GE Financial Services' 22

54 businesses – Commercial Real Estate and Corporate Finance (lever-
55 aged buyouts) – were not immune to the endemic problems in those
56 investment areas. Real estate produced only a small profit and LBOs
57 incurred a modest loss.

58 But enough of the numbers from '91. It's over. 1991 did, however,
59 once again remind us how absolutely critical productivity growth is
60 in the brutally Darwinian global marketplaces in which virtually all
61 of our businesses compete. We are aware, for instance, that if we had
62 the same productivity growth in '90 and '91 that we had in '80 and
63 '81, our '91 earnings would have been more like $3 billion rather
64 than $4.435 billion. We also are acutely aware that, without produc-
65 tivity growth, it is possible to lose in 24 months businesses that took
66 a half-century, or a century, to build. Productivity growth is essential
67 to industrial survival.

68 But to increase productivity, you first have to clear away all the im-
69 pediments that keep you from its achievement – primarily the man-
70 agement layers, functional boundaries and all the other trappings of
71 bureaucracy.

72 *Layers* ... insulate. They slow things down. They garble. Leaders in
73 highly layered organizations are like people who wear several sweat-
74 ers outside on a freezing winter day. They remain warm and com-
75 fortable but are blissfully ignorant of the realities of their
76 environment. They couldn't be further from what's going on.

77 We've been trumpeting the removal of bureaucracy and layers at GE
78 for several years now – and we did take our "sectors," "Groups"
79 and other superstructure – but much more remains; and unfortu-
80 nately, it is still possible to find documents around GE businesses that
81 look like something out of the National Archives, with five, 10 or
82 even more signatures necessary before action can be taken. In some
83 businesses, you might still encounter many layers of management in
84 a small area – boiler operators reporting to the supervisor of boilers,
85 who reports to the manager of plant services, who reports to the
86 plant manager, and so on.

87 Layers insulate. They slow things down. They garble. Leaders in
88 highly layered organizations are like people who wear several sweaters

89 outside on a freezing winter day. They remain warm and comfortable
90 but are blissfully ignorant of the realities of their environment. They
91 couldn't be further from what's going on.

92 Layers are symptoms of a century-old tradition at GE of rewarding
93 people with titles. Giving someone a "manager" title could be lik-
94 ened to issuing a building permit – the functional walls and manage-
95 ment floors begin construction, the procedural cement is poured, the
96 no-trespassing signs are posted. Today, more and more, we're cutting
97 back on useless titles, and we're rewarding people based on what
98 they contribute – the quality of their ideas and their ability to imple-
99 ment them – rather than on what they control.

100 We've made our most significant progress breaking down the hori-
101 zontal barriers that interrupt the flow within and among businesses.
102 We wrote last year of a remarkable method of compressing product
103 cycle times that we discovered in an appliance company in New
104 Zealand, tested in our Canadian affiliate and then brought to our
105 huge appliance operation in Louisville. That effort, which we call
106 Quick Response, has been an astonishing success in which every
107 function in the business – finance, distribution, consumer service,
108 marketing and manufacturing – worked together to reduce average
109 inventory by $200 million, to speed up the order-to-delivery cycle
110 time from 18 weeks to five weeks and to move that team closer to-
111 ward a shared vision – building appliances virtually to order – a
112 three-day cycle. And as this effort was unfolding, GE teams from all
113 of our other manufacturing businesses moved to Louisville for up to
114 a year, became deeply involved in the project and now are home us-
115 ing this experience to accelerate their own processes.

116 Barriers are coming down all around the Company. In Medical Systems,
117 our ultrasound technology is advancing rapidly because of an influx of
118 sonar experts from Aerospace, and scores of military aircraft engineers
119 have moved form Aircraft Engines to help Power Systems cope with the
120 explosive worldwide demand for our advanced gas turbines.

121 Finally, last year saw the transfer of leadership in four of our 13 big
122 businesses, with the new leaders coming from other GE businesses,
123 bringing with them fresh, recently tested ideas and proven team-
124 building skills.

125   *Speed ...* tends to propel ideas and drive processes right through
126   functional barriers, sweeping bureaucrats and their impediments
127   aside in the rush to get to the marketplace.

128   Whether the flow is people from Aerospace to Medical or technol-
129   ogy from Aircraft Engines to Power Systems or key management
130   transfers, the objective is the same – mining the enormous value that
131   exists all over the Company. GE's diversity creates a huge laboratory
132   of innovation and ideas that reside in each of the businesses, and
133   mining them is both our challenge and an awesome opportunity.
134   Boundaryless behaviour is what integrates us and turns this opportu-
135   nity into reality, creating the real value of a multibusiness company –
136   the big competitive advantage we call Integrated Diversity.

137   Boundary-busting does something else for us. It makes us **faster.**

138   There is something about speed that transcends its obvious business
139   benefits of greater cash flow, greater profitability, higher share due to
140   greater customer responsiveness and more capacity from cycle time
141   reductions.

142   Speed exhilarates and energizes. Whether it be fast cars, fast boats,
143   downhill skiing or a business process, speed injects fun and excite-
144   ment into an otherwise routine activity. This is particularly true in
145   business, where speed tends to propel ideas and drive processes right
146   through functional barriers, sweeping bureaucrats and their impedi-
147   ments aside in the rush to get to the marketplace. Speed helps force a
148   company "outside of itself" and prevents the inward focus that insti-
149   tutions tend to develop as they get bigger. In some businesses, the bu-
150   reaucracy can warp priorities to the point that a pat on the back
151   from the "boss" and a stick in the eye from a customer amount to a
152   pretty good day for an employee.

153   We say 'some' businesses – but not all. In 1991, we shared best prac-
154   tices with a number of great companies. We learned something ev-
155   erywhere, but nowhere did we learn as much as at Wal-Mart. Sam
156   Walton and his strong team are something very special. Many of our
157   management teams spent time there observing the speed, the bias for
158   action, the utter customer fixation that drives Wal-Mart; and despite
159   our progress, we came back feeling a bit plodding and ponderous, a

160 little envious, but, ultimately, fiercely determined that we're going to
161 do whatever it takes to get that fast.

162 And Work-Out is still the process that will help get us there.

163 Work-Out began three years ago with baby steps: a series of New
164 England-style town meetings with people of every conceivable rank
165 and function chipping away at the bureaucratic barnacles and non-
166 sense that develop on all institutions as they age and grow – wasteful
167 paperwork, duplication, unnecessary approvals and the like. After
168 the initial stages and modest progress, we began to move cautiously
169 into team analyzes of how specific functions and processes within
170 businesses could be done better and, above all, faster. Customers
171 were eventually invited into the process as were suppliers.

172 For a couple of years, we resisted the traditional GE predilection to
173 quantify and measure Work-Out, and, in truth, there was little be-
174 yond the anecdotal and atmospheric to report. For a year or so, indi-
175 vidual Work-Out environments seemed to just sit there, as one
176 observer noted, like popcorn kernels in a warm pan. The cynics no
177 doubt believed the warmth came only from the hot air of Company
178 rhetoric. **But all that time, trust was building, confidence was grow-**
179 **ing and teams were coming together.** Then, suddenly, things began to
180 pop, here and there, with big ideas, process breakthroughs; and to-
181 day they roar almost everywhere, with both radical transformations
182 in the way we do business and with tangible business results. The
183 Quick Response breakthrough at our Appliances operation would
184 still be years away – perhaps unreachable – without the cooperative
185 team approach Work-Out creates.

186 In Lynn, Mass., a century-old GE location that traditionally has been
187 a sore spot in labor-management relations, Work-Out has begun to
188 transform the climate into a much more productive atmosphere of
189 mutual respect and cooperation. "We versus them" is increasingly
190 coming to mean GE versus the competition. In 1987, at the Lynn
191 Plant, a combustor – a key part of a jet engine – took 30 weeks to
192 make. Through Work-Out, that process was down to eight weeks in
193 early '91; now its four weeks, and the teams that run it are talking
194 10 **days.** Hardware product cycles are now down an average of 20%
195 across the business, with 50% clearly in sight.

196 *Values* ... Too often all of us have looked the other way – tolerated
197 these 'type 4" managers because 'they always deliver" – at least in
198 the short term.

199 And in our Schenectady turbine plant, another site with a century-
200 old tradition of mistrust between labour and management, Work-
201 Out has grown a team effort that is improving productivity beyond
202 anything we ever envisioned. Just to name one area, in the critical
203 steam turbine bucket machinery center, teams of hourly employees
204 now run, without supervision, $20 million worth of new milling ma-
205 chines that they specified, tested and approved for purchase. The cy-
206 cle time for the operation has dropped 80%. It is embarrassing to
207 reflect that for probably 80 or 90 years, we've been dictating equip-
208 ment needs and managing people who knew how to do things much
209 better and faster than we did.

210 All around this Company in large plants like Schenectady, Lynn and
211 Louisville and in scores of smaller sites like Florence and Salisbury in
212 the Carolinas, Decatur, Alta., and in many other places, compulsive
213 managing and mutual mistrust are giving way to real teamwork. GE
214 has become faster and more energized than any of us ever thought
215 possible.

216 If one vignette typifies how Work-Out has transformed how we
217 work together in this Company, it is this: Late in '91 at a best prac-
218 tices session at our management school at Crotonville, N.Y., two of
219 the key lecturers on the subject of productivity were two of the
220 toughest union officers we face across any table. One of these leaders
221 told the group he used to have three clearly defined enemies in his
222 life – the IRS, Russians and GE management – but with the way
223 things changed, only the IRS retains that status. Both GE manage-
224 ment and the Russians are doing a lot better.

225 The transformation that is sweeping our Company is not complicated
226 in theory or even original. Much of the intellectual underpinning of
227 Work-Out consists of ideas like worker involvement, trust and em-
228 powerment – shopworn and even platitudinous concepts. The differ-
229 ence is that our whole organization is, in fact, living them ... every
230 day! Most of our 284,000-member Company are, in fact, using soft
231 concepts today as competitive weapons and are winning with them,
232 rather than just inscribing them on coffee mugs and T-shirts.

233 Yes, there are pockets where things haven't changed, and no, not ev-
234 eryone has been empowered, but the momentum in unmistakable,
235 and we are determined to make it irreversible.

236 This is a long road we are on, and a difficult one. Trust and respect
237 take years to build, and no time at all to destroy. In the first half of
238 the 1980s, we restructured this Company and changed its physical
239 make-up. That was the easy part. In the last several years, our chal-
240 lenge has been to change ourselves – an infinitely more difficult task
241 that, frankly, not all of us in leadership positions are capable of.

242 Over the past several years, we've wrestled at all levels of this Com-
243 pany with the question of what we are and what we want to be. Out
244 of these discussions, and through our experiences, we've agreed
245 upon a set of values we believe we will need to take this Company
246 forward, rapidly, through the 1990s and beyond.

247 *Leadership ...* we know that without leaders who "walk the talk",
248 all of our plans, promises and dreams for the future are just that –
249 talk.

250 In our view, leaders, whether on the shop floor or at the tops of our
251 businesses, can be characterized in at least four ways.

252 The first is one who delivers on commitments – financial or other-
253 wise – and shares the values of our Company. His or her future is an
254 easy call. Onward and upward.

255 The second type of leader is one who does not meet commitments and
256 does not share our values. Not as pleasant a call, but equally easy.

257 The third is one who misses commitments but shares the values. He or
258 she usually gets a second chance, preferably in a different environment.

259 Then there's the fourth type – the most difficult for many of us to
260 deal with. That leader delivers on commitments, makes all the num-
261 bers, but doesn't share the values we must have. This is the individ-
262 ual who typically forces performance out of people rather than
263 inspires it: the autocrat, the big shot, the tyrant. Too often all of us
264 have looked the other way – tolerated these "type 4" managers be-
265 cause "they always deliver" – at least in the short term.

266 GE **Values** ... GE Leaders throughout the Company:

267 • Create a clear, simple, reality-based, customer-focused vision and
268   are able to communicate it straightforwardly to all constituencies.
269 • Understand accountability and commitment and are decisive ... set
270   and meet aggressive targets ... always with unyielding integrity.
271 • Have a passion for excellence ... hate bureaucracy and all the non-
272   sense that come with it.
273 • Have the self-confidence to empower others and behave in bound-
274   aryless fashion ... believe in and are committed to Work-Out as a
275   means of empowerment ... are open to ideas from anywhere.
276 • Have, or have the capacity to develop, global brains and global
277   sensitivity and are comfortable building diverse global teams.
278 • Stimulate and relish change ... are not frightened or paralyzed by
279   it. See change as opportunity, not just a threat.
280 • Have enormous energy and the ability to energize and invigorate
281   others. Understand speed as a competitive advantage and see the
282   total organizational benefits that can be derived from a focus on
283   speed.

284 And perhaps this type was more acceptable in easier times, but in an
285 environment where we must have every good idea from every man
286 and woman in the organization, we cannot afford management
287 styles that suppress and intimidate. Whether we can convince and
288 help these managers to change – recognizing how difficult that can
289 be – or part company with them if they cannot will be the ultimate
290 test of our commitment to the transformation of this Company and
291 will determine the future of the mutual trust and respect we are
292 building. In 1991, we continued to improve our personnel manage-
293 ment to achieve much better balance between values and "num-
294 bers". That balance will change further in '92 and beyond, because
295 we know that without leaders who "walk the talk", all of our plans,
296 promises and dreams for the future are just that – talk.

297 In the first week of 1992, 450 men and women who lead our Com-
298 pany convened from around the world to share best practices and re-
299 view our course for the coming year. It was a very special event, with
300 a unique and spontaneous atmosphere – one we had never quite felt
301 before. It is striking that coming off one of the most brutal economic
302 years most of us can remember, the mood at that meeting was one of

303 exhilaration and boundless confidence. The commitment to speed
304 and boundaryless was at a new high.

305 We put our values, our people and our Company to the test in '91.
306 By our measure, at least, we passed with flying colors. We grew dur-
307 ing a bad recession, and as we see recovery on the horizon, it is diffi-
308 cult not be very, very optimistic about our future.

309 Thanks for your support.

310 John F. Welch, Jr.   Edward E. Hood, Jr.
311 Chairman of the Board and   Vice Chairman of the Board
312 Chief Executive Officer   and Executive Officer

Letter to Stockholders, 1940
Walt Disney Productions' Annual Report

To the Stockholders of Walt Disney Productions:

In April, 1940, Walt Disney Productions sought and obtained the participation of the public in its business through the sale of 155,000 shares of 6% Cumulative Convertible Preferred Stock, and the Board of Directors herewith submits its first annual report to the Company's new stockholders.

Included herein are financial statements of the Company for the fiscal year ended September 28, 1940, accompanied by the report of the Company's auditors, Messrs Price, Waterhouse & Co. We invite your attention to the notes which are attached to and constitute an integral part of the financial statements.

Your management believes that it will be of interest to our 1,800 stockholders to supplement the information shown in the financial statements with the following additional facts pertaining to the Company.

NEW STUDIO

At the time of the sale of the 6% Cumulative Preferred Stock, the Company was constructing and equipping its new studio. This studio was substantially completed and equipped and virtually all of the Company's production operations were transferred thereto by the end of May, 1940. As a result of the increased facilities, the Company has been able to augment its production of completed footage by more than 100% and has succeeded in lowering the cost of production per foot substantially. Therefore, the Company will be able to carry out its new policy of releasing two or more feature subjects each year as well as a large number of short subjects. As a result of the reduction in costs, short subjects are now being produced at a figure which the management believes will result in profitable releases even though sources of income in certain foreign countries now at war are no longer available.

EFFECT OF THE WAR

The effect of the war in Europe upon the affairs of your Company has been serious and the full measure thereof cannot yet be determined. It has been impossible to effect an orderly release of the Company's pictures in any of the countries at war and in many countries it has been impossible to effect any release whatsoever. In fact, in most of the territories dominated by the Axis Powers, the release of American pictures has been forbidden. In addition, currency restrictions and regulations, as well as fluctuations in foreign exchange rates, have served to reduce further the Company's income from such pictures as were already released in foreign countries.

PRODUCT

During the year, the Company delivered to RKO Radio Pictures, Inc., the organization currently distributing our pictures, one feature picture and ten short subjects and has in current production a number of other features and short subjects. Developments in connection with the Company's product are summarized as follows:

PINOCCHIO:
PINOCCHIO was first shown at the Center Theatre in New York on February 7, 1940, and at the Pantages and Hillstreet Theatres in Los Angeles on February 10, 1940. It was subsequently released for general exhibition on February 23, 1940. To the end of the Company's fiscal year, September 28, 1940, this picture had earned gross world film rentals of $1,673,956.54 of which $1,627,331.79 represented film rentals from the United States and Canada. The Company has received from its distributors as its net share of the world film rentals, $976,211.94. In addition, there have accrued to the credit of the Company, certain funds in Great Britain and Australasia amounting to £5818.7.5, which have been blocked by currency restrictions.

The Company has prepared Spanish and Portuguese language versions of this picture which are currently being shown in all the countries of Central and South America, as well as in the Philippine Islands and Portugal. No income from the Spanish and Portuguese language versions of PINOCCHIO is reflected in the above-mentioned film rentals as the picture was released in those countries too late for any such revenue to be included in the year ended September 28, 1940.

The total cost of producing PINOCCHIO was $2,595,379.66 and it is now anticipated that this amount will not be recouped under the conditions prevailing throughout the world. Accordingly, a charge of $1,000,000 has been made to provide for the excess of cost of this picture over the estimated total revenue.

The picture PINOCCHIO was planned and production was started prior to the outbreak of the European war. Consequently, it was budgeted on a program contemplating income from all countries where SNOW WHITE AND THE SEVEN DWARFS had been released. In addition, this production suffered from excessive cost which was a direct result of the transition period through which the Company passed when it changed its policy of making one feature in two years (SNOW WHITE was released in January, 1938), to a policy of producing from two to four features a year as presently projected. These excessive costs cannot be segregated as they very largely represent discarded work of untrained personnel. PINOCCHIO was produced during a period of development and expansion. These factors which included the schooling and training of personnel to meet the increased production needs, together with inadequate plant facilities at the old studios, contributed in no small measure to the high cost of this production.

FANTASIA:

FANTASIA was exhibited for the first time at the Broadway Theatre in New York on November 13, 1940. This picture is an innovation in the field of entertainment, featuring Leopold Stokowski and the Philadelphia Orchestra in a program of music as interpreted by Walt Disney and the Company's staff of artists and technicians. FANTASIA is being presented by methods never before employed in the exhibition of motion pictures. The exhibition of this production requires special sound equipment and the Company has contracted to purchase sufficient equipment so that the picture can be distributed simultaneously in twelve theatres. It is now planned to distribute the picture by the "road show" method in the first-run cities of the United States, Canada and other large centers. The management believes this method of distribution will result in an eventual realization of revenue in excess of that which would be realized by ordinary methods of distribution. However, this method of distribution will require a longer period of time for the Company to recoup the cost of the picture.

OTHER FEATURES:

Three other feature length pictures currently in production are planned for release during the fiscal year ending September 27, 1941. THE RELUCTANT DRAGON is a combination of animated cartoon and "live action" comedy, featuring the well-known humorist, Robert Benchley. BAMBI is a dramatization, through the medium of the animated cartoon, of the well-known book of the same name by Felix Salten. A distribution contract for both of the last-mentioned features has been entered into with RKO Radio Pictures, Inc. The name and basic story of the picture, DUMBO, THE FLYING ELEPHANT were purchased by the Company and are being developed by our staff into a feature length cartoon.

Among the features scheduled for release in 1942 are PETER PAN AND WIND IN THE WILLOWS.

SHORT SUBJECTS:

During the fiscal year ended September 28, 1940 the Company delivered to RKO Radio Pictures, Inc. a total of ten short subjects and contemplates delivery of twenty short subjects during the fiscal year 1941. These pictures continue in high popular favor and should prove to be a profitable part of the Company's business inasmuch as the increased efficiency made possible by the new plant has materially reduced production costs.

The Company has recently extended its releasing contract with RKO Radio Pictures, Inc. to cover a fourth series of eighteen short subjects.

The Company presently has twenty-eight short subjects in various stages of production.

OTHER ENDEAVORS

Names and characters created by the Company and licensed for use on merchandise, etc. continue to have a wide-spread appeal. Royalties from this source, from books and music, and revenue from comic strips and art sales, constitute a substantial portion of the income of the Company.

GENERAL

The inventory of pictures in process at the close of the fiscal year was the largest in the Company's history. The total cost of the feature length and short subjects in production was $3,650,256.67. These pictures represented a total film length of 44,490 feet. In addition there were 149 stories in our inventory on which we had spent $367,275.41. The system of budget control both as to cost and output was revised when the Company moved to the new studio, with the result that both feature pictures and short subjects are presently being completed on schedule and at their budgeted costs.

Your management has reduced expenses and has taken aggressive steps toward lowering production costs by increasing efficiency and eliminating dispensable activities.

In considering the profit and loss statement of the Company, it is worth while to repeat the following statement made in the prospectus offering the 6% Convertible Preferred Stock:

"The Company's principal income accrues according to the rapidity with which its features are exhibited in theatres and, accordingly, the relationship between dates of release and dates of accounting periods has in the past produced and will probably continue in the future to produce wide variations in earnings as they may from time to time be reported. This is made more pronounced by a program which contemplates the release of only one or two features per year. In connection with SNOW WHITE AND THE SEVEN DWARFS, the Company adopted a policy of writing off the entire cost of the picture against the first revenues received, and the Company may in the future follow this policy with respect to all of its feature productions. Consequently, if any given accounting period closes at a time when revenues have failed to exceed the costs incurred in connection with the production of a feature released during such period, it is possible that a loss may be reported in such period notwithstanding the fact that an actual profit may eventually be realized on such feature."

During the fiscal year ended September 28, 1940, the Company had only one new feature picture – PINOCCHIO – in release.

The Company also re-issued SNOW WHITE in the United States and Canada in July, 1940. This was released as the WALT DISNEY FESTIVAL in conjunction with four Walt Disney short subjects and is currently doing a satisfactory business.

During the next fiscal year ending September 27, 1941, the Company expects to have three new feature pictures in general release, in addition to its quota of new short subjects. These pictures should reflect the benefit accruing to the Company by reason of the training and skill acquired by the artists during the last three years. While the serious effect on the Company's business caused by the loss of foreign markets cannot be minimized, nevertheless your management now believes it has adjusted the Company's operations to a schedule of production and costs designed to be independent of those markets.

CAPITAL STOCK

At a meeting of the directors held on February 24, 1940, the capital stock of the Company was reclassified into 755,000 shares, of which 600,000 shares were designated as Common Stock (with a par value of $5 a share), and 155,000 shares were designated as 6% Cumulative Convertible Preferred Stock (with a par value of $25 per share). 300,000 shares of Common Stock ($5 par value) were thereupon issued in exchange for 150,000 shares of Common Stock ($10 par value) previously outstanding, and 45,000 shares of Common Stock were issued as a 15% stock dividend on the new amount of outstanding stock. 10,000 shares of Common Stock were issued to Walter E. Disney and Roy O. Disney in consideration of the cancellation of $200,000 indebtedness of the Company to them. 150,000 shares of preferred Stock were sold to the public through underwriters for net proceeds of $3,412,500 and 5,000 shares were sold to officers and employees for $125,000.

An initial dividend of 37 1/2c was paid July 1, 1940, to the Preferred stockholders of record June 15, 1940, and a regular quarterly dividend of 37 1/2c was paid October 1, 1940, to Preferred stockholders of record September 16, 1940. The regular quarterly dividend of 37 1/2c payable January 1, 1941, to Preferred stockholders of record December 16, 1940, was declared by the Board of Directors at a meeting held December 2, 1940. This dividend will be paid from the Company's initial surplus. No dividends were paid on the Common Stock.

DIRECTORS

During the year, Edward M. Francis resigned as a director of the Company and in his place the board elected Jonathan B. Lovelace as the representative of the Preferred stockholders in anticipation of Paragraph 9 of Article 5 of the Articles of Incorporation, as amended, which provides that:

"Holders of the Preferred Stock, voting separately as a class and entitled to one vote per share, shall be entitled at the first annual meeting of the

Corporation after the close of the fiscal year ending September 28, 1940, and annually thereafter, to elect one Director of the Corporation to hold office for a term of one (1) year and until his successor shall have been elected."

EMPLOYEES

At September 28, 1940, the organization consisted of a total of 1179 employees.

The Directors want to take this opportunity of thanking all members of the organization, whose loyalty and co-operation have contributed in such large measure to the continued progress of the Company.

FOR THE BOARD OF DIRECTORS
WALTER E. DISNEY, *President*

Letter to Stockholders, 1941 Walt Disney Productions' Annual Report

To the Stockholders of Walt Disney Productions:

We submit herewith as part of this annual report to stockholders financial statements of the Company for the fiscal year ended September 27, 1941, accompanied by the report of the Company's auditors, Messrs. Price, Waterhouse & Co. We direct your attention to the notes which are attached to and constitute an integral part of the financial statements.

FOREWORD

In our annual report to stockholders issued in December, 1940, and covering the fiscal year ended September 28, 1940, we stated, "the effect of the war in Europe upon the affairs of your Company has been serious and the full measure thereof cannot yet be determined." It was evident that the loss of foreign markets necessitated a sharp lowering in production costs in order to assure a profit from the remaining markets. The Company immediately took steps toward that objective. Since the date of that report there has been a further deterioration in the foreign markets and the Company again found it necessary to reduce materially its operating expenses and personnel in order to consolidate its position. As this program was being placed in effect, a strike was called by a minority group of the Company's employees. This development, discussed later in this report under the heading "Labor Relations," resulted in a retardation of our production schedule and interfered with the delivery and exhibition of product already completed.

Following is a summary of income account and balance sheet items taken from the financial statements published on pages 8 to 10 of this report, compared with corresponding figures in last year's report:

	Fiscal year		
Income Account	*1941*	*1940*	*Increase (decrease)*
Income from short subjects less amortization	$ 457,391.61	$ 131,668.88	$ 325,722.73
Income from royalties, comic strips, art work, licenses, etc., less costs	185,253.97	267,898.90	(82,644.93)
Income from "Snow White and the Seven Dwarfs"	139,173.23	103,526.10	35,647.13
Total	$ 781,818.81	$ 503,093.88	$ 278,724.93
Administrative and selling expenses	420,127.32	649,354.68	(229,227.36)
Balance	$ 361,691.49	$ (146,260.80)	$ 507,952.29
Interest expense	150,988.55	113,537.25	37,451.30
Profit (loss) before provision for losses on features	$ 210,702.94	$ (259,798.05)	$ 470,500.99
Provision for excess cost of features over estimated net income	1,000,000.00	1,000,000.00	
Balance (loss)	$(789,297.06)	$(1,259,798.05)	$ 470,500.99

	September	September	Increase
Balance Sheets	27, 1941	28, 1940	(decrease)
Cash and receivables	$ 156,020.52	$ 132,410.20	$ 23,610.32
Inventories at cost:			
Pictures in process, etc.	2,882,713.43	4,093,119.94	(1,210,406.51)
Unamortized picture costs	4,874,006.16	1,833,436.66	3,040,569.50
Total current and working assets, before deducting reserves	$7,912,740.11	$6,058,966.80	$1,853,773.31
Deduct provision for excess of cost over estimated net income from feature pictures	2,000,000.00	1,000,000.00	1,000,000.00
Current and working assets as per balance sheet	$5,912,740.11	$5,058,966.80	$ 853,773.31
Bank loans	$3,371,669.03	$1,932,992.24	$1,438,676.79

Income Account	Fiscal year		
	1941	1940	Increase (decrease)
Other liabilities, reserve for taxes and deferred income	907,273.30	841,499.11	65,774.19
Total liabilities	$4,278,942.33	$2,774,491.35	$1,504,450.98
Excess of current and working assets (as stated) over all liabilities	$1,633,797.78	$2,284,475.45	$ (650,677.67)
Deposits in foreign banks at current rates	1,060.61	1,088.70	(28.09)
Land, buildings and equipment at cost less reserve for depreciation	3,005,161.18	3,263,170.31	(258,009.13)
Copyrights, trademarks and patents less reserve for amortization	7,892.77	8,613.67	(720.90)
Deferred charges	234,186.31	230,297.68	3,888.73
Total net assets, as per balance sheet	$4,882,098.75	$5,787,645.81	$ (905,547.06)
Funds not taken into books representing blocked currencies at current official rates, approximately	$ 345,000.00	$ 22,000.00	$ 323,000.00

The comparative figures taken from the income account show the progress made in reduction of costs. The Company shows a profit, after all charges but before provision for excess cost of feature pictures over estimated net income therefrom, of $210,702.94 as compared with a loss of $259,798.05 in the fiscal year ended September 28, 1940. The income account does not reflect the reduction in costs of feature pictures as DUMBO was not released until after the close of the fiscal year. It does, however, reflect the working off of the inventory of high cost shorts and restoration of a satisfactory profit in that division. Last year the Company provided a reserve of $1,000,000 to write off the excess cost of PINOCCHIO. The Company has estimated its expectancy of return from all of its feature product, and as a result has set up a provision against a possible loss in the amount of $1,000,000.

The comparative figures taken from the Balance Sheet show that while pictures in process have decreased $1,210,406.51, the unamortized value of completed pictures has increased $3,040,569.50, giving a net increase in inventory (before reserve) of $1,830,162.99. This increase, which was largely financed by bank loans, is due primarily to the delay in the general release of FANTASIA, and to labor difficulties experienced at the time of release of THE RELUCTANT DRAGON. The Company now has two feature pictures ready for general release, DUMBO and FANTASIA. A third feature, BAMBI, is practically completed. With current operations reduced by 50% from last year, a steady reduction of the bank loan is anticipated.

Blocked currencies are not included in the Company's accounts until received. In October, 1941, the British Government entered into an agreement with the motion picture companies whereby 50% of the blocked currencies previously impounded in Great Britain was released. One-half of this amount was immediately payable and one-half is payable in April, 1942. The Company, since the date of this report, has received approximately $65,000 as part payment of its share of impounded funds. Australia and New Zealand have not yet released any of that portion of our revenue which those countries impounded.

PRODUCT

During the fiscal year under review the Company released its feature picture FANTASIA. Initially this picture was distributed directly by the Company through the medium of road shows using "Fantasound" rather than through normal distribution channels. The picture was presented in thirteen cities (New York, Boston, Los Angeles, Philadelphia, Detroit, Chicago, San Francisco, Pittsburgh, Cleveland, Buffalo, Minneapolis, Washington and Baltimore) and while a few of the engagements were disappointing, the aggregate results indicated a picture with wide appeal. The length of the New York and Los Angeles runs broke all existing records since the advent of sound.

Experience gained from the exhibition of FANTASIA in the above-mentioned cities demonstrated that a nation wide distribution of this picture with "Fantasound" was impractical. It was therefore decided to abandon "Fantasound" and generally release the picture through normal distribution channels. Our sound engineers succeeded in combining the various "Fantasound" tracks into one composite track, enabling the Company to present FANTASIA in motion pictures everywhere.

The company entered into an agreement with RKO Radio Pictures, Inc. for the distribution of FANTASIA throughout the world. Spanish and Portuguese versions have been prepared for the South American market, and the picture has already been released in Rio de Janeiro and Sao Paulo, Brazil; Montevideo, Uruguay and Buenos Aires, Argentina. FANTASIA is also being currently released in England and Australasia.

It is now planned to place FANTASIA in general distribution in the United States immediately following DUMBO. In preparation for this general release, test runs were made in representative small towns to guide in editing this picture.

THE RELUCTANT DRAGON

This picture was completed and delivered to RKO Radio Pictures, Inc. on April 17, 1941. It was first put into general release on June 20, 1941. Revenues obtained from this picture were seriously affected by the strike, due to picketing at various theatres throughout the country. It has been released in Great Britain and Australasia. Spanish and Portuguese versions have been prepared for the release of the picture in South America.

Although results to date have been disappointing, we are confident of the return to the Company of at least $500,000 and have provided in the inventory reserve for the balance of the cost.

DUMBO

DUMBO was completed and delivered to our distributor September 11, 1941. Because of selling conditions in the industry the picture was not generally released until the middle of December. The picture was pre-shown in the Broadway Theatre, New York, beginning October 23rd, and has been well received. In the trade and press it is getting excellent exploitation and publicity.

DUMBO is our first all-cartoon feature picture budgeted and produced subsequent to the outbreak of the European war and the loss of our foreign markets. The picture was produced at a cost well within present market possibilities and is of a quality that assures, in our opinion, a profitable return.

SHORT SUBJECTS

During the fiscal year ended September 27, 1941, the Company delivered to RKO Radio Pictures, Inc. a total of twenty-two short subjects. Our costs have been reduced to meet present market conditions and the pictures continue to be a profitable source of revenue.

Under date of April 11, 1941, the Company extended its releasing contract with RKO to cover a fifth series of eighteen short subjects.

The Company now has 22 short subjects in various stages of production.

BAMBI

The Company's feature picture BAMBI has been in work for over three years and is now practically completed. As now scheduled it will be delivered to

RKO Radio Pictures, Inc. on or about the first of February, 1942. Completion of this picture was delayed at least three months by the strike. It was the last of the feature pictures projected on the basis of the pre-war markets. Its cost will be substantially higher than DUMBO but will be approximately $1,000,000 less than the cost of PINOCCHIO. It is the consensus of opinion of those who have seen the picture that it is the best the Company has ever produced for entertainment value and quality of production.

FEATURES RELEASED IN PRIOR YEARS

During the fiscal year ended September 27, 1941, PINOCCHIO, which was first shown on February 7, 1940, returned a gross film rental of $554,730.74 of which the Company's share amounted to $387,100.12. This brought the total gross film rental on September 27, 1941, to $2,228,687.28 of which the Company's share was $1,363,312.06. The amount received in 1941 would seem to assure recoupment of the balance of the unamortized negative cost of $233,439.64 after giving effect to the reserve set up last year. The Company's share of blocked currencies resulting from the showings of PINOCCHIO had a value at official rates of approximately $240,000 at September 27, 1941. This amount is not included in the figures quoted above.

SNOW WHITE AND THE SEVEN DWARFS which was first shown in December of 1937 returned to the Company the sum of $139,173.23 in the fiscal year ended September 27, 1941.

OTHER ENDEAVORS

The licensing of names and characters created by the Company continues to have universal commercial appeal but revenue has fallen off during the year mainly because FANTASIA did not lend itself readily to such exploitation. Certain of our licensees also were beginning to feel the effect of defense priorities. However, royalties from this source and from books, music, comic strips and art sales continue to be substantial sources of income.

LABOR RELATIONS

For the first time in its history the company was, during 1941, beset by labor troubles. Early in May the Studio launched a program of reducing operating expenses and personnel, designed to bring output in line with results reasonably to be anticipated from the distribution of the Company's pictures under present world conditions. As this policy was being initiated, a strike was called (on May 28, 1941) by Screen Cartoonists Union, Local No. 852, an affiliate of the International Brotherhood of Painters, Paperhangers and Decorators of America (A. F. of L.). A majority of our employees stayed at work and during the nine weeks of the strike the Company's production proceeded satisfactorily. However, due to secondary boycotts and "hot cargo" activities on the part of sympathetic unions it became impossible to deliver and exhibit our product.

Repeated efforts by the Company to effect a settlement were unavailing. Finally, a commissioner from the National Conciliator's Office intervened; arbitration was agreed upon and an award was eventually rendered. Among other things, the award imposed the following: a close shop; reinstatement of all strikers; and 100 hours' retroactive pay for strikers. In relation to our proposed reduction of personnel, the award also imposed a formula under which a certain percentage of strikers had to be retained pro rata to non-striking employees. However, it required the Union to take in as a body without prejudice and at a nominal initiation fee employees in its classification who had remained at work during the strike.

After a period of four weeks of complete shutdown, necessitated by protracted negotiations, the Company resumed operations on September 15, 1941. The Studio is now operating under the terms of the award which, unfortunately, is in many respects very ambiguous and is silent on several disputed issues. However, the plant is now operating smoothly.

DIVIDENDS AND SINKING FUND REQUIREMENTS

In a letter addressed to the stockholders under date of June 14, 1941, you were advised of the reason for the omission of the preferred stock sinking fund payment due April 1, 1941, in the amount of $50,000 and of the deferment of the quarterly preferred dividend due July 1, 1941. The necessity for conserving working capital pending the orderly liquidation of the Company's inventory of completed feature pictures caused omission of the $100,000 preferred stock sinking fund payment due October 1, 1941, and deferment of the quarterly dividend on the preferred stock due on that date. Consideration will be given to resumption of payments when and as a comfortable working capital position has been re-established, but no prediction can be made in this respect at this time. The dividends on the preferred stock being cumulative, all arrearages in such dividends as well as fixed sinking fund payments must be paid before any dividends may be paid on the common stock.

GENERAL

Our principal problem now is one of orderly and satisfactory liquidation of feature product. Within the Studio production is going forward and costs are in keeping with present markets. The Company is operating with less than 50% of the personnel and pay roll of May, 1941. Our working capital position is strained because of the large amount of money tied up in feature negatives – DUMBO, FANTASIA and BAMBI. With proper liquidation of these three features, it is believed the Company will reduce its bank loan to a nominal figure or liquidate it completely and restore its working capital position to a satisfactory level. DUMBO and BAMBI are feature pictures which will have none of the problems of distribution presented by FANTASIA. Both are excellent pictures and should do satisfactory business.

For the current year, the Company is continuing its production of short subjects and has three feature subjects available for production, of which one would ordinarily be completed during the 1942 fiscal year. However, your management is making its facilities and equipment available for Army, Navy and other Government films in connection with national defense. We are now working on short subjects in cooperation with our Government's plans to promote hemispheric solidarity and are also producing a series of short subjects for the U. S. Navy and five short subjects for the Canadian Government. New feature product is being curtailed in favor of federal defense work. The volume of defense film work required of us will determine the extent of work done on feature subjects during the current year.

In summary, we are still in an adjustment period brought about by world conditions and the consequent loss of markets, but we believe we have sustained the major shocks of this adjustment. Pictures being projected will be properly budgeted and produced for present restricted markets. Our experience with DUMBO and our short subjects gives us every confidence in our ability to meet these conditions satisfactorily with respect both to cost and quality of our product.

FOR THE BOARD OF DIRECTORS
Walter E. Disney, *President*

Notes

INTRODUCTION

1 For example, the then Canadian National Railway CEO Paul Tellier, in a major speech delivered to the Canadian Railway Club in Montreal, Quebec, on 14 December 2001, expounded the need for Canada to replace its own currency with the American dollar and urged his fellow "leaders of the business community" to speak out on the issue.

2 Hegele and Kiesler 2001, 299.

3 Ibid., 301–2.

4 Slotkin 1985, 40.

CHAPTER ONE

1 Bacon 1891, 44.

2 Stackhouse 2001, A1.

3 Wells, for example, offers this plaintive lament over the dearth of corporate leadership during a crisis: "Today we are heading out on the hunt for leadership. These are parlous times. We want our hands held, our fears calmed, our hearts raised in hope" (2001).

4 Jönsson 1998, 11.

5 The power of language is illustrated in college teacher Carol Cohn's reflections on a year-long program on defense technology and arms control that she attended. Her exposure to the ambient, everyday

language used in the program led her to become "more and more engaged" with defense technology information and arguments, and she
found herself wondering, "How can *I* think this way? How can any of
us?" (1987, 688).

6 Morris 1946, 214.

7 It would be foolish to claim that all CEOs of large public companies assume sole responsibility for authoring the letter to stockholders, for example. Nonetheless, most CEOs who do not write such letters admit to
carefully briefing those who do – professional letter writers and public
relations staff – about the content and tone of the letters. CEOs usually
take an active role in editing drafts of these letters before endorsing the
contents by signature. Jack Welch, CEO of General Electric from 1981
to 2000, has publicly acknowledged that he took his CEO letters "seriously" and has expressed his gratitude "to Bill Lane, a guy who worked
with me on the annual report letters every year" (Welch 2001, 442). Indeed, CEOs are legally responsible for the statements made in the letters
they sign. And, in a somewhat perverse sense, whether or not a CEO is
actively involved in composing a letter to stockholders does not matter:
the words in the CEO's letter are symbolic and emblematic, and the
reader takes them to be the CEO's own.

8 See Lakoff and Johnson 1980; Lakoff 1993. Weick contends that
"what most people have missed is the use of writing as a tool for comprehension. If people know what they think by seeing what they say,
then the variety, nuance, subtlety, and precision of that saying will affect what they see, and then pursue" (1995, 196).

9 Fournier and Grey 2000, 11–12.

10 Speeches of CEOs have been analysed by Myers and Kessler (1980) and
Sussman, Ricchio, and Belohlav (1983). CEOs' letters to shareholders in
corporate annual reports have been the focus of Hyland (1998), Thomas (1997), Salancik and Meindl (1984), Bettman and Weitz (1983),
Hager and Scheiber (1990), Abrahamson and Amir (1996), Devinney
and Kabanoff (1999), Courtis (1998), and Prasad and Mir (2002),
among many others. Jones and Shoemaker (1994) summarize some of
this literature.

11 Weick 1995.

12 Welch 2001, 284, 375.

13 This notion of ideology, adopted by Weick (1995), is from Trice and
Beyer (1993, 33).

14 Slagell 1991, 155–6.

15 Martin 1990.

16 Boje 2001, 507ff.

17 Included among those who have followed this path are Bettman and Weitz (1983), Bowman (1984), Salancik and Meindl (1984), Hager and Scheiber (1990), Jones and Shoemaker (1994), Abrahamson and Amir (1996), Thomas (1997), Courtis (1998), Hyland (1998), and Devinney and Kabanoff (1999).

18 We did not choose the sampled texts through any rigorous or random- izing process; our choice was serendipitous and opportunistic. The mul- tiple-close-readings technique was demonstrated in the context of Internet sites by Amernic (1998).

19 Fournier and Grey 2000, 18.

20 Tinker 1985, 82.

21 For example, Barr, Stimpert, and Huff, in a comparative study of top- management adaptation and renewal over a period of twenty-five years at a successful versus an unsuccessful railway, were interested in "the interpretations of our sample firms' top managers, how these interpre- tations change, and the subsequent impact of these interpretations on organizational responses" (1992, 20–1). Their database was the set of stockholder letters written over the twenty-five-year period by the rail- ways' top managements. They explained that they used these letters "because we believe this document is too important not to be given close attention by top management." In another example, Geisler (a professor of rhetoric and composition) contends that since a company's annual report letter is placed on the public record and is a joint effort of various top managers, "at stake [is] the identity and control of the orga- nization itself" (2001). Geisler was commenting on research that fol- lowed closely the writing, power struggles, and rewriting of an annual report letter in an insurance company.

22 Counter-discourse seems sorely lacking in our society. Lively, open, and fair public debate – the very essence of what we think of as democracy – is often absent due to a lack of concepts that run counter to the prevail- ing orthodoxy – in short, due to a lack of words. Postman, in his *Build- ing a Bridge to the 18th Century*, argues on behalf of the power of words: "in discussing what words we shall use in describing an event, we are not engaging in 'mere semantics.' We are engaged in trying to control the perceptions and responses of others (as well as ourselves) to the character of the event itself. And that is why people who understand this fact wince when someone gets ready to 'tell it like it is.' No one can tell anything 'like it is.' In the first place, it isn't anything until someone names it. In the second place, the way in which 'it' is named reveals not

the way it *is* but how the namer wishes to see it or is capable of seeing it. And third, how it has been named becomes the reality for the namer and all who accept the name. But it need not be *our* reality" (2000, 165 [emphasis in original]).

23 This process of public education should be fundamental to any society that claims to be a democracy. It addresses directly Anderson and Prelli's (rhetorical) question of whether "public issues" may be discussed "from a wide and diverse variety of perspectives" (2001, 73). And, even more, it should be recognized as an essential aspect of university teaching.

24 Tinker 1985; Dillard and Nehmer 1990.

25 Eagleton 1991, xiii.

26 Weick 1995, 113. See also Trice and Beyer 1993, 33.

27 Harvey 1990, 355.

28 Postman 1993, 124.

29 EVA© is a registered trademark of Stern Stewart and Company.

30 The chief knowledge officer for Ernst and Young in Canada, Dave Pollard, is quoted as predicting that accountants will one day include EVA© and its acolyte, MVA (market value added), "on all balance sheets" ("Performance-Measurement" 1998).

31 Bauman 1999, 6.

32 Lye 1997.

33 Eagleton 1991, 9.

34 Lakoff 1996.

35 Myers 1999.

36 Burke 1961.

37 Klumpp 1999, 223.

38 Burke 1961.

39 Karim 2001, 117–18.

40 Ibid., 118.

41 Graham names this cyberspace utopia the "techno-Nirvana" (2001, 766).

42 All references in this paragraph are to Van Dijk (1993, 249, 257, 287). Harold Innis's concept of the "bias of communication" seems consistent with a rhetorical approach to analyzing the Internet and CEO-speak (1951). Comor asserts that "Innis' work provides valuable tools in efforts to assess what has become the focus of great interest almost fifty years after his death – the nature and implications of the Internet and more general digital technology developments" (2001, 286). Comor then poses analytical questions prompted by an Innisian perspective: "will such technologies serve to democratize communications, breaking the

monopoly of knowledge built up over the twentieth century by mostly large scale corporate entities? Or, will the context of capitalism and its complementary technological, organizational and institutional mediators suppress such potentials, thereby consolidating the power of capital in deeper and more expansive ways?" (2001).

43 Gibson 1996, 8.

44 Menzies 1996, 22 (drawing on Innis).

45 Gibbs 1994, 320.

46 Lakoff 1993, 203. Metaphor is an important influence on cognition and education (see Postman 1996, 174; Amernic and Craig 1999). The emergent theory of metaphor, summarized in Lakoff (1993), offers evidence of the metaphorical structure of human cognition. The modern theory of metaphor has been used to analyse the role of metaphor in legal reasoning (Winter 1989), American political discourse (Lakoff 1996), public education (Miller and Fredericks 1990), and management letters to stockholders in annual reports (Amernic and Craig 2000). Although Gibbs (1994) summarizes extensive empirical evidence supporting metaphor theory associated with (among others) Lakoff and Johnson (1980), there are many disparate views of the essential nature of metaphor and its cognitive, linguistic, and pragmatic character (see, for example, Glucksberg and McGlone 1999; Shen and Balaban 1999). Here we adopt Lakoff and Johnson's view of metaphor (1980) (see also Lakoff 1993).

47 Harrington 1995, 378.

48 Lakoff 1993; Cohn 1987.

49 Dunn 1990; Keenoy 1991.

50 Carrier 1997, 49.

51 Dunn 1990, 1.

52 Many of those who draw upon accounting even have a poorly developed understanding of accounting's *explicit* capacities. For example, industrial relations practitioners consistently regard accounting data as capable of providing objective and accurate characterizations of reality. There is a widespread belief that the numbers in financial statements preceded by monetary symbols (money of account) represent cold hard cash (material money). Understanding of accounting practices and the technical serviceability of accounting measurements for industrial relations purposes is often limited, despite the fact that this deficiency has been exposed by Clarke, Craig, and Amernic (1990) and Clarke and Craig (1992), among others. Labour educators Trumble and Tudor have asserted that "when labor leaders and others are trained in how to

read a financial report, a strategic plan, or annual report, they can understand the true health of the firm" (1996, 90). They invoke the metaphor of accounting as medical diagnostic tool, but their supporting argument is naive and induces profound skepticism that their particular doctor will ever "understand the true health of the firm" (1996).

53 Thus, we use the expression "about accounting" to encompass not only the mechanics and outputs of accounting, but also the processes and outputs of organizational accountability, and the contextual settings in which accounting and accountability function.

54 Eubanks 1999, 195.

55 The World Wide Web is rich in metaphors that possess "entailments": the metaphors of "surfing" and "superhighway" have entailments variously of health, vitality, wholesomeness, and efficiency (Amernic and Craig 1999).

56 See, for example, Cohn 1987.

57 Shen and Balaban 1999.

58 Johnson 1993; Lakoff 1996.

59 Johnson 1993, 41–50.

60 Landow 1996.

61 Angus 1998; Innis 1951; Lemke 1999.

62 Innis 1949, 5.

63 Angus 1998, 26.

64 Gibson 1996, 8.

65 In early 1999, several thousand people who "volunteered" to act as AOL "chat hosts" for free asked the US Department of Labor to investigate AOL's possible liability for back wages (Margonelli 1999).

66 Terranova 2000, 33.

67 Amernic, Losell, and Craig 2000; Amernic and Craig 1995.

68 Whitehead 1925.

69 For example, one that is based upon a respect for the rhythm of life, as envisioned by thinkers such as Alfred North Whitehead (1929).

CHAPTER TWO

1 At the time, the Enron Web site described the company as "one of the world's leading energy, commodities and services companies. The company markets electricity and natural gas, delivers energy and other physical commodities, and provides financial and risk management services to customers around the world" (accessed 7 February 2002, <www.enron.com>).

2 One especially good example is the treatment that the *Globe and Mail* gave Andersen managing partner and CEO Joseph Berardino after his appearance before the Financial Services Subcommittee of the US House of Representatives. On 6 February 2002 the paper ran the front-page headline "Enron Auditor Stonewalls" in forty-point font with a colour photo of a distressed-looking Berardino.

3 A press release (no longer accessible) on the Andersen Web site dated 7 February 2002 begins: "Statement of C.E. Andrews, Global Managing Partner, in response to Enron special committee report, February 2, 2002. The report issued today by Enron's special committee is troubling on many levels. Nothing more than a self-review, it does not reflect an independently credible assessment of the situation, but instead represents an attempt to insulate the company's leadership and the Board of Directors from criticism by shifting blame to others" (accessed 22 June 2004, <www.managementconsultancy.co.uk/news/1127644>).

4 Powers, Troubh, and Winokur 2002, 131.

5 Skilling 2002.

6 Bush 2002.

7 There were two versions of the Enron 2000 shareholders' letter: the Enron Web site version, and the annual report PDF version. They have identical text, but they differ in graphic and media design. The focus of our analysis here is the text, not the design, of the Enron letter. We recognize that there are rhetorical qualities beyond the text related to each version analysed. Nonetheless, we focus on text because it contains the words that Enron's top-management team chose as their language.

8 Tennyson, Ingram, and Dugan 1990, 395–6.

9 Lakoff and Johnson 1980; Weick 1995.

10 Indeed, when we analysed the letter with the computer-based content analysis software DICTION (see Hart 1997), it scored 4.21 standard deviations above a broad corpus of public texts on the "accomplishment" scale.

11 See Carrier, 1997.

CHAPTER THREE

1 The failure was that of Enron, which had rapidly evolved into a New Economy company. In the early 1990s, 80 per cent of its revenues came from the government-regulated gas pipeline business. By 2000, about 95 per cent of its revenues and 80 per cent of its reported profits came from trading energy and ownership positions in energy companies.

2 It was to become an even hotter potato with subsequent disclosures of political connections with the George W. Bush administration and the systematic shredding of Enron-audit-related documents by Andersen partner David Duncan in October and November 2001. But we focus here on the setting and what was publicly known when Berardino testified.

3 It could also potentially be used in future government investigations relating to the social usefulness of the accounting profession.

4 When adjustments are made for the errors, the reported profits are reduced by about $500 million.

5 Slocum 2001, 8.

6 Benoit 2001, 72.

7 Iyengar 1990.

8 Tversky and Kahneman 1981.

9 Emby and Finley 1997.

10 Benoit 2001, 70.

11 Entman 1993, 52.

12 Ibid., 52–3 (emphasis in original).

13 Daughton 1993.

14 Carrier 1997.

15 Tucker argues that "presence" is a fundamental idea in rhetoric, that it "is the property given by a speaker to a particular semantic 'shape' at the expense of the available others" (2001, 411). Berardino uses the words "complex" and "complexity" six times in his testimony: three times to describe the accounting (lines 13, 74, and 110), and three times to describe Enron as a company and a client (lines 213, 256, and 268).

16 Tucker 2001, 410.

17 Here, the term "accounting" encompasses financial statements such as income statements, cash flow statements, and balance sheets, as well as costs, budgets, and so on.

18 Indeed, even the conceptual frameworks adopted by many national accounting bodies assume, apparently unintentionally, that an objective "out there" is waiting to be "accounted for."

19 This might seem an extreme statement, but as historian Porter says, "Extremism in the deconstruction of accounting is no vice" (1992, 635).

20 Moore 1994, 583.

21 These issues are: consolidation of the "special purpose entities"; reclassification in the presentation of shareholders' equity; and Enron's disclosures regarding its off-balance-sheet transactions and related activities.

CHAPTER FOUR

1 There is ample support for such a contention. For example, after "a close analysis of the processes of Web reading," Bruce argued that there was a "heighten[ed] ... need for critical inquiry" into the World Wide Web as an information medium (2000, 109).

2 We are influenced strongly by the strategies adopted by Martin (1990); we use the device of close reading, which was demonstrated in the context of Internet sites by Amernic (1998).

3 Angus 1998, 26.

4 Access may be a feature characterizing internal corporate power struggles as well (Lemke 1999).

5 Van Dijk 1993, 257.

6 Ibid., 287.

7 Emphasis on "the significance of ... visual images ... in ... annual reports," especially analysis of alternative "ways of seeing" such images, resonates well with this focus (Preston, Wright, and Young 1996, 113).

8 Lakoff and Johnson 1980, 157. See also Amernic 1998; Amernic and Craig 2000.

9 Menzies 1996, 22 (drawing on Innis).

10 We accessed the Microsoft Web site on 4 May and 19 July 2000. On both dates it was indicated that most of the information had been last updated on 11 January 2000.

11 Microsoft's Web site was awarded the TechInvestor Poll's Best Overall Web Site Award in 1997.

12 It has done so through the use of moving images, multimedia inserts, access to sensitivity analysis tools, and so on.

13 The transitory nature of Web site disclosures is, in itself, a powerful rhetorical capability. Many Web site disclosures have no permanence – they are removed or otherwise rendered inaccessible after a brief period of availability.

14 Burbules 1998, 3.

15 Microsoft's main Web page was found at <http://www.microsoft.com>; for "Investor Relations," we went to <http://www.microsoft.com/msft>; for the 1999 annual report, we followed <http://www.microsoft.com/msft/ar.htm>.

16 Angus 1998, 22.

17 In a sense, rhetoric is unavoidable, but its existence and roles may be only dimly perceived and acknowledged.

18 Amernic 1998.

19 See, for example, Huizingh 2000.

20 Landow 1996; Gibson 1996.

21 Letiche 1995, 109.

22 Stabile 2000, 191.

23 Oliver 1991. See also Neu, Warsame, and Pedwell 1998.

24 Amernic 1998.

25 Amernic and Craig 1999, 441.

26 Ibid., 442.

27 But there might be an increasingly important feedback effect between corporate Web sites and the (allegedly) "real" corporation. Lemke observes that "a particular, novel discourse medium, the organization's Web site, seems to be playing a catalytic role in on-going processes of institutional change" (1999, 21). Thus, telepresence might become presence in ways that we now only dimly perceive.

28 http://www.microsoft.com/msft/ar99/any_tpd.htm

29 Indeed, "any time, any place, any device" appears to be Microsoft jingoism – a guiding mantra for the company and all those presumed to be "empowered" by Microsoft products. A word search of the phrase reveals fifteen instances on the Microsoft Web site.

30 Romei 2000, 35.

31 All quotations from Gates's 1999 letter to shareholders were found at <http://www.microsoft.com/msft/ar99/lts2.htm>.

32 McLuhan regarded such technologically facilitated extensions of reach as less than an unequivocal good, since, as "we approach the final phase of the extensions of man – the technological simulation of consciousness, when the creative process of knowing will be collectively and corporately extended to the whole of human society ... [it] affects the whole psychic and social complex" (1964, 3–40).

33 On many Web sites financial reporting is marginalized. The company's annual report is imbedded deeply as a minor component of a much more encompassing investor relations section.

34 Microsoft is not the only large corporation whose Web site is revealed through close reading to indulge in such gauche gender-based stereotypes. IBM's site was shown by Amernic and Craig to be similarly afflicted (2000).

35 Martin 1990, 342–3. Amernic provides an example of a conglomerate corporation whose CEO downplayed the fact that tobacco-related sales made a major contribution to corporate profits. The company masked the ugly reality by constructing a dichotomy of abstract "share portfo-

lio culture" language to represent itself as merely an efficient body seeking to optimize its shareholders' returns (1998).

36 For "Corporate Information," we went to <http://www.microsoft.com/
msft/ar99/lts6.htm>; "Fast Facts" was at <http://www.microsoft.com/
presspass/fastfacts.asp>.

37 One would expect financial data to play an important role in a company's overview of performance. However, "Fast Facts" marginalizes
financial information by focusing on highly aggregated figures for total
revenue, revenue growth, total income, and income growth. In the "historical" section the user is only able to view the time-series graph in
terms of revenue, not costs. Note too that there has been some questioning of Microsoft's earnings-management practices, especially as related to the efficacy of its accounting for unearned revenues.

38 "The Forest of Rhetoric: *Silva Rhetoricae*."

39 Orr 1989, 197.

40 Stabile 2000, 200.

41 Harvey 1990, 233.

CHAPTER FIVE

1 Mitchell 2000, 140.

2 This is a fundamental part of what we should be doing every day in a
society that claims to be a democracy. It addresses directly Anderson
and Prelli's (rhetorical) question as to whether "public issues" can be
discussed "from a wide and diverse variety of perspectives" (2001, 73).

3 Korten argues that part of the process of "corporate colonialism" involves the creation of "a world in which universalized symbols created
and owned by the world's most powerful corporations replace the distinctive cultural symbols that link people to particular places, values,
and human communities. Our cultural symbols provide an important
source of identity and meaning; they affirm our worth, our place in society. They arouse our loyalty to, and sense of responsibility for, the
health and well-being of our community and its distinctive ecosystem.
When control of our cultural symbols passes to corporations, we are essentially yielding to them to define the power of who we are. Instead of
being Americans, Norwegians, Egyptians, Filipinos, or Mexicans, we
become simply members of the 'Pepsi generation,' detached from place
and any meaning other than those a corporation finds it profitable to
confer on us. Market tyranny may be more subtle than state tyranny,

but it is no less effective in enslaving the many to the interests of the few" (1995, 158).

4 See Roscoe 1999.

5 Korten 1995, 104, 112.

6 Fairclough was writing specifically about "political and government processes," but his assertion is easily and fairly extended to corporations (2000, 167).

7 The AOLTimeWarner Inc. Joint Proxy Statement-Prospectus (form S-4/ A, registration statement), filed with the SEC on 19 May 2000, shows that the merged entity would have reported over $33 billion in revenues had the two companies been merged for the year ending 31 December 1999. On 12 January 2001, CNNfn (one of the newly merged entity's many holdings) reported that "Levin stood by the company's projection that its annual revenues are going to be above $40 billion, growing at 12 percent to 15 percent a year. Cash flow, a key measure of fiscal health used by media companies, is seen at $11 billion, growing at 25 to 30 percent" ("AOL Looks Ahead, But Stocks Drop" 2001).

8 Such a view of information is common. See Reddy 1993; Lakoff 1993.

9 Rohrer 1997; Amernic and Craig 1999.

10 Innis 1949; Comor 2001.

11 Angus 1998, 16–17.

12 Burke 1961.

13 DiMaggio, Hargittai, Neuman, and Robinson 2001.

14 Cheney, Garvin-Doxas, and Torrens 1999, 145.

15 Burke 1961.

16 As conceived by Burke (1961).

17 We wondered whether we should we use the collective singular or the plural for AOLTimeWarner, and we chose the collective singular ("it") for the sake of convenience, but that choice has rhetorical implications.

18 Lakoff 1993.

19 Dunn applied this metaphor to industrial relations, but it has much wider applicability (1990, 17–21).

20 McGee defines "ideograph" as "an ordinary-language term found in political discourse. It is a high-order abstraction representing collective commitment to a particular but equivocal and ill-defined normative goal. It warrants the use of power, excuses behavior and belief which might otherwise be perceived as eccentric or antisocial, and guides behavior and belief into channels easily recognized by a community as acceptable and laudable" (1980, 15).

21 Ibid.

22 Why was "involvement" chosen rather than some more neutral term?
   Every word choice is a rhetorical and therefore ideological act.

23 Who gets to do the determining, and what are the criteria?

24 Such dominance suggests that Internet policies achieving public acqui-
   escence will have implications well beyond the Internet. Public policy
   that enables the corporate colonization of the Internet will also facilitate the colonization of all public spaces, both virtual and real. Davis,
   whose interest is in the colonization of real public spaces, puts this process in historical context: "Both the textures of shared space and its potential for collective experience are being thoroughly revised. In the first
   half of the 20th century, the entertainment conglomerates were central
   in creating a nearly all-penetrating national and international mass culture, first through film and later through animation, popular music and
   televised sports. In the second half of the century, they have brought
   this largely American mass culture thoroughly and extensively into the
   home, to hundreds of millions of people. At the cusp of the 21st century,
   they are poised to weave the private realm together with the collective
   through the creation of dramatic and focused media-filled spaces. In the
   process ... the media conglomerates are changing the relationships between public and private experience" (1999, 436).

25 Innis 1949, 1951.

CHAPTER SIX

1 Accessed 22 May 1998, <http://www.ibm.com/FinancialGuide/>.

2 Chambers 1994, 3.

3 One example is the dispute between the Financial Accounting Standards Board and the US Federal Reserve (and others) over accounting
  for derivatives.

4 See, for example, Briloff 1972, 1981, 1990; Chambers 1973, 1994;
  Clarke, Dean, and Oliver 1997.

5 Heller 1994, 307. See also Carroll 1993, 1–7.

6 Chambers 1973; O'Connor 1973; Bird and McHugh 1977.

7 Ball and Brown 1968; Beaver 1968.

8 Beidleman 1973; Eckel 1981; Worthy 1984; Craig and Walsh 1989;
  Merchant and Rockness 1994.

9 Clarke, Dean, and Oliver 1997.

10 Greene 1986; Weberman 1986; Elliott and Shaw 1988; Walsh, Craig,
   and Clarke 1991.

11 See, for example, Briloff 1972, 1981; Chambers 1973; Tinker 1985.

12 On 7 April 1993, the *Wall Street Journal* ran a front-page story titled "Softer Numbers: As IBM's Woes Grew, Its Accounting Tactics Got Less Conservative" (Miller and Berton 1993). And dare we mention Enron?

13 Indeed, in the guide's glossary, "expenses" are defined as "Costs such as salaries, rent, office supplies, advertising, and taxes." Since there is no entry in the glossary for "costs," it seems inevitable that readers will not appreciate the distinction between expenses and cash outflows. Potential confusion is compounded when the guide says that "After a company deducts all costs and expenses ... from revenue ... the statement of earnings shows the net earnings (or loss)." This distinguishes two categories of deductions from revenues – costs and expenses – but the glossary had defined "expenses" as "costs."

14 Miller and Fredericks argued to this effect in analyzing the metaphors in the US government's influential education policy document *A Nation at Risk: The Imperative for Educational Reform* (1990, 67).

15 Postman 1996, 174.

16 In advocating a theory of visual rhetoric, Scott argues that advertisements containing pictures require consumers to "engage in metaphorical thought" (1994, 254). Forceville concludes that Black's interaction theory of metaphor can be used to describe and interpret pictorial metaphors (Forceville 1995; Black 1962, 1993). Forceville studied people's reactions to three billboard advertisements used by IBM in Holland. In each, the IBM logo, with its horizontal blue and white stripes, appeared beneath a photo of another item with horizontal blue and white stripes. One such advertisement used a photo of storm-tossed waters, above which was a beacon prominently displaying the IBM stripes, thus creating the visual metaphor "IBM is a beacon." A second advertisement used a close-up shot of a piano (a Steinway, a high-quality brand); a tuning fork in IBM's colours lay on top, just above the keyboard. This suggested that "IBM is a tuning fork" – that is, IBM helps everyone play in tune and act in harmony.

17 References in this paragraph are from Lakoff and Johnson 1980, 139, 157 (citing Charlotte Linde in conversation), 158.

18 Lakoff and Johnson 1980, 157.

19 For example, almost all the rhetorical terms that Lanham includes within the "balance, antithesis, and paradox" type are concerned with aspects of ordering – like "climax." Rhetorical terms that Lanham includes in other types, such as "amplification," may also involve an intentional ordering (1991, 184–5).

20 For example, we read that "The statement of financial position is like a snapshot" (and snapshots are created through the lens of a camera).

21 A visual form of this metaphor is used on the guide's opening page: numbers in a graphic are shown both in and out of focus; a lens brings them into focus and enlarges them.

22 Rosenau 1992; Angus 1998. Note that the objectivity of the camera lens itself is moot (Barthes 1967, 1981).

23 And there are still some other fundamental problems with the "basics" of this Web site – for example, its depiction of women.

CHAPTER SEVEN

1 Fox 2003, 64.

2 GE Web site, accessed 20 November 2001, <http://www.ge.com/fact-sheet.html>.

3 Hallett 2003, 133.

4 Newman 1953, 211.

5 Hill and Carley 1999.

6 Hegele and Kiesler 2001, 298.

7 See, for example, Greiner 2002; Hegele and Kiesler 2001.

8 Quoted in Byrne 1998, 90.

9 Skapinker 2003. The results were based on a poll of between 640 and 1,000 CEOs of major companies worldwide.

10 Fox 2003, 64.

11 Byrne 1998, 90.

12 Stein 2003.

13 Olive 2002.

14 Welch became GE's CEO on 1 April 1981, but he co-signed the 1980 CEO letter as "chairman-elect" with the then-CEO.

15 <www.ge.com>.

16 Jang and Barnett 1994, 55.

17 Wilson 2002, 42.

18 Ibid.

19 Welch and Byrne 2001, 442.

20 GE's board of directors had elected Welch to the post on 19 October 1980.

21 The next year, another photo of this trio appeared. In that one Welch is seated on a sofa, but he is still dominant, since the two vice chairs remain behind him.

22 Low cautions that "Generalizations from metaphoric utterances to social behavior or conceptual/mental organization should not be assumed

to be true; they need to be justified" (1999, 63). Thus, our claims here are suggestive.

23 Welch and Byrne 2001, 284, 375.

24 Bakan 2004.

25 CEOs of large corporations are human, and subject to the same cognitive limitations as the rest of us. So it is not surprising that they couch their perceptions of their huge, multi-faceted domains largely in accounting terms (Hines 1988).

26 Harvey 1990.

27 Welch demonizes bureaucracy, stigmatizing it as an "impediment" to achieving "productivity growth," therefore presuming that "productivity growth" is desirable. He performs this rhetorical move by writing, in the 1991 letter, "But enough of the numbers from '91. It's over. 1991 did, however, once again remind us how absolutely critical productivity growth is in the brutally Darwinian global marketplaces in which virtually all of our businesses compete. We are aware, for instance, that if we had the same productivity growth in '90 and '91 that we had in '80 and '81, our '91 earnings would have been more like $3 billion rather than $4.435 billion. We also are acutely aware that, without productivity growth, it is possible to lose in 24 months businesses that took a half-century, or a century, to build. Productivity growth is essential to industrial survival" (lines 58–67). Thus, "productivity growth" is set up not only as the cause of the good earnings number in 1991 but also as something "absolutely critical" in the "brutally Darwinian global marketplaces"; indeed, it is "essential to industrial survival." So, GE, the corporation-is-a-person, inhabits a "brutally Darwinian" world and absolutely must have "productivity growth" to survive. What a frightening metaphorical structure this is. It is a naive and superficial articulation of complex concepts involving international trade, competition, the marketplace, and the very concept of "productivity growth" itself. Welch connects "productivity growth" to "earnings" and "industrial survival" without interrogating these concepts.

28 *Merriam Webster's Collegiate Dictionary*, 10th ed., s.v. "layer."

29 The other values and beliefs are that companies must "relish change"; focus on "customer needs"; recognize size as a spur to innovation; annihilate bureaucracy; embrace self-confidence, simplicity, and speed; remove leaders who do not share the company's values; commit to advanced management training programs; employ the best people; adopt informality as "an operating philosophy as well as a cultural characteristic"; and become a "boundaryless" "global learning company."

30 Harris 2002.
31 Taylor 2003.
32 Grey 2003.

CHAPTER EIGHT

1 Boje 1995; Bryman 1995.
2 Attributing sole or substantial authorship unequivocally to Walt Disney is difficult. We cannot say with certainty that he personally drafted the 1940 stockholders' letter. However, in view of his reputation for keeping "a sharp eye on financial arrangements," his acute awareness of the "bottom line," and his obsession with detail (Capodagli and Jackson 1998, 7, 181–5), it seems likely that he was deeply involved. While acknowledging this lack of unequivocal proof of authorship, we do take into account the importance of the metaphoric "Walt." Schickel notes: "In the last analysis, Walt Disney's greatest creation was Walt Disney" (1968, 44). There is little doubt that the metaphoric Walt signed the letter and is accountable for it.
3 Garraty and Carnes 1988, 131 (quoting British cartoonist David Low).
4 Disney went bankrupt before moving from Kansas City to Los Angeles and achieving his initial successes in the late 1920s. Problems included decreasing profit margins on cartoons as efforts were made to effect technical improvements to satisfy markets. Unless otherwise noted, material in this and the following three paragraphs draws upon Bryman 1995.
5 "In 1930 the first international licensing contract for the sale of Mickey Mouse merchandise was signed," and "the first Mickey Mouse watch was sold by Ingersoll Watch Company in June, 1933" (Ellwood 1998, 19; see also *Walt Disney Company 1997 Fact Book*; de Cordova 1994).
6 Disney's plan to license his animated characters was highly successful: "in 1932 sales of Disney character articles had totaled $300,000, in 1937 they were $35,000,000" (Bristol 1938, 13–15). That success has been institutionalized. There is now a well-established and curiously seamless fusion of cinematic art and consumerism: "Every Disney animated film comes bundled with a complete marketing strategy for merchandise, interactive games and a line of children's books" (Ellwood 1998, 28).
7 He did so because "it was becoming increasingly difficult to combine the growing costs of animation … with the inherently limited returns that could accrue from shorts" (Bryman 1995, 9).

8 One wonders whether contemporary audiences would be receptive to a female hero so "young, virginal, pretty, sweet-natured and obedient," so unfazed by domestic drudgery, so absolutely convinced that "a handsome owning-class chap [would], someday soon, come and save her" (Maio 1998, 12).

9 In 1934 it had employed 187 people.

10 Among his vast array of admirers were Italian conductor Arturo Toscanini and Russian film director Sergei Eisenstein (Costantino 1991, 12).

11 Garraty and Carnes 1988, 130.

12 All references in this subsection are taken from "The Big Bad Wolf" (88–90, 146) unless otherwise indicated.

13 Ellwood 1998, 8.

14 Ibid.

15 As Boje has argued (1995).

16 Garraty and Carnes 1988, 131.

17 Ibid.

18 Ellwood 1998, 8.

19 Total assets reported on the balance sheet dated 28 September 1940 were $8.6 million. Of these, $4.9 million represented costs associated with feature films and short subjects (that is, "soft" assets). Stockholder equity was reported as $5,787,646.

20 *Time* magazine put it thus: "Last week, with its second full-length feature, *Pinocchio*, ready for a nation-wide Easter week opening, Walt Disney productions applied to the SEC for permission to sell 155,000 shares of $25 par, 6% cumulative convertible preferred stock. Purpose of the $3,875,000 offering: to pay off bank loans incurred in building the company's new studio at Burbank, Calif., and to provide working capital for four more features now in production: *Bambi, Wind in the Willows, Peter Pan, Fantasia*" (25 March 1940, 77).

21 Hollister 1940. As early as 1934, *Fortune* magazine reported that Disney was reinvesting profits "for the sole purpose of making his films more beautiful, more elaborate, more nearly perfect" ("Big Bad Wolf," 91).

22 "The $1,500,000 borrowed to make *Snow White* was repaid within three months" (Hollister 1940, 700).

23 "The average pay [was] higher than the average in any other Hollywood studio" (Hollister 1940, 700).

24 Although it provided significant support to Britain and its allies, the United States did not enter World War II until after the Japanese attacked Pearl Harbor on 7 December 1941.

25 According to Hollister, "Walt is the spark plug of production. No story starts toward a picture until Walt has bought or invented it, shaped it,

tried it out, and given it a push ... Throughout the production pattern of every picture Walt threads in and out like a guiding outline ... Walt knifes into the most minute step of the most microscopic element" (1940, 700).

26 Hollister 1940.

27 Weick 1995, 13.

28 Lanham 1991, 11.

29 Ibid., 70.

30 Barry and Elmes 1997.

31 Salancik and Meindl 1984.

32 Lanham 1991, 191.

33 The financial statement footnotes in the 1940 annual report show that the accounting method was doubly conservative. Not only were profits from an animated feature not admitted to the company's accounting system until all of a feature's production costs had been recovered, but also Disney did not account for any revenues until cash had been received from a film's distributor.

34 For example, we might have explored more deeply the argument schemes apparent in the letter (Warnick and Kline 1992) or the ways in which the letter dealt rhetorically with its composite audiences (Myers 1999); or we might have analysed text structure and metadiscourse (Hyland 1998).

35 This resonates with Bakan's interpretation of the corporation (2004).

36 Summarized in Boje 1995; Schickel 1968; and Watts 1997.

37 Boje 1995, 1014–5.

38 Ellwood 1998, 8.

CHAPTER NINE

1 Den Tandt 2001.

2 Nortel reported revenues of US$22 billion in 1999. Former parent BCE's common-share ownership had been rapidly reduced to about 3 per cent, so Nortel was no longer beholden or accountable to BCE.

3 Nortel Networks Corporation 1999, 10.

4 Ibid., 3.

5 Tsing 2000, 118.

6 The shares traded at about CDN$10 from June 2001 to January 2002.

7 See also Thrift 2001. Thrift argues that "the new economy was a rhetorical fiction, which, through the ability of stakeholders like the cultural circuit of capital, was able to define what the facts consisted of and to train up bodies that bent to those facts. This fabrication could

therefore produce regularities in the world. In the first instance, the chief beneficiary was the financial sector, which was able to use the new economy rhetoric to engineer a financial bubble. But, even after the inevitable crash, the new economy has left a legacy which should not be scoffed at" (2001, 412).

8 Our speculations regarding the rhetorical power of Accounting and English are sobering in light of the detritus that invariably accompanies investment frenzies. Recent history is rife with examples, such as the losses sustained by employees who invested in Enron as part of their retirement planning, and the environmental abomination in Kalimantan, Indonesia, associated with the Bre-X mining scams.

9 Welch served as GE's CEO from 1981 to 2001 (see chapter 7).

10 Hamilton and Cribb 2001a.

11 Buckler 2001, 27.

12 Tuck 2001.

13 Hamilton and Cribb 2001a.

14 Shiller 2000.

15 Hamilton and Cribb 2001b.

16 Kostera and Glinka 2001, 647–82.

17 Curiously, although the letter was labelled "Open Letter to Shareholders" on Nortel's Web site, the version published in the *Toronto Star* on 9 March 2001 was labelled "Nortel Networks™ CEO Letter to Shareholders."

18 For example, one appeared in the *Toronto Star* on 9 March 2001; interestingly, there was no indication that it was an advertisement.

19 Edwards 2000, 53.

20 Wicks, Berman, and Jones 1999, 99.

21 All references in this paragraph, unless otherwise noted, are from Orbuch 1997, 455–78.

22 Ochs and Capps 1996, 19–43.

23 Cheney 1998, 29.

CHAPTER TEN

1 This bragging was short-lived. A day later, Alcoa announced that it intended to regain the title of "world's largest aluminium company" by acquiring Reynolds, and it completed the transaction soon afterwards. The impressive size of each of the three merging companies is shown in this table drawn from the companies' annual reports (amounts are in US dollars):

	Alcan	Pechiney	Alusuisse
1998 Revenues	7.8 billion	10.9 billion	6.4 billion
1998 Net income	399 million	679 million	333 million
Employees	40,000	33,085	29,000

2 However, in a news release dated 13 April 2000, the three companies announced that the merger would not proceed, at least partly due to concerns of the European Commission. Alcan and Algroup (Alusuisse) forged ahead with a new, two-way merger, without Pechiney.

3 Huxley's book and the world it describes is part of our society's broad cultural knowledge, and this is a necessary precondition for such a metaphoric evocation.

4 The US Financial Accounting Standards Board has since banned the pooling method. Instead it advocates the purchase method of accounting because it reveals the "real cost of the transaction and gives investors the valuable information they need to make investment and capital allocation decisions" (US Financial Accounting Standards Board 2000). The standards board of the Canadian Institute of Chartered Accountants has also since banned the pooling method.

5 EVA©, which stands for "economic value added," is a concept of economic income that measures the excess of net operating profit after taxes over the opportunity cost of the capital invested.

6 Many other metaphors might also be elicited: for example, "the company is a building" is suggested by the first sentence of paragraph 10, and "the strict father" metaphoric model introduced by Lakoff is suggested throughout (1996).

7 Harrington 1995, 372.

8 Cheney 1998, 29.

9 Dunn 1990, 21.

10 Over 11,000 employees will lose their jobs; customers will be affected by reduced competition and choice; shareholders will see some dilution in their shareholding and they will have less clout in the much larger company; governments will have less power to control this now geographically liberated entity.

CHAPTER ELEVEN

1 Miller and Simmons 1998, 529.

2 The actual term used was not "privatization" but "commercialization." The governing Liberal Party regarded the term "privatization" as "so detestably Tory they refused to use it. They talked instead about the 'commercialization' of CN" (Bruce 1997, 3).

3 CN was sold to underwriting companies on 16 November 1995 for CDN$2.2 billion. Its shares were traded for the first time the following day. The IPO was grossly oversubscribed – eight times, by one account (Bruce 1997, 140).

4 Critchley 1995.

5 Leger 1995, 6.

6 See Critchley 1995. CN's first newsletter on privatization for employees and pensioners, titled *On a New Course for the Future* and published in May 1995, cites the following as one of two reasons "Why CN Is Ready for Privatization": "During the past two years, CN has taken the measures required to perform according to private sector operating and financial standards. Fiscal year 1994 earnings of $245 million reflect the progress being made" (CN 1995).

7 Bruce 1997, 11.

8 It has become routine to the extent that consultants now proffer advice on how to privatize, and unions publish annual reports intended to create awareness of privatization as a process that "is fundamentally changing the nature of ... society, undermining the public services that bind us together and underpin the foundations of ... democracy" (Darcy 1999).

9 Shaoul 1997, 479.

10 Serious questions have been raised about the mechanisms and conflicts of interest in some privatizations. There has, for example, been debate over the privatization of Medway ports in the UK (Arnold and Cooper 1999); individual employee health and well-being as a result of privatizations (Cunha and Cooper 1998); the imposition of deficient management control systems in newly privatized companies (Ogden and Anderson 1999); and the economic performance of companies post-privatization (Shaoul 1997).

11 We consider the during-privatization period to be from 27 February 1995 to 17 November 1995, and the post-privatization period to be from 18 November 1995 to the present.

12 We chose to read the July-August 1992 through the January-February 1995 issues.

13 Bruce 1997, 3, 11, 13.

14 Bruce provides further evidence. In 1994, when Tellier was engaged in merger discussions with CP Rail CEO William Stinson, Tellier said to Stinson, "All that matters to me is the bottom line" (Bruce 1997, 38).

15 *Keeping Track*, December 1992, 1. Such use by corporate leadership of accounting language, and thus this language's cognitive world view, is not surprising. Accounting is the reductionist "language of business" (Lavoie 1987), and it helps structure the way managers make sense of their world (Weick 1995; Hines 1988).

16 *Keeping Track*, February-March 1993, 1.

17 Bruce 1997, 32.

18 Railway companies often publicly report their achieved operating ratios and their target operating ratios. Such public announcements of accounting-based targets provide "a common language" and help "create shared beliefs about the value and logic of action" (Swieringa and Weick 1987, 306). Technically, a railway company's operating ratio is constructed as railway operating expenses divided by railway operating revenues.

19 Bruce 1997, 26.

20 All quotations in this paragraph are from *Keeping Track*, May 1993, 1, 3.

21 Bruce 1997, 32.

22 The issue is not the GAAP treatment (which requires recording in the year of restructuring even if the expenditures are in future years; separate disclosure is also required), but rather the fact that the GAAP number is irrelevant to Tellier's comparison. He should have used a basis of comparison that examined both the actual CN and the imagined (privatized) CN on the same footing. But instead he chose to use the GAAP numbers, not because he was uninformed in an accounting sense, but because he was astute rhetorically. He exploited GAAP's patina of respectability by using the reported bottom line number, even though (as we maintain) the number was technically irrelevant.

23 For a fuller understanding of "big bath accounting," the use of extraordinary items to effect it, and the managerial motives for its implementation, see Walsh, Craig, and Clarke 1991.

24 Another defensible treatment would have been to regard the "workforce reduction charges" as arising from poor management practices in the pre-1992 years and to allocate those charges as adjustments to profits over a range of years prior to 1992. That is, these charges would be ignored entirely in profit comparisons in the years 1992, 1993, and 1994. That Tellier did not contemplate such an accounting treatment is understandable for two reasons: first, the rhetorical power of the GAAP-based 1992 net loss number was the result of the application of GAAP and an external audit; and second, the magnitude of the "loss." But it seems blatantly wrong to use accounting charges in this way. They were created by CN's Crown corporation mandate and activities and by the 1992 decision of CN top management and board of directors to radically downsize the

company. They were ammunition with which to seduce CN employees to accept the apparently natural necessity of all that management intended to do to get that balance sheet "ready." This is similar to an Alice-in-Wonderland use of (accounting) language, and it also shows that corporate leadership often involves the practice of seduction (Calás and Smircich 1991).

25 *Keeping Track*, September 1993, 3.

26 *Keeping Track*, October 1993, 3.

27 *Keeping Track*, November 1993, 3.

28 *Keeping Track*, December 1993, 3.

29 For a definition of "ideograph," see McGee 1980, 15 or chapter 5, note 20. It seems plausible to contend that "balance," as both a social and personal goal, is an ideograph.

30 Tellier's use of "balance" in accounting also recalls the balanced-accounts feature of double-entry bookkeeping, which was prized rhetoric for medieval tradespersons (Aho 1985).

31 *Keeping Track*, January-February 1994, 3.

32 *Keeping Track*, July-August 1994, 3.

33 Carrier 1997.

34 Bauman 1999, 6.

35 Delaney 1994, 514.

CHAPTER TWELVE

1 Bakan 2004; Estes 1996.

2 Bakan 2004, 110.

3 A possible exception is AOLTimeWarner's Internet-based corporate Internet policy statement.

4 Weick 1995, 196.

5 Gwyn 2002, A15.

6 Dobbs 2002.

7 Weick 1995; Searle 1969.

8 Bush 2002. Regulations requiring such vouching have followed.

9 Boje 2001, 507ff.

10 See Craig and Amernic 2002.

11 Power 1997.

References

Abrahamson, E., and E. Amir. 1996. "The Information Content of the President's Letter to Shareholders." *Journal of Business Finance and Accounting* 23, no. 8: 1157–82.

Aho, J. 1985. "Rhetoric and the Invention of Double Entry Bookkeeping." *Rhetorica* 3, no. 1: 21–43.

Amernic, J.H. 1998. "'Close Readings' of Internet Corporate Financial Reporting: Towards a More Critical Pedagogy on the Information Highway." *The Internet and Higher Education* 1, no. 2: 87–114.

Amernic, J.H., and R.J. Craig. 1995. "Accounting Images and the Resolution of Labor Contract Costing Conflict." *Journal of Collective Negotiations in the Public Sector* 24, no. 2: 131–51.

– 1999. "The Internet in Undergraduate Management Education: A Concern for Neophytes among Metaphors." *Prometheus* 17: 437–50.

– 2000. "Accountability and Rhetoric during a Crisis: An Analysis of Walt Disney's 1940 Letter to Stockholders." *Accounting Historians Journal* 27, no. 2: 49–86.

Amernic, J.H., D.L. Losell, and R.J. Craig. 2000. "Economic Value Added as Ideology through a Critical Lens: Towards a Pedagogy for Management Fashion?" *Accounting Education* 9, no. 4: 343–67.

Anderson, F.L., and L.J. Prelli. 2001. "Pentadic Cartography: Mapping the Universe of Discourse." *Quarterly Journal of Speech* 87, no. 1: 73–95.

Angus, I. 1998. "The Materiality of Expression: Harold Innis' Communication Theory and the Discursive Turn in the Human Sciences." *Canadian Journal of Communication* 23: 9–29.

"AOL Looks Ahead, But Stocks Drop." 2001. *CNN Money*, 12 January. <http://money.cnn.com/2001/01/12/deals/new_aol/>.

Arnold, P.J., and C. Cooper. 1999. "A Tale of Two Classes: The Privatisation of Medway Ports." *Critical Perspectives on Accounting* 10, no. 2: 127–52.

Bacon, F. 1891. "The Proficience and Advancement of Learning, Divine and Human." In *The Advancement of Learning*. Edited by W. Aldis Wright. Oxford: Clarendon Press.

Bakan, J. 2004. *The Corporation: The Pathological Pursuit of Profit and Power*. Toronto:Viking Canada.

Ball, R., and P. Brown. 1968. "An Empirical Evaluation of Accounting Income Numbers." *Journal of Accounting Research* 6, no. 2: 159–78.

Barthes, R. 1967. *Elements of Semiology*. Translated by Annette Lavers and Colin Smith. London: Jonathan Cape.

– 1981. *Camera Lucida*. Translated by Richard Howard. New York: Hill and Wang.

Barr, P.S., J.L. Stimpert, and A.S. Huff. 1992. "Cognitive Change, Strategic Action, and Organizational Renewal." *Journal of Strategic Management* 13: 15–36.

Barry, D., and M. Elmes. 1997. "Strategy Retold: Toward a Narrative View of Strategic Discourse." *Academy of Management Review* 22, no. 2: 429–52.

Bauman, Z. 1999. *In Search of Politics*. Stanford: Stanford University Press.

Baxter, S. 2004. "Power Couple in Successful Merger." *Australian*, 19 April.

Beaver, W.H. 1968. "The Information Content of Annual Earnings Announcements." *Journal of Accounting Research* 6: 67–92.

Beidleman, C.R. 1973. "'Income Smoothing': The Role of Management." *Accounting Review* 48, no. 4: 653–67.

Benoit, W.L. 2001. "Framing through Temporal Metaphor: The 'Bridges' of Bob Dole and Bill Clinton in Their 1996 Acceptance Speeches." *Communication Studies* 52, no. 1: 70–84.

Bettman, J.R., and B.A. Weitz. 1983. "Attributions in the Board Room: Causal Reasoning in Corporate Annual Reports." *Administrative Science Quarterly* 28: 165–83.

"The Big Bad Wolf." 1934. *Fortune*, 10 November.

Bird, R., and A. McHugh. 1977. "Financial Ratios – Why?" In *Capital, Income, and Decision-Making*. Edited by I. Tilley and P. Jubb. Sydney: Holt, Rinehart and Winston.

Black, M. 1962. *Models and Metaphors*. Ithaca: Cornell University Press.

– 1993. "More about Metaphor." In *Metaphor and Thought*. Edited by A. Ortony. Cambridge: Cambridge University Press.

Boje, D.M. 1995. "Stories of the Storytelling Organization: A Postmodern Analysis of Disney as 'Tamara-Land.'" *Academy of Management Journal* 38, no. 4: 997–1035.

– 2001. "Corporate Writing in the Web of Postmodern Culture and Postindustrial Capitalism." *Management Communication Quarterly* 14, no. 3: 507–16.

Bowman, E.H. 1984. "Content Analysis of Annual Reports for Corporate Strategy and Risk." *Interfaces* 14: 61–71.

Briloff, A.J. 1972. *Unaccountable Accounting*. New York: Harper and Row.

– 1981. *The Truth about Corporate Accounting*. New York: Harper and Row.

– 1990. "Accountancy and Society: A Covenant Desecrated." *Critical Perspectives on Accounting* 1, no. 1: 5–30.

Bristol, G.T. 1938. "Inanimate Characters becoming a New Force in Merchandising." *Dun's Review*, April.

Bruce, B.C. 2000. "Credibility of the Web: Why We Need Dialectical Reading." *Journal of Philosophy of Education* 34, no. 1: 97–109.

Bruce, H. 1997. *The Pig That Flew: The Battle to Privatize Canadian National*. Vancouver and Toronto: Douglas and McIntyre.

Bryman, A. 1995. *Disney and His Worlds*. London: Routledge.

Buckler, G. 2001. "Nortel's Optical Illusion." *Journal of Business Strategy* 22, no. 5: 27–8.

Burbules, N.C. 1998. "Aporia: Webs, Passages, Getting Lost, and Learning to Go On." In *Philosophy of Education 1997*. Edited by Susan Laird. Urbana, IL: Philosophy of Education Society.

Burke, K. 1961. *The Rhetoric of Religion: Studies in Logology*. Berkeley: University of California Press.

– 1966. *Language as Symbolic Action*. Berkeley: University of California Press.

Bush, G.W. 2002. "The President's Ten-Point Plan." Washington, DC, 7 March. <www.whitehouse.gov/infocus/corporateresponsibility/index2.html>.

Byrne, J.A. 1998. "Jack: A Close-up Look at How America's Number 1 Manager Runs GE." *Business Week*, 8 June.

Calás, M.B., and L. Smircich. 1991. "Voicing Seduction to Silence Leadership." *Organization Studies* 12, no. 4: 567–602.

Capodagli, B., and L. Jackson. 1998. *The Disney Way: Harnessing the Management Secrets of Disney in Your Company.* New York: McGraw Hill.

Carrier, J.G. 1997. Introduction. In *Meanings of the Market: The Free Market in Western Culture.* Edited by J.G. Carrier. Oxford: Berg.

Carroll, P. 1993. *Big Blues: The Unmaking of IBM.* New York: Crown.

Chambers, R.J. 1973. *Securities and Obscurities: A Case for Reform of the Law of Company Accounts.* Melbourne: Gower.

– 1994. "Pacioli 500 Years On." Opening address at the Accounting and Finance Association of Australia and New Zealand conference, Wollongong, Australia, July.

Cheney, G. 1998. "'It's the Economy, Stupid!' A Rhetorical-Communicative Perspective on Today's Market." *Australian Journal of Communication* 25, no. 3: 25–44.

Cheney, G., K. Garvin-Doxas, and K. Torrens. 1999. "Kenneth Burke's Implicit Theory of Power." In *Kenneth Burke and the 21st Century.* Edited by B.L. Brock. Albany: State University of New York Press.

Clarke, F.L., and R.J. Craig. 1992. "Juridical Perceptions of the Relevance of Accounting Data in Wage Fixation." *British Journal of Industrial Relations* 29, no. 3: 463–83.

Clarke, F.L., R.J. Craig, and J.H. Amernic. 1990. "Misplaced Trust in Reliance on Published Accounting Data for Wage Negotiation: An International Perspective." *International Journal of Accounting* 25, no. 4: 184–201.

Clarke, F.L., G.W. Dean, and K. Oliver. 1997. *Corporate Collapse: Regulatory, Accounting and Ethical Failure.* Melbourne: Cambridge University Press.

CN. 1995. *On a New Course for the Future,* May.

Cohn, C. 1987. "Sex and Death in the Rational World of Defense Intellectuals." *Signs* 12, no. 4: 687–718.

Comor, E. 2001. "Harold Innis and 'The Bias of Communication.'" *Information, Communication and Society* 4, no. 2: 274–94.

Costantino, M. 1991. *Fashions of a Decade: The 1930s.* London: Batsford.

Courtis, J.K. 1998. "Annual Report Readability Variability: Tests of the Obfuscation Hypothesis." *Accounting, Auditing and Accountability Journal* 11, no. 4: 459–71.

Craig, R., and J. Amernic. 2002. "Accountability of Accounting Educators and the Rhythm of the University: Resistance Strategies for Postmodern Blues." *Accounting Education* 11, no. 2: 121–71.

Craig, R., and P. Walsh. 1989. "Adjustments for 'Extraordinary Items' in Smoothing Reported Profits of Listed Australian Companies: Some Empirical Evidence." *Journal of Business Finance and Accounting* 16, no. 2: 229–45.

Critchley, B. 1995. "Ottawa Made All the Right Moves in CN Sale." *Financial Post*, 25 November.

Cunha, R.C., and C.L. Cooper. 1998. "Privatisation and the Human Factor." *Journal of Applied Management Studies* 7, no. 2: 201–10.

Darcy, J. 1999. Introduction. *CUPE Annual Report on Privatization 1999*. <http://cupe.ca/www/arp1999>.

Daughton, S.M. 1993. "Metaphorical Transcendence: Images of the Holy War in Franklin Roosevelt's First Inaugural." *Quarterly Journal of Speech* 79: 427–46.

David, C. 2001. "Mythmaking in Annual Reports." *Journal of Business and Technical Communication* 15, no. 2: 195–222.

Davis, S.G. 1999. "Space Jam: Media Conglomerates Build the Entertainment City." *European Journal of Communication* 14, no. 4: 435–59.

de Cordova, R. 1994. "The Mickey in Macy's Window." In *Disney Discourse*. Edited by E. Smoodin. New York: Routledge.

Delaney, K.J. 1994. "The Organizational Construction of the 'Bottom Line.'" *Social Problems* 41, no. 4: 497–518.

Den Tandt, M. 2001. "What We Have Here, Mr. Roth, Is a Failure to Communicate." *Globe and Mail*, 10 March.

Devinney, T., and B. Kabanoff. 1999. "Doing What They Say or Saying What They Do? Australian Organisations' Signals of Performance and Attitudes." *Australian Journal of Management* 24, no. 1: 59–75.

Dillard, J.F., and R.A. Nehmer, 1990. "Metaphorical Marginalization." *Critical Perspectives on Accounting* 1, no. 1: 31–52.

DiMaggio, P., E. Hargittai, W.R. Neuman, and J.P. Robinson. 2001. "Social Implications of the Internet." *Annual Review of Sociology* 27: 307–36.

Dobbs, L. 2002. "Business Reforms Should Include a Close Look at Executive Compensation." CNN.com, 16 April. <www.cnn.com>.

Dunn, S. 1990. "Root Metaphor in the Old and New Industrial Relations." *British Journal of Industrial Relations* 28, no. 1: 1–31.

Eagleton, T. 1991. *Ideology: An Introduction*. London: Verso.

Eckel, N. 1981. "The Income Smoothing Hypothesis Revisited." *Abacus* 17, no. 1: 28–40.

Edwards, B.A. 2000. "Chief Executive Officer Behavior: The Catalyst for Strategic Alignment." *International Journal of Value-Based Management* 13: 47–54.

Elliott, J.A., and W.H. Shaw. 1988. "Write-offs as Accounting Procedures to Manage Perceptions." *Journal of Accounting Research* 26: 91–119.

Ellwood, W. 1998. "Inside the Disney Dream Machine." *New Internationalist*, 7-10 December.

Emby, C., and D. Finley. 1997. "Debiasing Framing Effects in Auditors' Internal Control Judgments and Testing Decisions." *Contemporary Accounting Research* 14, no. 2: 55–77.

Entman, R.M. 1993. "Framing: Towards Clarification of a Fractured Paradigm." *Journal of Communication* 43, no. 4: 51–8.

Estes, R. 1996. *Tyranny of the Bottom Line*. San Francisco: Berrett-Koehler.

Eubanks, P. 1999. "Conceptual Metaphor as Rhetorical Response: A Reconsideration of Metaphor." *Written Communication* 16, no. 2: 171–99.

Fairclough, N. 2000. "Discourse, Social Theory, and Social Research: The Discourse of Welfare Reform." *Journal of Sociolinguistics* 4, no. 2: 167.

Federal Communications Commission. 2001. "Statement of FCC Chairman William E. Kennard on Conditioned Approval of AOLTime Warner Merger," 11 January. <http://www.fcc.gov/Speeches/Kennard/Statements/2001/stwek101.html>.

Forceville, C. 1995. "IBM Is a Tuning Fork: Degrees of Freedom in the Interpretation of Pictorial Metaphors." *Poetics* 23: 189–218.

"The Forest of Rhetoric: *Silva Rhetoricae*." <http://humanities.byu.edu/rhetoric/silva.htm>.

Fournier, V., and C. Grey. 2000. "At the Critical Moment: Conditions and Prospects for Critical Management Studies." *Human Relations* 53, no. 1: 7–32.

Fox, J. 2003. "What's So Great about GE?" *Fortune*, 4 March.

Garraty, J.A., and M.C. Carnes, eds. 1988. *Dictionary of American Biography, Supplement Eight, 1966–1970*. New York: Charles Scribner's Sons.

Geisler, C. 2001. "Textual Objects: Accounting for the Role of Texts in the Everyday Life of Complex Organizations." *Written Communication* 18, no. 3: 296–325.

Gibbs, R.W., Jr. 1994. *The Poetics of Mind: Figurative Thought, Language, and Understanding*. Cambridge: Cambridge University Press.

Gibson, S. 1996. "Is All Coherence Gone? The Role of Narrative in Web Design." *Interpersonal Computing and Technology: An Electronic Journal for the 21st Century* 4: 7–26.

Glucksberg, S., and M.S. McGlone. 1999. "When Love Is Not a Journey: What Metaphors Mean." *Journal of Pragmatics* 31: 1544–58.

Graham, P. 2001. "Space: Irrealist Objects in Technology Policy and Their Role in a New Political Economy." *Discourse and Society* 12, no. 6: 761–88.

Greene, R. 1986. "Big Bath? Or a Little One?" *Forbes*, 6 October.

Greiner, L. 2002. "Steve Kerr and His Years with Jack Welch at GE." *Journal of Management Inquiry* 11, no. 4: 343–50.

Grey, C. 2003. "The Fetish of Change." *Tamara* 2, no. 2: 1–19.

Gwyn, R. 2002. "Greed Sullies Neo-Con Creed about Rules of the Market." *Toronto Star*, 14 April.

Hager, P.J., and H.J. Scheiber. 1990. "Reading Smoke and Mirrors: The Rhetoric of Corporate Annual Reports." *Journal of Technical Writing and Communication* 20, no. 2: 113–30.

Hallett, T. 2003. "Symbolic Power and Organizational Culture." *Sociological Theory* 21, no. 2: 128–49.

Hamilton, T., and R. Cribb. 2001a. "John Roth Speaks Out." *Toronto Star*, 8 December.

– 2001b. "Nortel Inflated Sales, Suit Claims: 'Pulled Forward $500 Million US,' Documents Say." *Toronto Star*, 13 December.

Harrington, A. 1995. "Metaphoric Connections: Holistic Science in the Shadow of the Third Reich." *Social Research* 62, no. 2: 357–85.

Harris, M. 2002. Notes for a speech to the Toronto Board of Trade, 5 March. Accessed 24 March 2002, <www.gov.on.ca>.

Hart, R. 1997. *DICTION: The Text Analysis Program*. Thousand Oaks, CA: Sage.

Harvey, D. 1990. *The Condition of Postmodernity*. Oxford and Malden, MA: Blackwell.

Hegele, C., and A. Kiesler. 2001. "Control the Construction of Your Legend or Someone Else Will: An Analysis of Texts on Jack Welch." *Journal of Management Inquiry* 10, no. 4: 298–309.

Heller, R. 1994. *The Fate of IBM*. London: Little Brown.

Hill, V., and K.M. Carley. 1999. "An Approach to Identifying Consensus in a Subfield: The Case of Organizational Culture." *Poetics* 27: 1–30.

Hines, R.D. 1988. "Financial Accounting: In Communicating Reality, We Construct Reality." *Accounting, Organizations and Society* 13, no. 3: 251–61.

Hollister, P. 1940. "Walt Disney." *Atlantic Monthly*, December.

Huizingh, E. 2000. "The Content and Design of Web Sites: An Empirical Study." *Information and Management* 37: 123–34.

Hyland, K. 1998. "Exploring Corporate Rhetoric: Metadiscourse in the CEO's Letter." *Journal of Business Communication* 35, no. 2: 224–45.

Innis, H.A. 1949. "The Bias of Communication." *Canadian Journal of Economics and Political Science* 15, no. 4: 457–76.

– 1951. *The Bias of Communication*. Reprint, Toronto: University of Toronto Press, 1991.

Iyengar, S. 1990. "Framing Responsibility for Political Issues: The Case of Poverty." *Political Behavior* 12: 19–40.

Jang, H-Y, and G.A. Barnett. 1994. "Cultural Differences in Organizational Communication: A Semantic Network Analysis." *Bulletin de méthodologie sociologique* 44: 31–59.

Johnson, H.T., and R.S. Kaplan. 1987. *Relevance Lost: The Rise and Fall of Management Accounting*. Boston: Harvard Business School Press.

Johnson, M. 1993. *Moral Imagination*. Chicago: University of Chicago Press.

Jones, M.J., and P.A. Shoemaker. 1994. "Accounting Narratives: A Review of Empirical Studies of Content and Readability." *Journal of Accounting Literature* 13: 142–84.

Jönsson, S. 1998. "Relate Management Accounting Research to Managerial Work." *Accounting, Organizations and Society* 23, no. 4: 411–34.

Karim, K.H. 2001. "Cyber-Utopia and the Myth of Paradise: Using Jacques Ellul's Work on Propaganda to Analyze Information Society Rhetoric." *Information, Communication and Society* 4, no. 1: 113–34.

Keenoy, T. 1991. "The Roots of Metaphor in the Old and the New Industrial Relations." *British Journal of Industrial Relations* 29, no. 2: 313–28.

Klumpp, J.E. 1999. "Burkean Social Hierarchy and the Ironic Investment of Martin Luther King." In *Kenneth Burke and the 21ˢᵗ Century*. Edited by B.L. Brock. Albany: State University of New York Press.

Korten, D.C. 1995. *When Corporations Rule the World*. San Francisco: Kumarian Press, Berrett-Koehler.

Kostera, M., and B. Glinka. 2001. "Budget as Logos: The Rhetorics of the Polish Press." *Organization* 8, no. 4: 647–82.

Lakoff, G. 1993. "The Contemporary Theory of Metaphor." In *Metaphor and Thought*. Edited by A. Ortony. Cambridge: Cambridge University Press.

– 1996. *Moral Politics*. Chicago: University of Chicago Press.

Lakoff, G., and M. Johnson. 1980. *Metaphors We Live By*. Chicago and London: University of Chicago Press.

Landow, G.P. 1996. "Newman and the Idea of an Electronic University." In *The Idea of a University*. Edited by F.M. Turner. New Haven: Yale University Press.

Lanham, R.A. 1991. *A Handlist of Rhetorical Terms*. Berkeley: University of California Press.

– 1993. *The Electronic Word*. Chicago: University of Chicago Press.

Lavoie, D. 1987. "The Accounting of Interpretation and the Interpretation of Accounts: The Communication Function of 'The Language of Business.'" *Accounting, Organizations and Society* 12, no. 6: 579–604.

Leger, K. 1995. "A Fine Way to Run a Railroad." *Financial Post* 23–25 December.

Lemke, J.L. 1999. "Discourse and Organizational Dynamics: Website Communication and Institutional Change." *Discourse and Society* 10, no. 1: 21–47.

Letiche, H. 1995. "Researching Organization by Implosion and Fatality." *Studies in Cultures, Organizations and Societies* 1, no. 1: 107–26.

Low, G. 1999. "Validating Metaphor Research Projects." In *Researching and Applying Metaphor*. Edited by L. Cameron and G. Low. Cambridge: Cambridge University Press.

Lye, J. 1997. "Ideology: A Brief Guide." <www.brocku.ca/english/jlye/ideology.html>.

Maio, K. 1998. "Disney's Dolls." *New Internationalist,* 12–14 December.

Margonelli, L. 1999. "Inside AOL's 'Cyber-sweatshop.'" *Wired*, October.

Martin, J. 1990. "Deconstructing Organizational Taboos: The Suppression of Gender Conflict in Organizations." *Organization Science* 1: 339–59.

McGee, M.C. 1980. "The 'Ideograph': A Link between Rhetoric and Ideology." *Quarterly Journal of Speech* 66, no. 1: 1–16.

McLuhan, M. 1964. *Understanding Media: The Extensions of Man.* Reprint, Cambridge: MIT Press, 1994.

Menzies, H. 1996. *Whose Brave New World? The Information Highway and the New Economy.* Toronto: Between the Lines.

Merchant, K.A., and J. Rockness. 1994. "The Ethics of Managing Earnings: An Empirical Investigation." *Journal of Accounting and Public Policy* 13, no. 1: 79–94.

Miller, H.T., and J.R. Simmons. 1998. "The Irony of Privatization." *Administration and Society* 30, no. 5: 513–32.

Miller, M.W., and L. Berton. 1993. "Softer Numbers: As IBM's Woes Grew, Its Accounting Tactics Got Less Conservative." *Wall Street Journal*, 7 April.

Miller, S.I., and M. Fredericks. 1990. "Perceptions of the Crisis in American Public Education: The Relationship of Metaphors to Ideology." *Metaphor and Symbolic Activity* 5, no. 2: 67–81.

Mitchell, G.R. 2000. "Placebo Defense: Operation Desert Mirage? The Rhetoric of Patriot Missile Accuracy in the 1991 Persian Gulf War." *Quarterly Journal of Speech* 86, no. 2: 121–45.

Moore, D.C. 1994. "Feminist Accounting Theory as a Critique of What's 'Natural' in Economics." In *Natural Images in Economic Thought*. Edited by P. Mirowski. Cambridge: Cambridge University Press.

Morris, C.W. 1946. *Signs, Language and Behavior.* Englewood Cliffs, NJ: Prentice Hall.

Myers, F. 1999. "Political Argumentation and the Composite Audience: A Case Study." *Quarterly Journal of Speech* 85: 55–71.

Myers, R.J., and M.S. Kessler. 1980. "Business Speaks: A Study of the Themes in Speeches by America's Corporate Leaders." *Journal of Business Communication* 17, no. 3: 5–17.

Neu, D., H. Warsame, and K. Pedwell. 1998. "Managing Public Impressions: Environmental Disclosures in Annual Reports." *Accounting, Organizations and Society* 23, no. 3: 265–82.

Newman, W.H. 1953. "Basic Objectives which Shape the Character of a Company." *Journal of Business of the University of Chicago* 26, no. 4: 211–23.

Nortel Networks Corporation. 1999. *1999 Annual Report 10-K.*

Ochs, E., and L. Capps. 1996. "Narrating the Self." *Annual Review of Anthropology* 25: 19–43.

O'Connor, M.C. 1973. "On the Usefulness of Accounting Ratios to Investors in Common Stock." *Accounting Review* 48, no. 2: 339–52.

Ogden, S.G., and F. Anderson. 1999. "The Role of Accounting in Organisational Change: Promoting Performance Improvements in the Privatised UK Water Industry." *Critical Perspectives on Accounting* 10, no. 1: 91–124.

Olive, D. 2002. "Finding Cracks in the Brand That Jack Built." *Toronto Star*, 26 January.

Oliver, C. 1991. "Strategic Responses to Institutional Processes." *Academy of Management Review* 15: 145–79.

Orbuch, T.L. 1997. "People's Accounts Count: The Sociology of Accounts." *Annual Review of Sociology* 23: 455–78.

Orr, L. 1989. "The Post-turn Turn: Derrida, Gadamer and the Remystification of Language." In *Deconstruction: A Critique*. Edited by P. Rajnath. London: Macmillan.

Osborne, J.D., C.I. Stubbart, and A. Ramaprasad. 2001. "Strategic Groups and Competitive Enactment: A Study of Dynamic Relationships between Mental Models and Performance." *Strategic Management Journal* 22: 435–54.

"A Performance-Measurement Takeover Bid?" 1998. *CA Magazine* January/February, 15.

Poe, R. 1994. "'Can We Talk?' CEOs Speak Frankly in the New Breed of Annual Reports." *Across the Board*, May, 16–23.

Porter, T.M. 1992. "Quantification and the Accounting Ideal in Science." *Social Studies of Science* 22: 633–52.

Postman, N. 1993. *Technopoly: The Surrender of Culture to Technology.* New York: Basic.

– 1996. *The End of Education.* New York: Vintage.

– 2000. *Building a Bridge to the 18th Century: How the Past Can Improve Our Future.* Toronto: Random House Vintage.

Power, M. 1997. "Expertise and the Construction of Relevance: Accountants and Environmental Audit." *Accounting, Organizations and Society* 22, no. 2: 123–46.

Powers, W.C., Jr, R.S. Troubh, and H.S. Winokur Jr. 2002. *Report of Investigation by the Special Investigative Committee of the Board of Directors of Enron Corp (Powers Report).* 1 February. <http://news.findlaw.com/hdocs/docs/enron/sicreport/sicreport020102.pdf>.

Prasad, A., and R. Mir. 2002. "Digging Deep for Meaning: A Critical Hermeneutic Analysis of Shareholder Letters to Shareholders in the Oil Industry." *Journal of Business Communication* 39, no. 1: 92–116.

Preston, A.M., C. Wright, and J.J. Young. 1996. "Imag[in]ing Annual Reports." *Accounting, Organizations and Society* 21, no. 1: 113–37.

Rajnath, P. 1989. *Deconstruction: A Critique.* London: Macmillan.

Reddy, M.J. 1993. "The Conduit Metaphor: A Case of Frame Conflict in Our Language about Language." In *Metaphor and Thought.* Edited by A. Ortony. Cambridge: Cambridge University Press.

Rohrer, T. 1997. "Conceptual Blending on the Information Highway: How Metaphorical Inferences Work." *Proceedings of the International Cognitive Linguistics Conference,* vol. 2. Amsterdam: Johns Benjamin.

Romei, S. 2000. "Boiling Billy Blames Blues on Billionaires." *Weekend Australian* August 5–6, 35.

Roscoe, T. 1999. "The Construction of the World Wide Web Audience." *Media, Culture and Society* 21: 674–84.

Rosenau, P.M. 1992. *Post-modernism and the Social Sciences.* Princeton: Princeton University Press.

Salancik, G.R., and J.R. Meindl. 1984. "Corporate Attributions as Strategic Illusions of Management Control." *Administrative Science Quarterly* 29: 238–54.

Schickel, R. 1968. *The Disney Version.* Reprint, Chicago: Ivan R. Dee, 1997.

Scott, L.M. 1994. "Images in Advertising: The Need for a Theory of Visual Rhetoric." *Journal of Consumer Research* 21: 252–73.

Searle, J.R. 1969. *Speech Acts.* New York: Cambridge University Press.

Shaoul, J. 1997. "A Critical Financial Analysis of the Performance of Privatised Industries: The Case of the Water Industry in England and Wales." *Critical Perspectives on Accounting* 8: 479–505.

Shen, Y., and N. Balaban. 1999. "Metaphorical (In)coherence in Discourse." *Discourse Processes* 28: 139–53.

Shiller, R. 2000. *Irrational Exuberance.* Princeton: Princeton University Press.

Skapinker, M. 2003. "Different Game, Same Winners." *Financial Times,* 17 January.

Skilling, J. 2002. Testimony before the US Congress Energy and Commerce Committee, Financial Collapse of Enron Corp. Subcommittee on Oversight and Investigations, 7 February. <http//:energycommerce.house.gov/107/Hearings/02072002hearing485/hearing.htm>.

Slagell, A.R. 1991. "Anatomy of a Masterpiece: A Close Textual Analysis of Abraham Lincoln's Second Inaugural Address." *Communication Studies* 42, no. 2: 155–71.

Slocum, Tyson. 2001. "Blind Faith: How Deregulation and Enron's Influence over Government Looted Billions from Americans." *Public Citizen,* December. <http://www.citizen.org/documents/Blind_Faith.pdf>.

Slotkin, R. 1985. *The Fatal Environment: The Myth of the Frontier in the Age of Industrialization, 1800–1890.* New York: Antheneum.

Stabile, C. A. 2000. "Nike, Social Responsibility, and the Hidden Abode of Production." *Critical Studies in Media Communication* 17, no. 2: 186–204.

Stackhouse, J. 2001. "Operation Careful Rhetoric." *Globe and Mail,* 21 September.

Stein, N. 2003. "America's Most Admired Companies: Why GE Isn't No. 1." *Fortune,* 18 February.

Sussman, L., P. Ricchio, and J. Belohlav. 1983. "Corporate Speeches as a Source of Corporate Values: An Analysis across Years, Themes, and Industries." *Strategic Management Journal* 4: 187–96.

Swieringa, R.J., and K.E. Weick. 1987. "Management Accounting and Action." *Accounting, Organizations and Society* 12, no. 3: 293–308.

Taylor, S. 2003. "Dissolving Anchors: Acid Management on Mars." *Tamara* 2, no. 4: 1–6.

Tennyson, B.M., R.W. Ingram, and M.T. Dugan. 1990. "Assessing the Information Content of Narrative Disclosures in Explaining Bankruptcy." *Journal of Business Finance and Accounting* 17, no. 3: 391–410.

Terranova, T. 2000. "Free Labor: Producing Culture for the Digital Economy." *Social Text* 63, vol. 18, no. 2: 33–58.

Thomas, J. 1997. "Discourse in the Marketplace: The Making of Meaning in Annual Reports." *Journal of Business Communication* 34, no. 1: 47–6.

Thrift, N. 2001. "'It's the Romance, Not the Finance, That Makes the Business Worth Pursuing': Disclosing a New Market Culture." *Economy and Society* 30, no. 4: 412–32.

Tinker, T. 1985. *Paper Prophets.* New York: Praeger.

Trice, H.M., and J.M. Beyer. 1993. *The Cultures of Work Organizations.* Englewood Cliffs, NJ: Prentice Hall.

Tsing, A. 2000. "Inside the Economy of Appearances." *Public Culture* 12, no. 1: 115–44.

Trumble R., and T. Tudor. 1996. "Equitable Collective Bargaining through Publicly Accessible Financial Data." *Journal of Collective Negotiations in the Public Sector* 25, no. 2: 89–99.

Tuck, S. 2001. "Roth's Legacy One of Triumph, Failure." *Globe and Mail,* 3 October.

Tucker, R.E. 2001. "Figure, Ground and Presence: A Phenomenology of Meaning in Rhetoric." *Quarterly Journal of Speech* 87, no. 4: 396–414.

Tversky, A., and D. Kahneman. 1981. "The Framing of Decisions and the Psychology of Choice." *Science* 211: 453–58.

US Financial Accounting Standards Board. 2000. "Chairman Jenkins Testifies at House Hearing," 4 May. <http://www.fasb.org/news/nr5400.shtml>.

Van Dijk, T. 1993. "Principles of Critical Discourse Analysis." *Discourse and Society* 4, no. 2: 249–83.

Walsh P., R. Craig, and F. Clarke. 1991. "'Big Bath Accounting' Using Extraordinary Adjustments: Australian Empirical Evidence." *Journal of Business Finance and Accounting* 18, no. 2: 173–89.

Walt Disney 1997 Fact Book. 1998. Burbank, CA: Walt Disney Company.

Warnick, B., and S.L. Kline. 1992. "The New Rhetoric's Argumentation Schemes: A Rhetorical View of Practical Reasoning." *Argumentation and Advocacy* 29: 1–15.

Watts, S. 1997. *The Magic Kingdom.* New York: Houghton Mifflin.

Weberman, B. 1986. "Rumpelstilzchen Accounting." *Fortune,* 24 February.

Welch, J., and J.A. Byrne. 2001. *Jack: Straight from the Gut.* New York: Warner.

Wells, J. 2001. "Milton Fails Leadership Test in Airline's Time of Crisis." *Toronto Star,* 29 September.

Weick, K.E. 1995. *Sensemaking in Organizations.* Thousand Oaks, CA: Sage.

Weissman, R. 2001. "Global Management by Stress." *Multinational Monitor* 22, nos 7–8.

111111111116111

Whitehead A.N. 1925. *Science and the Modern World*. Reprint, New York: Free Press, 1953.

– 1929. *The Aims of Education and Other Essays*. Reprint, New York: Free Press, 1957.

Wicks, A.C., S.L. Berman, and T.L. Jones. 1999. "The Structure of Optimal Trust: Moral and Strategic Implications." *Academy of Management Review* 24, no. 1: 99–116.

Wilson, I. 2002. "Blunt Welch." Review of *Jack: Straight from the Gut*, by J. Welch and A. Byrne. *Strategy and Leadership* 30, no. 1: 41–2.

Winter, S.L. 1989. "Transcendental Nonsense: Metaphoric Reasoning and the Cognitive Stakes for Law." *University of Pennsylvania Law Review* 137, no. 4: 1105–237.

Worthy, F.S. 1984. "Manipulating Profits: How It's Done." *Fortune*, 25 June.

Index

accountability: for CEO-speak 137–44; of companies, 67; documents, 87; missing principle, 29; morphing, 42; need to take seriously, 141; to stakeholders, 12, 67

accountants: ethics of, 19, 142

accounting: accrual-based, 69; assistance in narrative conspiracy, 107; authority of, 96; big bath, 68, 131; cash-based, 69; complexity of, 37; conservative, 96–7; curious, 132; curricula reform, 143; distorted view of, 67; of Enron, 75; as an explicit technical practice, 13; "feral," 68; fuzzy, 76; fictions and solecisms, 16, 71; generic problems, 68; hidden ideologies, 16, 46; ideological overtones, 7; language, x, 12, 81, 103, 125; language of business, 13, 104, 138; for mergers, 117–18; policy choice, 68; rhetoric, 36–8; as a social engine, 104–8; socially constructed, 36; standards, 66, 142; techno-babble, 37; as a way of thinking, 12

agency: lack of, 31; of shareholders, 79

Alcan, xi, 3, 116–17

Ali, Muhammad, 24

Alusuisse, xi, 116

American Accounting Association, 36

American Federation of Labor, 99

America Online, 51

anaphora, 93

Andersen, xi, 3, 19, 20, 28–38; accusations against, 29; errors of judgment, 35; litigation settlements, 29; remarks of Joseph F. Berardino to US House of Representatives Committee on Financial Services, 153–64

antanagoge, 49

AOLTimeWarner, xi, 3, 51–64; and consumers, 56–64; humanized, 60; hypocrisy of, 63; Internet policy, 53, 55–64; Internet Policy Statement, 165–73; as a juggernaut, 53, 62; merger, 55; SEC filings, 54; Web site, 51

apomnemonysis, 96–7

audit[ors]: reform of curricula, 141; role, 68, 104; wake-up call, 141

Bacon, Francis, 3

balanced scorecard, 14

balance sheet(s), 3, 12–13, 29, 97, 118; of IBM, 68, 71; readiness for privatization, 128

Bambi, 88